Modern Scholarship on
European History

HENRY A. TURNER, JR.
General Editor

REAPPRAISALS OF
FASCISM

REAPPRAISALS OF
FASCISM

EDITED WITH AN INTRODUCTION BY HENRY A. TURNER. JR.

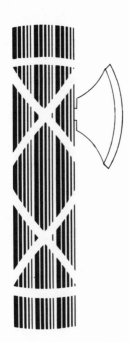

NEW VIEWPOINTS
A Division of Franklin Watts, Inc.   New York, 1975

REAPPRAISALS OF FASCISM

Library of Congress Cataloging in Publication Data
Main entry under title:
REAPPRAISALS OF FASCISM.
    (Modern scholarship on European history)
    Bibliography: p.
    CONTENTS: The interpretation of Ernst Nolte:
Epstein, K. A new study of fascism. Nolte, E. The
problem of fascism in recent scholarship.—Subsequent
re-interpretations: Allen, W. S. The appeal of
fascism and the problem of national disintegration.
Cassels, A. Janus: the two faces of fascism.
Sauer, W. National socialism: totalitarianism or
fascism? Turner, H. A., Jr. Fascism and modernization.
[etc.]
    1. Fascism—Addresses, essays, lectures.
I. Turner, Henry Ashby.
D726.5.R33   320.5′33   75-6626
ISBN 0-531-05372-5
ISBN 0-531-05579-5 pbk.

Manufactured in the United States of America
6 5 4 3 2

TABLE OF CONTENTS

PREFACE

During the strife-ridden decade between 1963 and 1973, two terms that had largely dropped out of everyday usage in most languages experienced a remarkable revival: "fascism" and "fascist." Those words were, in fact, hurled about during that decade with considerable heat in an often bewildering fashion. Israelis accused Arabs of being fascists; Arabs denounced Israelis as fascists. Chinese Communists branded the government of the Soviet Union as fascist; the Soviets called the Chinese rulers fascists. Rebellious students in Western democracies labeled their societies as fascist, only to be charged in turn with being red fascists. Countless elected public officials in democratically governed countries were accused of being fascists. Nor was use of the terms "fascism" and "fascist" limited to the realm of politics. They were adapted as well to the sphere of esthetics, so that one read of fascist films, psychedelic fascism, and the fascism of music. Not even that most basic of human problems—the relationship between men and women—was spared, as charges were heard of sexual fascism. Whatever these formulations were intended to mean, the response of those persons at whom the terms "fascism" and "fascist" were directed was almost invariably one of enraged indignation. Clearly, these are among the relatively few remaining all-purpose, international epithets that still carry a painful sting—a fact that undoubtedly contributed to the conspicuous growth in their popularity during a troubled and anxious time.

By coincidence, at about the same time that the terms "fascism" and "fascist" were being revived as epithets in politics, the popular press, and common speech, scholars in widely scattered parts of the world were—much less stridently and conspicuously—subjecting those same terms to renewed scrutiny after a long period of neglect. The product of their endeavors is a now sizable body of critical and analytic re-examinations of fascism as a generic phenomenon, that is, as a multi-national movement that assumed varying forms in different places at different times but which can be regarded as fundamentally similar wherever it existed or, in the opinion of some, still exists. Many of these scholarly re-assessments of fascism have appeared in the form of articles in learned journals, so that it is difficult to assemble and compare them. The intent of this volume is to make some of these articles more accessible and thus to encourage further thought and inquiry about the still unresolved riddle of fascism.

One aspect of the volume deserves explanation: the absence of Marxist analyses. It proved impossible to find even one interpretation from that point of view of a quality comparable to that of the contributions published here. The explanation for this is twofold, involving "orthodox" Marxists on the one hand and "non-orthodox" on the other. As is mentioned in a number of the contributions to this volume, those "orthodox" Marxists who have adhered to the Moscow-dictated party line of international communism have for nearly forty years been shackled to the simplistic "agent theory" promulgated by Stalin's Comintern in 1933, according to which the fascist movements were mere tools and lackeys of "finance" or "monopoly" capitalists. Recently, there have been signs that the bonds of this ideological straitjacket are being loosened. But the result thus far has been that even the most venturesome of Soviet analysts of fascism merely concedes what has long been regarded as self-evident in non-Communist circles: that fascism was a sociologically complex phenomenon which enjoyed in most countries a high degree of autonomy in its actions before and after gaining power.[1] The most recent and emancipated Communist scholarship has, that is, thus far managed only to arrive at what is essentially the point of departure for the contributions in this volume. Although this apparent relaxation of ideological controls is a hopeful sign, orthodox

Marxist-Leninist scholarship has yet to contribute in noteworthy fashion to the reassessment of fascism. Indeed, it has failed even to reattain the degree of sophistication and insight that marked the often perceptive, if impressionistic and non-empirical, analyses of the Communist intellectuals of the 1920s whose voices Stalin and his henchmen were to stifle.[2] As for the "non-orthodox" Marxist writers of today, their interpretations of fascism as a generic phenomenon are indeed in some cases quite sophisticated, if often rather scholastic in their reasoning. Almost without exception, however, these writings suffer, as do those of "orthodox" Marxists, from over-reliance on questionable, if not fraudulent scholarship, and from egregious misrepresentation of factual information. Until such independent Marxists who write about fascism acquaint themselves with the most recent findings of empirical scholarship and develop more scrupulous habits in their use of factual data, they cannot expect their position to receive a full hearing in the forum of international scholarship.[3]

[1] Alexander Galkin, "Capitalist Society and Fascism," in *Social Sciences* (Akademiia nauk SSSR. Otdelenie obshchnestvennykh nauk), I (1970), 128–138.

[2] See John M. Cammett, "Communist Theories of Fascism, 1920–1935," *Science and Society*, XXXI (1967), 149–163; Ernst Nolte (ed.), *Theorien über den Faschismus* (Cologne and Berlin, 1967).

[3] See, for example, Nicos Poulantzas, *Fascisme et Dictature* (Paris, 1970); Ernest Mandel, "Introduction" to Leon Trotsky, *The Struggle Against Fascism in Germany* (New York, 1971); Reinhard Kühnl, *Formen bürgerlicher Herrschaft. Liberalismus—Faschismus* (Reinbek bei Hamburg, 1971); Manfred Clemenz, *Gesellschaftliche Ursprünge des Faschismus* (Frankfurt, 1972).

ACKNOWLEDGMENTS

The editor wishes here to express his gratitude to those who have made this volume possible:

To Princeton University Press, as well as to the author's widow and father, for permission to republish Klaus Epstein's "A New Study of Fascism," *World Politics*, XVI, no. 2 (copyright © 1964 by Princeton University Press): pp. 302–321.

To Ernst Nolte, for permission to translate and publish his "Der Faschismus als Problem in der wissenschaftlichen Literatur der jüngsten Vergangenheit," which first appeared in *Fašismus a Evropa* (2 vols., Prague, 1969), I. pp. 17–46, and was also published in Professor Nolte's *Der Nationalsozialismus* (Berlin, 1970).

To William Sheridan Allen, for permission to publish his "The Appeal of Fascism and the Problem of National Disintegration."

To Alan Cassels and the Canadian Historical Papers for permission to republish Professor Cassels' "Janus: The Two Faces of Fascism," in *Historical Papers 1969*, pp. 166–84.

To Wolfgang Sauer for permission to republish his "National Socialism: Totalitarianism or Fascism?", *The American Historical Review*, LXXIII (1967), pp. 404–422.

To Princeton University Press for permission to republish my "Fascism and Modernization," *World Politics*, XXIV, no. 4 (copyright © 1972 by Princeton University Press): pp. 547–564.

To Stanley G. Payne for permission to republish his "Span-

xiii

ish Fascism in Comparative Perspective," *Iberian Studies*, II (1973), pp. 3–12.

To Hans Rogger and The University of Chicago Press for permission to republish Professor Rogger's "Was there a Russian Fascism?—The Union of Russian People," *The Journal of Modern History*, XXXVI (1964), pp. 398–415.

To George Macklin Wilson and Cambridge University Press for permission to republish Professor Wilson's "A New Look at the Problem of 'Japanese Fascism,' " *Comparative Studies in Society and History*, X (1968), pp. 401–412.

To Renee Winegarten and the Wiener Library for permission to republish Mrs. Winegarten's "The Fascist Mentality—Drieu la Rochelle," *The Wiener Library Bulletin* (Winter, 1967–68), pp. 37–43.

I

THE INTERPRETATION OF
ERNST NOLTE

Without question, the single most important contribution to the reappraisal of fascism is Ernst Nolte's book, *Three Faces of Fascism,* which was originally published in German in 1963 with a quite different title, *Der Faschismus in seiner Epoche* (Fascism in its Era). Nolte's book deserves to be read in entirety by anyone seriously concerned with the problem of fascism as a generic phenomenon, so no attempt has been made here to reproduce excerpts from it. The first selection is thus one of the most trenchant and insightful analyses of Nolte's book, which was written in 1964 by the late Klaus Epstein, who was professor of history at Brown University when his tragic death in 1966 at the age of forty prematurely ended what promised to be a brilliant career. Epstein's analysis will serve as an informative introduction for those who have not yet read Nolte's book and a thought-provoking stimulus for a re-examination of it for those who have. The second selection is an essay by Nolte himself which was prepared for an international symposium on fascism held in Prague in August 1969, and which has never before been published in English. In it Professor Nolte reflects in illuminating fashion upon his own work and gives his views on the interpretations of a number of others who have sought to grapple with the problem of fascism. Ernst Nolte currently is professor of history at the Free University of Berlin.

1

I

A New Study of Fascism

BY KLAUS EPSTEIN

I

Ernst Nolte's *Three Faces of Fascism* is a work of exceptionally broad range that combines description, comparison, and interpretation in an admirable manner. It attempts three major tasks requiring skills rarely combined in a single historian: a general classification of fascist systems aiming at a typology; a special examination of the main features of one pre-fascist (*Action Française*) and two fascist movements (in Mussolini's Italy and in Hitler's Germany); and an overall interpretation, in both historical and philosophical terms, of fascism as the dominant force of the period of European history extending from 1919 to 1945.

A general characterization of Nolte's book is appropriate before discussing its specific content. To avoid disappointment it will be best to begin with a brief listing of the things that the book does *not* attempt—for while Nolte is broad in his subject matter, he is explicitly and self-consciously selective in his approach. Readers must not expect a conventional political history of the movements headed by Maurras, Mussolini, and Hitler, or a specific analysis of why and how fascism triumphed in particular countries at particular times. The author provides only incidentally a sociological description of the groups supporting fascism, and there is very little analysis of how fascist systems actually worked from an institutional point of view. Nolte has little to say on such previously investigated topics as fascist police repression, propaganda techniques, or economic policies. His work is based exclusively upon

2

published sources, and does not aim at uncovering "new facts" either through archival research or through interviews with survivors.

Nolte has aimed at something far more important than these tasks of "conventional history" (whose value he of course does not deny)—namely, to define the position of fascism in modern history; to analyze its constituent elements with reference to an empirically derived but theoretically elaborated "ideal type"; and, above all, to explore the "phenomenology" of fascism in terms of its ideology and *self*-understanding. This final aim has led him to include first-rate intellectual biographies of Charles Maurras, Benito Mussolini, and Adolf Hitler in which he argues convincingly that their personal outlook largely shaped the movements they led. Nolte is well aware of the criticism likely to be directed against this biographical approach, but it is one of his major theses that "great men" *do* matter even in an age when politics is often interpreted as the clash of impersonal forces.

Nolte's preoccupation with the ideology of fascism is rooted in the thesis (convincing to this reviewer) that fascist ideas were crucial in determining the motives and shaping the structures of at least some fascist movements. This thesis will be unacceptable on *a priori* grounds to those who believe that ideology is never anything *but* "rationalization" of material interests; it may be questioned more plausibly by pointing to the primitive crudeness of fascist ideas. To this Nolte replies that crudeness does not preclude conviction (on the contrary, crude men have a natural affinity for crude ideas), and that the intellectual caliber of two of his protagonists—Maurras and Mussolini—has been too often underrated. He insists, moreover, that fascism constitutes the culmination of the reaction against the ideas of 1789; it reckons among its forerunners the entire European "conservative tradition," going back to Maistre and Bonald. Nolte brilliantly describes the French current of this tradition in his survey of the roots of Maurras' thought, thus giving fascism a distinguished intellectual pedigree not usually found in studies of the subject. The establishment of this pedigree is far more subtle and convincing than the once-popular pastime of rummaging through German intellectual history for possible forerunners of nazism: a procedure that usually resulted in twisting thinkers (wholly or in part) out of their contemporary context and interpreting German fascism as the "inevitable" result of Germany's national history, thereby distracting attention from the *universal* roots of modern fascism.

A special feature of the book is its "objectivity"; a quality made possible by the fact that fascism, while still a powerful memory, is no longer a significant political force. Nolte seeks to approach it as the historian would any other "dead" historical period—say, the Renaissance or the Counter-Reformation—and succeeds to a remarkable extent in this self-appointed task. He does not deny fascism the minimum of "sympathy" that is necessary for "understanding" it: "sympathy" in terms of recognizing that the fascists (though often criminals) genuinely wrestled with the major problems of our exceedingly perplexing age. Nolte seeks to understand them both as they understood themselves and as they appear *sub specie aeternitatis;* their statements are taken seriously unless obviously made with an *ad hoc* purpose; the record of their deeds is studied without political or personal bias. It should be stressed that this attitude does not involve any moral obtuseness on Nolte's part, for he is poignantly aghast at such a phenomenon as the Nazi destruction of Europe's Jews: but he shows his historical perspective by viewing this destruction as the (objective) *logical consequence* of certain ideas, not merely the (subjective) *personal wickedness* of certain individuals. He completely avoids (what some might expect from a German author) the apologetic tendency potentially inherent in a comparative approach to fascism by stressing on repeated occasions that the most abhorrent aspects of nazism, such as the destruction of the Jews, were peculiar to itself and find no analogue in other fascist systems.

The scope of the subject matter and the objectivity of treatment are only two of the qualities that give Nolte's book a claim to the rare attribute of greatness. One can also admire his combination of courage and judiciousness in tackling the most unpleasant aspects of his topic. To give only one example, deliberately selected for its provocativeness: Nolte does not hesitate to point out certain parallel features of Nazi and (of all things) Zionist ideology:

4

extreme racialism, disregard for the historic rights of others, drive for *Lebensraum*, and fear of extinction. He hastens, however, to add a commentary on the last parallel: ". . . for the Jews everything was reality which for the National Socialists were the imaginings induced by pathological fear." [1] The author shows superb craftsmanship in his scholarly apparatus (unhappily placed at the end of the book). Nolte's scholarship is admirable, yet it is never only an end in itself; he is deeply stirred by the importance of his subject matter—important in itself and for the light it throws upon the predicament of modern man—and seeks to *explain* as well as merely to *document*. This is not to say that description, sometimes colorful description, is missing; see, for example, the account of the terroristic practices of the Italian Fascists in 1921 or of the Nazi party rally at Nürnberg in 1937. [2] His special talent, however, lies in *analysis*, especially the analysis of various doctrines, and *interpretation*, especially the metaphysical interpretation of fascism in the concluding section. All these qualities make Nolte's book, in the opinion of this reviewer, one of the half-dozen most important historical works to appear in Germany since 1945.

A word of warning to the reader is, however, necessary about some obvious weaknesses of *Three Faces of Fascism*. Some great books are difficult to read, and this is certainly one of them. All authors have the defects of their qualities—in this case, the list begins with the style; although it conveys the author's meaning clearly and precisely, it is often more suitable to a philosophical treatise than a work of history. The exposition is studded with technical terms that are not always satisfactorily explained. The analysis is sometimes on an intolerably abstract level; certain sections (for example, the important last section on "Fascism as a Metapolitical Phenomenon") must be read at least twice before the drift of the argument emerges. The historical sections are marred by an occasional allusiveness that may either flatter or irritate; the interpretive sections can easily breed an inferiority complex in those who have not enjoyed the rigorous philosophical training of the author. Nolte errs (unlike most historians) in *thinking* too much rather than too little; one suspects, for example, that there is a good portion of Nolte in what purports to be merely a systematic statement of the philosophical foundations of Maurras' doctrine.[3] The attempt to establish a typology of fascism (to be discussed below) shows a tendency to impose *a priori* constructions upon empirical facts. These defects are by no means inconsiderable. It should be stressed, however, that (if this reviewer's experience is any guide) Nolte's book is very much worth the struggle required to master it. It is merely difficult, not intrinsically obscure; and the persevering reader will be rewarded by profound insights not only into the nature of fascism *per se*, but also into the historical configuration of the tragic period of European history of which fascism was part cause and part effect.

II

Nolte's introductory section, "Fascism and the Era of World Wars," describes the historical prerequisites of fascism, classifies its miscellaneous varieties, differentiates between fascism and communism, and defines fascism as a "significant unit of historical study."

What were the historical prerequisites of Europe's Age of Fascism, a period Nolte dates from 1919 to 1945? First and foremost was the pulverizing impact of the First World War upon the predominantly liberal society of nineteenth-century Europe. The war caused not only untold suffering but shook the moorings of a still largely intact traditionalism; both effects intensified the demand of the broad masses for a higher material and psychological stake in the community. This demand provoked a near-hysterical fear of social revolution on the part of the established classes. They were frightened and puzzled by the rise of the Communist world movement, with its elaborate organization, ideology, and mass appeal; they welcomed fascist movements that developed a successful counter-ideology and a counter-organization with similar appeal. The *international* character of the Communist challenge suggested the advantage of a *national* response in an age when nationalism was still burning (if properly stoked) with an explosive intensity. The unspent force of imperialism could also be mobilized, with its suggestion that internal problems could be solved through external conquest. The "scientific rationalism" of communism provoked a counter-appeal to the "irrational currents" that had played an influential role in European culture since the turn of the century. It should not be thought, however, that fascism was exclusively shaped by its hostility to communism; it was equally hostile to the democratic parliamentary system that the liberal nineteenth century had considered the "normal" type of government for a modern industrialized community. This system was denounced as degenerate, corrupt, and incapable of dealing with current problems— a charge that was, unhappily, not totally devoid of substance. Fascism claimed that it would restore the vigorous and effective government needed to deal with the Communist challenge and the many problems left unresolved by "liberal civilization."

Nolte is excellent not only in describing the general political, social, and intellectual situation in which fascism developed in Europe; he also defines the international situation that permitted it to become a major world phenomenon. We know today that the "European Age" of history ended irrevocably in 1917 with the almost simultaneous epochal events of the Russian Revolution and the American entry into the World War. This fact was obscured for contemporaries, however, by two powerful forces whose temporary character was not understood: the revival of American isolationism in the 1920s and the Russian concentration upon building "socialism in one country." These factors created a final opportunity for "autonomous" European development, an opportunity used by the fascist forces to establish a European hegemony that could be overthrown only by the reentry of America and Russia into European affairs in 1941.

The most interesting part of Nolte's introductory section is his taxonomy of the different types of fascism. He defines four different stages under the labels "pre-fascist," "early fascist," "normal fascist," and "radical fascist." Where any given movement belongs depends upon the compound answer to several questions:

(1) What is the movement's relationship to traditional authority, religion, and class structure? There are very traditionalist "pre-fascist" regimes (e.g., Horthy, Pilsudski, Alexander of Yugoslavia, Salazar), less traditionalist "early fascist" regimes (e.g., Franco), non-traditionalist "normal fascist" regimes (e.g., Mussolini), and outright anti-traditionalist "radical fascist" regimes (e.g., Hitler—

though this fact was concealed for opportunistic reasons until the Second World War). Traditionalist regimes are more concerned with defending the past than with constructing a totalitarian future. They lack any basic hostility to such traditional institutions as the monarchy, the church, the army, or the aristocracy. The answer to this first question is crucial in classifying any given example of fascism; much can also be learned, however, from the answer to the following additional questions.

(2) What is the relationship among Caesarist, elitist, and socialist features in a regime? Much depends upon the personal style of the Leader, a fact made obvious when one looks at the very different personalities of, say, Franco and Hitler. The formation of a distinctively fascist elite, standing apart from the traditional upper classes, presents a further criterion of radicalization. The "socialist" features in fascism are in some ways the most fascinating problem of all: the "state socialist" goals of the period prior to the seizure of power tend to be forgotten when power is achieved, only to revive in the period of "racical fascism" under the impact of external misfortune. Mussolini's "Republic of Salo" was more "socialist" than the pre-1943 regime; Hitler became a "Bolshevist of the Right" only in the phase of "total mobilization" as he confronted military defeat.

(3) What is the relationship between particular and universalist elements in ideology and practice? Fascism is, on the one hand, aggressively nationalist (although its elitist conception of rule is quite contrary to the traditional nationalist emphasis upon the unity and homogeneity of the nation), yet it frequently advances a racial doctrine that transcends national borders. The relationship to other fascisms also raises problems, especially in the case of those fascists (Quisling, for example) who secured power only as the result of German occupation. Quisling (assuming that he was not a mere opportunist) presumably believed that allegiance to "world fascism" was a higher allegiance than that owed to the national independence of Norway—though fascists are usually fanatical champions of national independence.

(4) What is the social composition of a given fascist move-

8

ment? There is an invariable lower middle-class core; the crucial question is how far it also reaches into the upper classes, the peasantry, and the proletariat.

(5) What is the real purpose or function of a given fascist regime? Its leaders generally seek power and prestige for themselves, and frequently loot as well. These common motives are not unknown in other regimes and cannot serve the purposes of taxonomy. Nolte finds that fascist regimes may have four types of motivation. They usually begin as dictatorships restoring order in the midst of anarchy, real or alleged (*Festigungsdiktatur*). They subsequently justify themselves by the impetus they give to modernization through a developmental dictatorship (*Entwicklungsdiktatur*). They are not, however, satisfied for long with the peacetime laurels of establishing order and creating prosperity, but begin to show a tendency to embark upon foreign conquest (thus becoming *Raumeroberungsdespotien*). The final motive, fully reached only in the case of Hitler, is to bring salvation to a suffering world by freeing it from a Jewish (or Marxist, or plutocratic) illness. (Nolte calls this *Weltheilungsdespotie*.)

An intransigent hostility to the revolutionary movement of the Left (interpreted as the spearhead of what Nietzsche called the "revolt of the slaves" against the "natural" aristocratic order of society) is characteristic of all fascist movements. This antagonism is rarely one of contemptuous hostility, for a weak enemy would deprive the regime of much of its *raison d'être*. It is often accompanied by a more than grudging respect, as witness Hitler's envious admiration for Stalin (especially after the conspiracy of July 20, 1944, which showed that the Russian dictator had more skill in handling his generals than Hitler) and Mussolini's lifelong fascination with Lenin. Fascism's hostility to communism is shared by democratic and traditionalist regimes, but it differs from both of the latter in the quality and intensity of its response. Fascists meet the danger of Communist ideology by developing a radical counter-ideology, whereas democratic regimes remain pluralist-libertarian, and traditionalist regimes merely reiterate their traditional values. Fascists meet the danger of Communist organization by developing counter-organizations, whereas democratic regimes rely upon the good sense of their citizens,[4] and traditionalist regimes upon intensified police work.

It is a notorious fact that fascist regimes take on many of the features of the Communist enemy they combat (for example, the use of terror, concentration camps, single-party dictatorship, and destruction of man's "private sphere"). Yet it is important to keep communism and fascism sharply distinct for analytical purposes. They differ in their avowed aim, ideological content, circumstances of achieving power, and the groups to which they appeal. Fascists seek the greatness of the nation (which need not exclude a racialist internationalism); Communists, the world triumph of the working class (which need not exclude a strong Russian nationalism). Fascists stand in avowed revolt against the ideas of 1789; Communists pose as the heirs and executors of those ideas. Fascism has a miscellaneous and heterogeneous ideological content; communism prides itself upon the all-embracing logic of its *Weltanschauung*. Fascism glories in an irrational world of struggle; communism aims ultimately at a rational world of peace and harmony (which does not preclude some pride in the violent methods required prior to the final achievement of utopia). Fascism has triumphed in some highly developed communities through abuse of the electoral process (e.g., Germany); communism typically achieves power through military occupation or successful use of violence in backward communities demoralized by prolonged military strains (Russia, Yugoslavia, China). Fascism has special appeal to the lower middle class and sections of the frightened upper class; communism generally finds its greatest resonance in sections of the working class, peasantry, and intelligentsia. Fascism consists, finally, of a series of national movements lacking centralized overall direction, while communism is a centralized world movement in which each member party obeys the orders emanating from a single center. (At least this was true until the Moscow-Peiping split.) For all these reasons, Nolte stands justified in selecting fascism as a "significant unit of historical study" instead of following the current fashion—valid on the level of political science—of exploring the broader phenomenon of "totalitarianism."

10

Nolte delimits his subject matter by the following working definition: "Fascism is anti-Marxism which seeks to destroy the enemy by the evolvement of a radically opposed and yet related ideology and by the use of almost identical and yet typically modified methods, always, however, within the unyielding framework of national self-assertion and autonomy.[5] This definition is obviously geared primarily to the phase of "normal fascism" in the four-phase classification mentioned above; it does not apply to pre-fascism (where ideology and organization remain embryonic) or radical fascism (where the framework of the national state is easily transcended, as in Hitler's racialism). It may be observed that the four types of fascism noted by Nolte—which are *not* necessarily stages that develop in sequence—are sufficiently variegated to obviate the charge that he has imposed his own systematic definition upon heterogeneous phenomena. The line between pre-fascism and (non-fascist) mere traditionalism is obviously fluid; only one fully developed example of the species of "radical fascism" is as yet known (nazism) and can therefore be described by its unique qualities. Nolte is too good a historian to become a prisoner of any general definition (his own included), although his definition performs the useful function of identifying the essential common features of a great number of known fascisms.

Nolte buttresses his view of fascism as a single phenomenon (whose many species are subordinated to a genus) by an appeal to the consensus among previous writers. The most dissimilar authors, advancing the most heterogeneous interpretations, are agreed on the existence of a single fascism that requires explanation. Nolte provides an admirably fair-minded survey of all the general interpretations of fascism hitherto advanced, including the Marxist (e.g., Franz Neumann), liberal (e.g., Luigi Salvatorelli), Christian (e.g., Luigi Sturzo), conservative (e.g., Herman Rauschning), psychoanalytical (e.g., Ignazio Silone), and sociological (e.g., Talcott Parsons).[6] The consensus concerning a "unitary fascism" is reenforced by the sense of solidarity to be found among fascists themselves; sympathy for fellow-fascists was frequently responsible for actions that obviously violated self-interest, as Nolte shows by examples drawn from the careers of Maurras, Mussolini, and Hitler.

11

The conclusion to be derived from the author's classification, definition, and methodological observations is that fascism is a meaningful unit of study, and that it has been the dominant phenomenon of the historical period just preceding our own (with 1945 as the historical watershed). Nolte realizes that to cover fascism exhaustively would mean nothing less than to write a history of the entire period of 1919–1945; even to study the various fascist movements in depth would obviously exceed the strength and linguistic capacity of any single author. He has wisely confined himself, therefore, to sketching out in his introductory section what might become the research program for a future International Center for the Study of Fascism. Having set forth this overall program, he devotes the bulk of his book to a detailed examination of the three important cases of the *Action Française*, Italian Fascism, and German Nazism.

III

No attempt can be made here to discuss the many individual themes developed in the three case studies that form the bulk of *Three Faces of Fascism*. Each of them is a solid monograph based upon impressive mastery of a vast printed literature; each of them seeks to answer particular problems and avoids becoming a mere narrative of generally known facts. A certain want of chronological proportion is the inevitable accompaniment of Nolte's selective method. To give only one example: the history of Italian Fascism before it seized power (three years, 1919–1922) is covered in 94 pages, while Fascism in power (23 years, 1922–1945) is compressed into 43 [in the original German edition—ed.]. This disproportion is fully justified, however, by the important theses that Nolte develops about the young Mussolini and his problematic relationship to the early Fascist Party (both to be discussed below), whereas he has little that is new to say about the years of power. The book is notable for its excellent overall organization. Each of the three sections on the *Action Française*, Italian Fascism, and German Nazism is subdivided into chapters dealing with the history of the movement (including the biography of the Leader), its traditions (i.e., roots in the cultural heritage of the respective countries), its practices (i.e., organizational setup before achieving power, institutional development thereafter), and its doctrine. Nolte is above all interested in the interaction of these four factors, which he finds through his comparative approach to be very different in the three cases studied.

The best way to convey an impression of the richness of Nolte's study is to present some of the results of his comparative approach. The treatment of the three leaders—Charles Maurras, Benito Mussolini, and Adolf Hitler—is a superb study in similarities and contrasts. Each was born in the provinces as a scion of the Catholic petty bourgeoisie and possessed the confidence of the self-made man; each succeeded to a remarkable extent in imposing his personal style upon the movement he headed, though this was less true of Mussolini than of the two others. They differed fundamentally, however, in their personality, political aptitude, and intellectual outlook. Maurras combined a sensitive artistic nature with a complete inflexibility in his substantive opinions after he had reached thirty. His rigidity made him all the more convincing a teacher for those attracted by his views; but it made him an impossible political leader, since he could neither compromise nor adapt to changing circumstances. His inflexibility brought him to the tragically false position of the years 1940–1945 and hence to his post-Liberation trial and imprisonment. Maurras had in fact never collaborated with the Germans in *subjective* intent; he simply had not understood that his anti-Semitic tirades assumed a new significance through the new circumstance that the Gestapo was now hunting Jews in occupied France.

Mussolini was, by contrast, an eminently practical man with great flexibility and adaptability. It is easy to denounce him as a mere opportunist, but Nolte shows that at least his most controversial change of position—the shift from socialist internationalism to nationalist interventionism in 1914—was contrary to his personal interests: he abandoned a position of great influence in the Socialist Party to enter upon years of uncertainty and isolation. Nolte succeeds, in one of the most brilliant sections of the book, in depicting Mussolini's intellectual development with considerable sympathy by identifying a consistent socialist strain through all the stages of

Mussolini's career. Before 1914 he was a fervid Marxist, though one accessible to the "philosophy of life" exemplified by Nietzsche (who influenced him far more than either Bergson or Sorel). Nolte shows that Mussolini's pre-1914 views often strained the limits of what could still be considered orthodox Marxism (exactly as in the comparable case of Lenin), yet never unmistakably went beyond them.[7] The decision to support Italy's intervention in the 1914 war could be covered by the Marxist formula of permissible wars of liberation; in Mussolini's eyes, it was part of the necessary task of freeing Italian Marxism from its doctrinaire rigidity. He aimed, in his own words, "To reaffirm socialist ideals and review them in the light of the criticism under the present terrible lesson of facts." [8] He annoyed many of his followers in 1921 by declaring the education of the Socialists to "national responsibility" to be one of the primary goals of the Fascist Party; he contemplated a parliamentary coalition with the Socialists and Popolari that year; and there is some reason to believe that he wanted to take Turati, the Socialist leader, into his government as late as 1925. His dictatorship was, at least until 1935, predominantly a developmental one (*Entwicklungsdiktatur*) with great achievements in the modernization of Italy. Nolte notes, finally, the explicitly socialist program of the "Republic of Salo" in 1943–1945: Mussolini at that time openly repented of the concessions made to monarchy and plutocracy in the heyday of his power.

How different a figure was Hitler! In treating him Nolte is forced to abandon his favorite method of "intellectual biography" for a psychological approach which emphasizes the monomanic, infantile, and fear-obsessed sides of Hitler's personality. His systematic doctrine (if his crude ideas can be dignified with this name) had all the static consistency of Maurras' system, while being of course on a much lower intellectual level. Hitler's basic premise was fear for the future of the German race, which he saw as mortally threatened by a Jewish world conspiracy; this obsessive fear constituted the never-changing keynote of his outlook from the earliest political utterances in Vienna to his final testament written in the crumbling Berlin Chancellery.[9] Hitler must be described as an "honest fanatic" in his anti-Semitic convictions: what makes his career so

14

grisly is that he combined this fanaticism with the tactical flair necessary to seize power, and used that power to translate his intellectual obsessions into the physical destruction of all Jews within his grasp. He pursued this program with fanatical tenacity as long as he could, and bequeathed it as a legacy to his followers just before his suicide.

The mode of death of the three leaders is, incidentally, symptomatic of much of their careers. Maurras retained his inflexibility in prison (1946–1952) but returned to Catholicism just before his death: a sign that he had not completely lost touch with that Christian conservatism which had stood at the cradle of his kind of prefascism. Mussolini showed, on the other hand, a flexibility almost indistinguishable from weakness, and explicable only by his personal disintegration. He allowed himself (quite unnecessarily, it seems) to be "legally" deposed from power after the famous meeting of the Fascist Grand Council on July 25, 1943; he consented in his Salo period to become a puppet of the Germans, whom he had always hated (although sometimes hypnotized by their power and achievement); he allowed himself, finally, to be arrested disguised in a German uniform, and to be killed under circumstances that showed no regard for his historical position. He showed that he was *not*, in the last resort, a man of fanatical conviction who could impose himself upon his environment. Hitler's death was very different: he chose suicide after keeping unchallenged control of Germany's governmental apparatus until the end; his manner of death precluded an abuse of his corpse similar to that of the murdered Mussolini, who was exhibited like a slaughtered pig in Milan; and he bequeathed a strident testament to his followers that he believed might yet develop historical efficacy. Hitler's last days saw only a further exaggeration of the pathological sides of his personality: they remained unrelieved by the slightest trace of self-examination, let alone repentance.

The three movements analyzed had very different relationships to the national traditions of their respective countries. The *Action Française* was a not unimpressive synthesis of the strains of three French schools of thought: Christian conservatism (Maistre, Bonald), critical liberalism (Comte, Le Play, Renan, Taine,

15

Fustel de Coulanges), and radical conservatism (de La Tour du Pin, Drumont, Barrès). It was firmly rooted in one part of the national tradition, while rejecting completely that greater part symbolized by the ideas of 1789. Italian Fascism was, on the other hand, confronted by only *one* vital national tradition, the *Risorgimento:* it could never make up its mind whether to interpret itself as the continuation, fulfillment, or repudiation of that glorious period of Italian history. At any rate there can be no question that Fascism was never deeply rooted in Italian soil: the nation's rather mixed but essentially irrepressible traditions of Catholicism, radicalism, and anarchism made it immune to thorough fascistization (a point insufficiently stressed by Nolte). Nazism was rooted in an anti-Semitic tradition that was international rather than distinctively German in character (Gobineau, Vacher de Lapouge, Chamberlain), though it probably had more—and, above all, more fervid—followers in Germany than in the other Western European countries. In the opinion of this reviewer, Nolte does not stress adequately the *indirect* roots of Nazism in certain factors of German history, for example, the anachronistic survival of the authoritarian state (*Obrigkeitsstaat*). While *not* proto-Nazi in nature (as believed by Shirer and his school), it nonetheless prevented the mature development of those modern forces—liberalism, democratic socialism, left-wing Catholicism, responsible conservatism—alone capable of offering effective resistance to a fascist onslaught. (This point will be discussed in detail below.)

The most interesting comparisons are to be made in the field of *practice*, both before and after the fascist achievement of power. Nolte shows brilliantly how the *Action Française* anticipated, in a way sometimes embryonic, sometimes rarefied, many of the institutional features of fascism: the *Camelots du Roi,* the storm troopers; the *Nouvelle Librairie Nationale,* the *Eher Verlag;* the *Institut d'Action Française,* the Nazi *Ordensburgen.* The value of the *Action Française* for comparative purposes is, however, limited by the fact that it never won power, whereas Fascism and Nazism offer an endless field for historical comparisons. Both Mussolini and Hitler won control of the state when the upper classes panicked in the face of the Communist danger and thought a fascist government necessary

16

to preserve the social *status quo;* they also trusted that the Duce or Führer would put a leash upon their own extremist followers, and relieved their uneasiness at fascist rowdyism by the belief that power generally breeds responsibility. There were, however, considerable differences in the circumstances under which that power was attained. The Italy of 1920–1922 was in a genuine situation of civil war; Germany in 1930–1933 knew only sporadic—though for a civilized community quite intolerable—violence. Mussolini continued to experience organized opposition for several years and long remained a contested figure even within the Fascist movement; the early German opposition to Hitler was paralyzed by the fact that the majority of the German people succumbed in 1933 to an euphoric mood of national revolution. The Nazis established a totalitarian dictatorship in a matter of months, acting in accordance with plans clearly conceived in advance; Mussolini, on the other hand, was for some years satisfied to head a multiparty coalition and was driven into totalitarianism as much by the intransigence of his opponents (who refused to confine their criticism to detail, but struck at the foundations of this system) as by the extremism of his followers. The antagonism between party members and storm troopers (so important in the early history of Nazism) was almost unknown in early Fascism, where membership in the party and in the combat units was nearly identical. Hitler aimed at converting men to his *Weltanschauung* through public meetings, and valued the SA primarily for the removal of alien elements that might break the emotional communion between Leader and followers; when Röhm tried to turn the SA into an auxiliary army he aroused Hitler's suspicion. Mussolini had no cohesive *Weltanschauung* to preach, hence public meetings did not play the central role in his movement; the *squadristi* did not perform the limited functions of the SA, and arose in fact quite independently of Mussolini in the civil war that raged in several parts of Italy from 1919 to 1922.

The differences between Fascism and Nazism become especially striking after the seizure of power. Both regimes rested upon a potent combination of spontaneous consent, propaganda, and terror; there was, however, nothing in Italy comparable to the openly sanctioned terror that broke out in Germany on June 30, 1934.

Both regimes aimed at foreign conquest, but differed significantly in opportunity and ultimate intent. Mussolini headed a nation with only a marginal Great Power potential; he could conquer Ethiopia and Albania only through skillful exploitation of an international situation not of his own creation. Hitler controlled a Great Power still capable of starting and sustaining (though not winning) a major war. The war unleashed in 1939 was from the beginning far more than a conventional "war of national restitution," aiming to break the remaining shackles of Versailles; it was even more than a conventional "war of conquest," since it aimed at the decimation of Slavic peoples for the sake of *Lebensraum* in the East. It was, in fact, the culmination of Hitler's obsession with the "Jewish illness" which he sought to cure through the total elimination of European Jewry. Hitler was able to impose his fantastic policies, derived from his personal obsessions and applied with a systematic rigor rare in history, only because he ruled over a remarkably docile people. There was nothing comparable to this in Italian Fascism, though one must not minimize the odious mistreatment of the conquered Ethiopians or the introduction (apparently without strong German pressure) of anti-Semitic legislation in 1938.

It is a weakness of Nolte's book—rooted, I believe in the fact that he is more interested in a systematic than a historical treatment of fascism—that he does not provide an adequate explanation of why fascism took on a unique form in Germany. It would be absurd to suggest that the vast majority of the German people approved (or even knew) of the horrors perpetrated in their name; but it must be said that there was altogether too much acquiescence in what was done *because* it was done by duly constituted authority, and a widespread desire *not to want to know*. Nolte says in a notable passage that few Germans *had* to know the full horror of the Nazi policies, but nearly all were *able* to know a significant part of the truth.[10] The cause for their attitude is to be sought primarily in human nature in general, from which it is unreasonable to expect either great political insight or moral courage; moreover, one must always remember that the slightest protest against Nazi atrocities had ruinous consequences not only for oneself but one's family: those of us who have never been in a comparable situation should

18

avoid pharisaism in judgment. It is true, nonetheless, that acquiescence to the policies of a criminal government was partly due to *German* human nature as it had been shaped (of course not for all time, but for the period here considered) by the facts of Germany's exceptionally unhappy modern history. Bismarck, who had reason to know, once deplored the want of civic courage (*Zivilcourage*) among his fellow-countrymen; it is certain that this was part of a tradition that created the prerequisites for a government that was surely the most monstrous of recorded history. These considerations clearly go beyond what can be treated in a review article; suffice it to say that Nolte *describes* the unique features of German fascism but—contrary to his usual practice—makes too little attempt to *explain* them.

IV

Nolte has achieved (despite the last reservation) impressive results in the comparative study of fascism, and is fully aware of (indeed, stresses) the highly developed individuality of the three systems examined; yet his main interest is the interpretation of fascism as a *general* phenomenon. This is the purpose of his final section, "Fascism as a Metapolitical Phenomenon": it provides a comprehensive theory which incorporates many elements drawn explicitly from the thought of Karl Marx, Friedrich Nietzsche, and Max Weber. The theory may be outlined as follows: The dominant fact of modern history is the evolution of "bourgeois society," a term that Nolte uses to describe essentially what Marx dealt with in the famous section of the Communist Manifesto hailing the achievements of the bourgeoisie: the destruction of the confining *particular* ties of class, nation, religion, etc., as society becomes characterized by a high degree of *universality*. Nolte calls this trend (of which industrialization is the key element) "practical transcendence"—i.e., transcending *in this world* the particularities which had previously limited man's freedom. The yearning of man for freedom from particular ties is, of course, far older than the modern process of industrialization; it has, indeed, been one of the main themes of Western history since the philosophical position of idealism was first formulated in ancient Greece by Parmenides.

19

Nolte calls the idealist position, with its confrontation between the world of things (limited by the laws of number, space, and time) and the world of "true Being" (or "the One," or "Nature," or God—all expressing what is unitary, infinite, and eternal), "theoretical transcendence"—i.e., transcending the particularities of this world by entering into a supramundane world of theory. The schism between things and true Being is mirrored in human nature in the schism between our particular concrete existence and our capacity for universal, abstract thought. The latter allows us to enter the world of "true Being" and to derive from it general ideals that are then used to criticize the particular world of things. The result is a *demand* that the world be changed and a *belief* that change is possible: this has proved one of the factors behind the modern "emancipatory process," and in this sense theoretical transcendence is one of the factors behind practical transcendence. The realization of practical transcendence is one of the greatest events in history, for it means that "philosophy and religion are no longer taken for granted as offering the sole possibilities of relating to the whole." [11] The possibility now exists that man can become emancipated from particular ties in *this* world—this at least is the utopian vision of Marx, who believed that the residual particular fetters which still confined man in bourgeois society (exploitation, subjection to the division of labor, and political domination) could be eliminated with the establishment of socialism; theoretical transcendence would then no longer be necessary, since man's striving for freedom would be fully satisfied through the triumph of practical transcendence. [12]

    This paraphrase of Nolte's philosophical framework surely bears out what he says himself with a tinge of self-irony: "The discussion seems to have moved a long way from fascism into the undemonstrable realm (*Unanschaulichkeit*) of metaphysical terminology." [13] It is improbable that Nolte shares Marx's vision of the perfectly free man fully integrated into a world of practical transcendence (though the final paragraph of the book has a *prima facie* utopian ring)—but he clearly affirms the inevitability of the "advance" to practical transcendence. His condemnation of bolshevism is comparatively lenient because—however great its vices—it at least promotes practical transcendence, though its use of compulsion and repression of criticism produce many unpleasant features. It is the glory of bourgeois society that it encourages spontaneous "advance" to the accompaniment of much self-criticism—the danger being that this criticism degenerates easily into downright hostility. Criticism within the limits of overall acceptance of transcendence is laudable and can play a humanizing role; downright hostility Nolte finds understandable, but he insists that it only serves further to complicate problems already intrinsically difficult to solve.

The process of transcendence inevitably arouses fears, for it not only threatens but brings about the loss of much that is dear and familiar to man. It must be remembered that man not only yearns for freedom but also clings to the particularities that both confine and shelter him. The pulverizing process of practical transcendence inevitably arouses opposition: an opposition that first crystallized in conservatism, only to become invigorated and vulgarized in fascism. Nolte gives the following interpretative definition of "radical fascism" to supplement his earlier empirical definition of "normal fascism": "National Socialism was the death throes of the sovereign, martial, inwardly antagonistic group. It was the practical and violent resistance to transcendence" [14]—a process that was leading inevitably to a world of internationalism, pacifism, and equality. Fascism furthermore did not limit itself to the struggle against practical transcendence; it also opposed theoretical transcendence because the yearning for the universal stood in the way of fascism's idolization of the particular. The most characteristic feature of fascist doctrine was the belief that the progress of transcendence was *not* an inevitable development, but rather the result of a Jewish conspiracy that could still be stopped if sufficiently brutal methods were employed. The Nazi resistance to the inevitable had all the violent futility characteristic of death struggles.

Nolte shows in an especially brilliant chapter [15] that the essence of fascism—resistance to transcendence—was anticipated by Friedrich Nietzsche. He far from supports the once popular doctrine that Nietzsche "caused" nazism; but *his* Nietzsche is nonetheless very different from the transfigured Nietzsche known to most American scholars from the important work of Walter Kaufmann. The "slave revolt" that so horrified the German philosopher took place in the name of a morality rooted in "theoretical transcendence." Nietzsche scarcely knew the work of Marx, yet he himself constituted the antipode of the latter's conviction that the world can and should be changed. Nietzsche opposed the desirability of change by the idolization of the existing world, as joyously mastered by the overman in the Here and Now. He did not hesitate to call for an alliance between military castes and intellectuals to defend the *status quo;* his main purpose was the "nontranscendental self-assertion of the sovereign, martial, and inwardly antagonistic group" [16]—exactly what Nolte interprets as the essence of fascism. Maurras and Hitler were devoted to the same purpose, though their outlook (especially the latter's) was of course infinitely more primitive intellectually, and both (especially Hitler) used methods that would have made Nietzsche shudder.

It is difficult to pass a definite judgment on Nolte's interpretation of fascism, both because of its abstractness and because it is part of a general interpretation of man's modern history—and indeed man's fate!—which can only be sketched out in a review article. It is paradoxical that the interpretation of fascism he offers applies least well to the Italian Fascism that has given the genus its name. If Mussolini in fact headed a developmental dictatorship (*Entwicklungsdiktatur*) promoting industrialization (a key feature of practical transcendence), he clearly does not belong among the antitranscendentalists; it can be argued, of course, that the "really" fascist character of his Fascism emerged only with the Ethiopian conquest (1935) and the anti-Semitic legislation (1938). It appears to this reviewer that Nolte's overall interpretation is more impressive in its scope than helpful in its exploration of the concrete phenomenon that was fascism. The proof of this is to be found in the excellence of Nolte's preliminary empirical survey of fascism and his individual treatment of the *Action Française,* Italian Fascism, and German Nazism; both are virtually unaffected by his excursion into the metapolitical in his concluding section. Their value will be appreciated by the many readers who will fail to agree with (or, more likely, fail to understand) Nolte's concluding section.

What makes Nolte's book great despite its unhelpful metaphysical abstractions is the range of subject matter covered, the pioneering comparative treatment, the thoroughness of the scholarship, and the moral seriousness of the author. A deep compassion for the predicament of twentieth-century man often breaks through the most abstract pages and the most heroic (and remarkably successful) efforts at "objectivity." The author's meticulous scholarship gives firm support to many challenging theses developed throughout the book. The value of the comparative approach has been indicated above; the fact that it has been employed here for the first time in depth is a deplorable commentary on the still widespread compartmentalization of history along national lines. The author has succeeded in his primary task of establishing the *epochal* character of fascism for the period 1919–1945 and defining its historical prerequisites. His empirical survey of the varieties of fascism, and his theoretical construction of a fascist "ideal type," constitute a valuable prolegomena to all future studies in fascism. It is to be hoped, but scarcely to be expected, that future works will reach the same level of scholarly precision, explicitly elaborated theoretical concepts, and the right mixture of objectivity and engagement.

[1] *Three Faces of Fascism* (New York, Chicago, San Francisco, 1966), p. 531; (New York and Toronto, 1969), p. 652; *Der Faschismus in seiner Epoche* (Munich, 1963), p. 608. Hereafter page references to the two American editions will be indicated thusly: p. 531/p. 652. The pagination of the first American edition corresponds to that of the British edition of *Three Faces of Fascism* (London, 1966).

[2] *Three Faces*, p. 382 ff./pp. 482 ff; *Der Faschimus*, pp. 464 ff.

[3] *Three Faces*, pp. 135–41/pp. 182–89; *Der Faschismus*, pp. 183–90.

[4] Such is, at least, the ideal case. In practice, even democratic regimes frequently fall into fascist practices when combating communism, as the United States did in the McCarthy period. Is it needless to add that there is a world of difference between fascist practices *within* a predominantly liberal system, and fascism *per se?*

[5] *Three Faces*, pp. 20–21/p. 40; *Der Faschismus*, p. 51.

[6] Nolte finds considerable merit in all these interpretations, while adding his own in the concluding section. He has no use, on the other hand, for the "anti-German" interpretation (e.g., William L. Shirer's) that sees Nazism only as the extreme manifestation of a perennially wicked German national character. Even if true, this approach is of no value in interpreting fascism as a *general* phenomenon—indeed, it precludes fruitful generalization by being hypnotized by the particular German case, which, while an especially odious species, can nonetheless be subsumed under the general genus of "fascism."

[7] This theme is enlarged in a valuable article by Ernst Nolte, "Marx und Nietzsche im Sozialismus des jungen Mussolini," *Historische Zeitschrift*, Vol. 191 (1960), 249–335.

[8] *Three Faces*, p. 172/p. 226; *Der Faschismus*, p. 225.

[9] Nolte has discovered an important new source that documents the central role of anti-Semitism in Hitler's Weltanschauung: Dietrich Eckart, *Der Bolschewismus von Moses bis Lenin. Zwiegespräch zwischen Adolf Hitler und mir* (Munich 1924). Nolte gives an excellent analysis in "Eine frühe Quelle zu Hitlers Antisemitismus," *Historische Zeitschrift*, Vol. 192 (1961), 584–606.

[10] *Three Faces*, p. 359/p. 453; *Der Faschismus*, p. 438.

[11] *Three Faces*, p. 432/p. 541; *Der Faschismus*, p. 519.

[12] Nolte gives an excellent account of Max Weber's criticism of the utopian strain in Marxism in a special chapter (*Three Faces*, pp. 446–50/pp. 558–63; *Der Faschismus*, pp. 535–40). He notes—I think, with a tone of reproach—that Weber faced bourgeois society in a spirit of hesitating courage. His view of Weber is expressed at length in an important article: "Max Weber vor dem Faschismus," *Der Staat*, II (1963), 1–24. Nolte shows in a provocative fashion that some of Weber's

substantive views (e.g., his Freiburg *Antrittsrede* in 1895) possess a remarkable similarity to Hitler's and that his ambivalence towards the process of modernization might have proved a source of weakness in the face of fascism; he does not question, of course, that Weber would have become a foe of fascism if he had lived until 1933. Nolte also demonstrates that Weber's sociology shows little anticipation of fascism, and that the concept of charisma is misunderstood when applied to the Hitler-Mussolini type of leadership—facts indicating that fascism was "one of the least expected phenomena of political history and therefore one of the most difficult to explain" (p. 24).

[13] *Three Faces*, p. 434/p. 543; *Der Faschismus*, p. 521.

[14] *Three Faces*, p. 421/p. 529; *Der Faschismus*, p. 507.

[15] *Three Faces*, pp. 441–46/pp. 551–58; *Der Faschismus*, pp. 529–34.

[16] *Three Faces*, p. 446/p. 558; *Der Faschismus*, p. 535.

2

The Problem of Fascism
in Recent Scholarship

BY ERNST NOLTE

It is not easy to determine precisely when the concept of fascism became a problem in post-war scholarly literature; what is certain is that for many years fascism was first regarded as self-evident and then, in the western world, as a tabu. Thus the study *Fascism in Action*, which appeared under American auspices in 1947, reflects an official interpretation, according to which the Second World War was a struggle of "democracy" against the "fascist powers," among which not only Germany and Italy but also Japan were unhesitatingly included.[1]

The onset of the Cold War altered this situation fundamentally. In the new atmosphere, the concept of totalitarianism, which in the writings of Sigmund Neumann[2] and Franz Neumann[3] had been chiefly oriented toward fascism, was transformed in 1951 by Hannah Arendt. The unmistakable thrust of her book, *The Origins of Totalitarianism*, was to equate Nazism and Stalinism and to subsume Italian Fascism, along with Franco's Spain and Horthy's Hungary, under the rubric of mere authoritarianism.[4] This approach prevailed in western historical writing during the next decade, even though it was subjected to numerous variations.[5] That the concept of fascism was accorded at most a subordinate role is obviously attributable to its unmistakably disturbing implications for western society at a time when the virtues of western democracy seemed so evident. As a result, the old and new attempts to identify imperialism with fascism, which held sway in the literature of the "East Bloc," were dismissed as mere propaganda; to be sure, unless I am mistaken, this attempt at identifying imperialism with fascism has yet to find expression in a significant scholarly work.[6]

Thus it was that the problem of fascism became virtually an Italian specialty. All too often it was handled in a simplistic fashion under the reconciling banner of a broad "anti-fascism," with the primary aim being to rescue the national tradition of the Italian state by drawing the sharpest possible line between the Risorgimento and Fascism. The efforts of those who placed primary emphasis on the relationship between the German past and National Socialism—and who shared the latter topic with the totalitarianism school—were directed in exactly the opposite direction, namely toward establishing the derivation of Nazism from the German national tradition. Because of the prevalence of these approaches, it was impossible for the concept of fascism to gain recognition as a problem, except in a marginal fashion, within the framework of the dominant schools of interpretation.

It is perhaps permissible to regard the years 1959 and 1960 as the beginning of a change, a change that was certainly related to an alteration in the world situation characterized by a relaxation in the Cold War, the onset of polycentrism in the East, and a renewed readiness for self-criticism in the West. In 1959, after a long hiatus, the concept of fascism once again appeared in the title of a book, if not a scholarly one.[7] In the same year, Dante L. Germino published a book in which he employed the concepts of Carl J. Friedrich and concluded that Italian Fascism was a fully developed totalitarianism and thus should not be regarded in a different light than Nazism.[8] Starting from very different presuppositions, Seymour Martin Lipset published, also in 1959, an article in which he re-introduced class analysis into the discussion of fascism, thus again raising the question of its relationship to western society.[9] In 1960 Ralf Dahrendorf published an article on democracy and social structure in Germany which, although framed basically in terms of a search for the roots of Nazism in the German past, went beyond the confines of German history, thus following the examples of Dahrendorf's predecessors, Lipset and Talcott Parsons.[10] In the same year, my article on the influence of Marx and Nietzsche on

27

Mussolini's early thought appeared, announcing my intention to subject the concept of fascism to historical analysis on the basis of newly discovered source materials.[11] Thereafter, the concept of fascism rapidly gained acceptance so that by the end of the 1960's it could be regarded as a newly established field of scholarly inquiry; in addition, the word "fascism" had by then been revived as a widely used political battle-cry. Although the list of publications is not yet boundless, it is already necessary to exclude certain categories of writing in order to deal with the subject of fascism in a short essay. It should be recognized that such exclusions are unavoidably somewhat arbitrary, since the boundaries between categories of writings are seldom sharply delineated and since there are few books on modern politics which do not assume and discuss one concept or another of fascism. Still, in this essay the following categories of publications will not be considered: polemical and apologetic writings; historical descriptions of one or more fascist movements; analyses of single aspects of fascism; biographical works; essays by scholars whose main interests lie elsewhere; theoretical works written before 1945; and studies dealing with "neo-fascism."

This essay will thus deal only with studies primarily concerned with the concept of fascism as a generic phenomenon or those in which the legitimacy of that concept is either explicitly endorsed or assumed. One such study is the article by Lipset mentioned above. Its point of departure is the most generally accepted yet at the same time most vague thesis of all about the nature of fascism: that it was an extremism of the middle class. According to Lipset, the middle class is democratic as long as democracy protects and furthers its interests, but it turns to populist extremism whenever it is threatened by an economic crisis. This is in no respect limited to Germany or to the inter-war era. A considerable part of Lipset's article is devoted to post-war phenomena such as the Italian neo-fascist party, the *Movimento Soziale Italiano*, and to the Poujadist party in the fourth French Republic. Still, Lipset draws his crucial evidence from the German election statistics for the years prior to the Nazi take-over. Those statistics leave no doubt that the Nazis' electoral successes must be attributed mainly to the votes of former supporters of the liberal parties or special interest parties such as the "Economy party" (*Wirtschaftspartei*). However, in the course of his analysis Lipset casts considerable doubt on the validity of this extremely simple model, which attempts to explain modern history in terms of a tripartite social structure—upper class, middle class, working class—and a neat duality according to which each of these three social groups expresses itself politically in normal times in a moderate, democratic fashion that is different for each class, while in times of crisis each responds with a distinctive form of anti-democratic extremism. From his assumptions, for example, it follows that the traditional upper class has its own form of extremism which must necessarily be essentially different from that of the middle class. Lipset sees this upper-class extremism embodied in the authoritarianism of Franco, Horthy and DeGaulle. But is not this authoritarianism the oldest and most obvious tradition of the European Right? And what is the democratic alternative of the Right, which in normal times should, according to Lipset's model, replace the authoritarianism of periods of crisis? What Lipset seems to have in mind here is nothing more than the rightist liberalism of the upper middle class, which has always tended to align itself with the traditional authoritarianism of the old upper class (as opposed to a new authoritarianism spawned by crisis). Moreover, it is obvious that Nazi ideology had more in common with that of the conservative, upper-class German Right than with the Jacobin-like populism of the Poujadist movement. There can be just as little doubt that in Germany and Italy the "extremism of the middle class" allied with the "extremism of the upper class" in violently opposing what Lipset describes as the "extremism of the lower class," namely communism. However, Lipset also classifies as such an "extremism of the lower class" the Peronism of the 1940's and 1950's, which in many ways manifested sympathy for and emulated fascism. Is it not conceivable that fascism is a phenomenon which can bridge all three of Lipset's classes, even if it cannot eliminate their conflicts of interest? What needs to be explained is not that the Nazi Party consisted predominantly of members of the middle class (a group whose upper and lower boundaries have never been established with any accuracy) but rather that the party attracted so many workers and noteworthy figures from the upper class. The rigidity of Lipset's sociological model thus does damage to the overarching elements of historical unity involved, that is, those aspects of fascism that cannot be contained in the categories of the model. Similarly, this model proves inadequate to the historical complexities. It is, for example, clear in Lipset's own analysis that factors other than class were of great significance in the rise of Nazism, factors such as religious denomination, region, sex, generation. Catholic members of the middle class voted Nazi in much smaller numbers than did their Protestant counterparts; East Prussia—cut off from the rest of the country territorially by the Polish Corridor—tended to be more rightist than Hesse, secure in the center of Germany; married women were far more conservative than their husbands; the younger generation turned to Nazism in greater numbers than did their elders. The war and the general intellectual climate, moreover, receive virtually no attention from Lipset, although it is entirely conceivable that these factors were more fundamental causes of the emergence of fascism than class interests and provide a better explanation for the elements of both unity and complexity which elude Lipset's sociological model.

To grasp the *historical* essence of fascism was the intent of my book, as expressed in the original German title, which can be translated as "Fascism in its Era." If there was in fact an "era of Fascism," then it would not be possible for the "same" sociological configuration in a different period and under other world conditions to produce an historically relevant phenomenon that can qualify as fascism, at least not—as spelled out in another of my studies [12]—in the form of European national fascism, which is all I am concerned with in my book. On the other hand, fascism is in my book in no respect severed from the societies within which it grew. It is, as the title indicated, conceived of as generic and thus international. Its sociological dimension is implicit throughout the book; it is explicitly discussed in the last sub-chapter, "Outline of a Transcendental Sociology of this Period," as well as in the first section of my book on the crisis of the liberal system and the fascist movements.[13] What is vitally important to note is that the society which makes fascism possible cannot be accounted for with an abstraction such as "capitalism." The history of Europe has produced a multifarious social order, in which the most disparate institutional structures and ideologies exist side by side. It is the public and political resolution of the contradictions in this multifarious society that can result in a reconciling and unifying process, which in the economic sphere is called "capitalism." This "capitalism" is no static institution but rather a perpetually evolving phenomenon whose simple and easily comprehended early phases of production and exchange contrast paradoxically with a future which promises to be one of concentrated interdependence of a sort that can no longer be described as "capitalistic."

This sort of development is not a process of nature that takes place without the knowledge or participation of mankind. From a certain point on, it challenges human thought to become the force that establishes coherence and points the way to the future—a fragile and fallible force which shapes the process of change and leads it in peculiar directions as soon as that process becomes a matter of everyday life and begins to affect people in an organized fashion. This organizing, or ideological, thought arises from objective, material factors and is never free of dependence upon them. But its relationship to objective, material factors is not a simple one: it neither determines the course of events in an absolute sense nor does it merely mirror them. Instead, human thought is ultimately the essence of the process of history. My initial definition of fascism is thus derived from this historical-ideological point of departure: "Fascism is anti-Marxism which seeks to destroy the enemy by the evolvement of a radically opposed and yet related ideology and by the use of almost identical and yet typically modified methods, always, however, within the unyielding framework of national self-assertion and autonomy." [14]

This definition would have remained an empty construct had it not been anchored in the historical record, so my book is an attempt to combine theoretical formulations with detailed historical analysis. Precisely this is the phenomenological method; a detached and therefore critical, although not polemical, description of a social phenomenon, all of whose multifarious aspects are allowed, as it were, to gain expression, forcing one to come to grips with the

31

uniqueness of the phenomenon in a manner impossible if one merely attempts to describe it in terms of other phenomena. This self-portrayal of a phenomenon must, however, take place in a framework of the widest scope of possibilities, and ultimately the phenomenon must be viewed in terms of the historical process bursting its own bounds, that is, in terms of transcendence. This explains the inclusion in my book of the *Action Française* and the significance of my third and final definition of fascism as "practical and violent resistence to transcendence." [15] That definition in no sense reduces fascism to mere "reaction," since the accent is meant to be on the adjectives and since that definition applies in full only to National Socialism as the most radical manifestation of a phenomenon marked by internal gradations.

If one takes as a basis the categories spelled out in the introduction to my volume on theories about fascism,[16] the mode of interpretation in my *Three Faces of Fascism* is one that conceives of fascism as a generic and autonomous force, one that is metapolitical and phenomenological. It describes fascism as regressive, but not simply reactionary, and attributes its appearance neither to chance nor necessity, but rather to that "necessity of chance" that is the distinguishing feature of historical phenomena.

This description is, however, obviously too abstract, even if it succeeds in taking into account the factor of individuality. Following its publication in German in 1963, *Three Faces of Fascism* had the remarkable fate of being accepted as a primarily scholarly achievement only in the United States. In Europe it was regarded as a basically political work which nevertheless was accorded praise from one end of the political spectrum to the other, from the radical Left to the radical Right, although none of these camps lay claim to it unreservedly in order to buttress its own position. It is in fact a book that is not easy to classify.

The influence of Marxism on *Three Faces of Fascism* is unmistakable, even though the "absence of the economic dimension" has been criticized by Marxists. The latter dimension is absent, however, only in the form of trivial or questionable details and the even more trivial or questionable assignment of a causal role in politics to certain economic processes. The economic dimension occupies a fundamental place in my analysis in the form of "practical transcendence," the most simple and at the same time most comprehensive designation for those "productive forces" whose allegedly boundless capacity for ever higher achievement is a mystical focal point of Marxist doctrine. Furthermore, the historic-ideological approach of my book was obviously influenced by the role which the ideology of Marxism has played in recent history. But the conclusions are anything but Marxist. To the contrary, Marxism's contention that it alone possesses the ability to predict the future is decisively refuted by the fact that the era of fascism began precisely at a time when according to Lenin and virtually all other Marxist theoreticians only two political alternatives remained: "bourgeois democracy" and "the dictatorship of the proletariat."

It can hardly be denied that *Three Faces of Fascism* is basically liberal in the sense of affirming the liberal social order of the West. This affirmation is, however, far removed from love or admiration. Indeed, the underlying question seems to be how dynamism can be sustained by the coexistence in the West of political traditions that no longer have their original vitality. On the other hand, there is an unmistakable respect for the Communist parties as organizing and disciplining forces, although the state socialist regimes are regarded as flawed contrivances whose only goal is the achievement of a temporarily heightened efficiency.

Obviously, a book that accords a central role to practical transcendence cannot be conservative. Still, it is impossible not to notice conservative overtones in *Three Faces of Fascism*, since transcendence is assigned neither positive nor negative valuation, being assigned a thoroughly ambivalent status far removed from any glorification of "progress." Indeed, I emphasize at the end of the book that transcendence is not the earthy place of repose for a mortal humanity but rather its "throne of glory and its martyr's cross." [17]

Finally, my refusal to concede that theoretical transcendence can be replaced by practical transcendence places *Three Faces of Fascism* squarely in the tradition of Christianity and the ancient world. But the consequence of my refusal is not hope but a skepticism which, while not denying the efficacy of worldly activity, sets limitations to its powers of achievement.

33

It is hardly correct to conclude that *Three Faces of Fascism* is nothing more than a book that sets forth a theory about fascism. But a final verdict on the book must await an answer to the question of whether it is eclectic or synthetic. Until now, however, this question has not even been asked of the book.

Eugen Weber's *Varieties of Fascism* also demonstrates that any serious theory about fascism must of necessity be an interpretation of a whole era and thus something distinct from both conventional historical treatments of the inter-war period and Marxist orthodoxy. In contrast to my study, Weber takes the revolutionary rather than the conservative aspect of fascism as his point of departure, setting Charles Maurras, whom he classifies among the "true reactionaries," in sharp contrast to fascism.[18] Weber's characterization of fascism as a kind of collectivistic nationalism comes close to giving it the appearance of a form of socialism more appropriate to its time than the international version of socialism, whose failure was no accident. For Weber, as for Lipset, fascism is a populism, but a populism which stood up for the workers and whose following was drawn to no small extent from the ranks of the workers. Weber, moreover, displays a remarkable degree of detached understanding for the racism of the Rumanian Iron Guard and the Hungarian Arrow Cross, showing that this racism derived from the disproportionate over-representation of the Jewish minority in certain occupations. In his frame of reference, Nazism represents not a radical form of fascism but rather a kind of hypertrophy which departed fatefully from the pragmatic cast of Italian Fascism by according a primacy to doctrine. The result was that Nazism dug its own grave. Because of its doctrinal rigidity, it proved incapable of exploiting even potentially advantageous opportunities, such as an alliance with the Ukrainians against the Communists after the invasion of the Soviet Union. It ended by committing an ideologically motivated outrage which resembled a senseless nightmare more than a crime committed for any rational and profitable purpose: "The Germans murdered a people for a dream, a strange dream which fanatical purpose turned to nightmare." [19] In the case of the Iron Guard as well, Weber concludes that "high ideals" were turned "into a sordid doom." [20] Yet on the whole, Weber's final verdict—"Fascism looks much like the Jacobinism of our time" [21]—is not without positive overtones that distinguish his interpretation from the unqualified and all-encompassing moral condemnation that characterized studies of fascism during the early post-war period.

Equally noteworthy is George L. Mosse's article, "The Genesis of Fascism," which is just as free of any apologetic taint as is Weber's book.[22] According to Mosse, fascism's roots lay in the same spirit of rebellion which gave birth to expressionist art and literature. It was a kind of youth movement, an attempt to end the alienation of mankind. For Mosse, neither racism, nor anti-Semitism, nor mass terror were essential components of European fascism. The sociological fact that the bulk of its adherents came from the petty bourgeoisie is for him not an adequate basis for a definition of fascism, especially since some fascist movements successfully relied on the support of workers and farmers. Fascism thus emerges from Mosse's analysis as nothing less than one of the great European movements of renewal. The final triumph of its negative side is attributed by Mosse to the in no respect necessary or essential pre-eminence which German National Socialism attained toward the end of the 1930's.

The tendency of these interpretations is obviously to retrieve fascism from the so-to-speak extraterrestrial exile to which the catastrophe of 1945 had consigned it and to re-integrate it into history, if only into history up to the end of the Second World War. Hugh Trevor-Roper makes this explicit in his recent article on the subject: "now, when fascism is dead . . . our need is not to oppose but to understand." [23] It is difficult, to be sure, to reconcile this statement with Trevor-Roper's definition of fascism: "European fascism, then, is the political response of the European bourgeoisie to the economic recession after 1918—or rather, more directly, to the political fear caused by that recession. Before all else, it was anti-communist." [24] There is still, after all, a European bourgeoisie, as is the case with communism, and the possibility of economic recession is never to be ruled out. Why, therefore, if the prerequisites are unaltered, should there be any assurance that fascism cannot recur? Trevor-Roper's strongest counter-argument is his emphasis on the collapse of Germany as a great power. He thus combines in curious fashion his initial, completely generic concept of fascism with a second, thoroughly particularized theory: "In fact, we may say that, in this respect [anti-Semitism], 'fascism' was simply the means of generalizing, in a reluctant Europe, the pathological attitudes of German society. . . . It was German power, and that alone, which gave a hideous similarity to national anti-communist movements. . . ." [25]

Marxist theorists as well have not been completely immune to a tendency to relate Nazism to German national traditions, but in general Marxists have accorded pre-eminence to a more tangible factor—"capitalism"—and in this way reintegrated fascism into the historical process. For if the capitalist social order as such is increasingly likely to give birth to fascism the higher the stage of development it attains and the more acute the threat becomes from the masses who demand "democracy" or "socialism," then the reappearance of fascism cannot be ruled out as long as capitalism survives. For according to Marxist theory fascism is nothing more than the nakedly exposed inner nature of capitalism: domination, force, exploitation, repression. In West Germany it was primarily the journal *Das Argument* that once again gave currency to this interpretation. In his article on "bourgeois society and its state" in a 1966 issue of that journal Johannes Agnoli writes: "If in both cases—fascism and liberal rule—the goal is the same, the path in both instances repressive, the methods to be sure terroristic in one case, constitutional in the other yet in both instances manipulative, one can thus conclude that the two paths are both open and that only exceptional circumstances and conditions force bourgeois society onto the path of fascism. The controllers of capital do not always need fascism. But the continuity between the repressive character of the liberal and neo-liberal state and the terroristic methods of the fascist state should not be overlooked." [26] This interpretation without question re-integrates fascism into the historical process much more completely and immediately than do those of Weber or Mosse, while at the same time it preserves the totally negative evaluation of the immediate post-war period. The validity of the Marxist interpretation, however, stands and falls with two

THE INTERPRETATION OF ERNST NOLTE

implicit premises: first, that "capitalism" as such, and not some combination of capitalist and pre-capitalist forces, is decisive for the emergence of fascism; and second, that a society that is non-repressive and free of state power, in which "individuals" exercise authority, is an actual possibility in the modern world. The Marxist theory about fascism thus to some extent resembles a process of reasoning that would be compelling for Catholics: the distinction between organic and non-organic being is insignificant, since both are material or dependent upon material substances; therefore, only God's purely spiritual form of existence is worthy of the designation "life" in its true sense. If the premises on the basis of which such distinctions seem insignificant are not accepted, then the distinctions assume fundamental importance. In the case of Marxist theories about fascism, a rejection of the premises leads to an interesting insight. If the existence of a liberal society—that is, one based on public but peaceful resolution of differences—is the prerequisite for fascism, then it is to an even greater extent the prerequisite for extreme leftism. Moreover, liberal society is only subjected to the "allures of fascism" if the Left refuses to abide any longer by the rules that exclude a resort to violence. To this extent, the theory of the Left about fascism bears the character of a self-fulfilling prophecy and proves to be itself the most important of all the prerequisites for fascism.

The most recent and explicit rejection of the first of the two implicit premises of Marxist theories about fascism is found in the book by John Weiss, *The Fascist Tradition*. For Weiss, it is precisely the pre-capitalist, conservative components of an incompletely liberalized society which are responsible for fascism. "Fascism was not the 'last gasp of monopoly capitalism'," he writes. "If anything, it was the last gasp of conservatism." [27] Weiss is therefore only being consistent with this view when he denies that fascism came to an end in 1945 and expresses the opinion "that the greatest potential for fascism lies not in the liberal West, but rather in the dialectical polarities even now increasing in non-Western or underdeveloped societies." [28] Weiss thereby places himself in the long tradition of self-assurance characteristic of western liberalism. To be sure, in his case that self-assurance can manifestly compete with

37

its negative counterpart, Marxism, in producing unhistorical simplifications.

Barrington Moore's book, *The Social Origins of Dictatorship and Democracy*, occupies an unusual and significant middle ground in the debate about fascism. A leftist himself, Moore subjects to devastating criticism the most hallowed legends of the Left, for example, the belief that revolutionary social groups have had "progressive" intentions and belonged to the "rising" component of society. Without question a foe of fascism, Moore nevertheless concedes that it can be a modernizing force. Anything but an anti-Communist, he sees greater similarities between fascism and Stalinism than do the latest anti-anti-Communist interpretations, which are exclusively concerned with the ideological factor of "goals." The explanation for Moore's views is that, in contrast to Marx, he is concerned with examining not the relationship of capitalists to proletarians but rather the relations between landlords and peasants. It is in those relations that he discerns one of the world's most potent impetuses for revolution. But Moore finds that the peasant revolutions arose from thoroughly conservative motivations, and where they succeeded the peasants were the most important victims of the industrialization carried out by the new Communist ruling group. For Moore there can thus be no hedonistic, repression-free modernization of the kind which Agnoli assumes is possible and which serves as the basis of the latter's criticism of liberal capitalist society. Instead, according to Moore there are only three basic routes from the pre-industrial to the modern world: the western route of a bourgeois "revolution from below"; the German and Japanese route of a "revolution from above," which in the last resort leads to fascism; and, finally, the Communist route via peasant revolutions in undeveloped countries. Each of these routes is characterized by repression, if not of the same sort. Although Germany, Italy and the Soviet Union are not dealt with directly, the goal of the author is obviously a re-evaluation of the concepts democracy, fascism and communism against the background of the revolutionary unrest of a thoroughly reactionary class: the peasantry, which is everywhere exploited and finally condemned to extinction. In this colossal death struggle, fascism, unlike democracy and communism, is only a temporarily modernizing force which is itself doomed to extinction by virtue of being inextricably linked with the peasantry. Fascism is for Moore a form of that "catonism" which in the ancient world extolled the peasant as the backbone of society, demanded strict morals, accorded a high place to militarism, detested foreigners and preached anti-intellectualism. The point of departure for Moore's interpretation is not any existing social order, not the "dictatorship of the proletariat," but rather "the ancient Western dream of a free and rational society." [29] To this ideal Moore clings, even though he is uncertain whether it may not be only a chimera.

Moore's book is another that is difficult to classify, perhaps because so little of it is concerned directly with a theory of fascism.

Just how broad the frame of reference must be in which fascism finally might find its place is shown by a much less detailed book in which the word "fascism" hardly appears: Cyril E. Black's *The Dynamics of Modernization*. For Black, modernization is a universal and inevitable process which no society in the world can escape. Yet that process, which consists of the adaptation of historically-evolved institutions to rapidly changing functions in response to the "scientific revolution," is extremely complex. There can be protracted resistance to modernization, as for generations was the case in China; there can be a defensive form of modernization, as in the Russia of Peter the Great; there can be a rapid and forced modernization, as in the Soviet Union; and there is the original kind of modernization which took shape in the western societies. In no instance is this process a matter of simple progress; instead, it involves great distress and brings in its wake atomization, alienation, loss of individuality. Soviet modernization, according to Black, was achieved "at the highest relative human cost previously experienced by a modernizing society." [30] In western societies, too, the transition from traditional to modern leadership was ordinarily effected by force. Black thus portrays a great race among states and societies in which what is decisive is not the antithesis of "capitalism and socialism" but rather the timing of the start of the modernizing process and the degree of "integration of society"—in the sense of a great expansion of the middle reaches of society—achieved by that process. Black designates the position of various societies in this race in a rather pedantic fashion. While in the first two "patterns" the Anglo-Americans and the French stand isolated with fully integrated societies, the Soviet Union emerges as a straggler in the fifth pattern, still lacking social integration along with Iran and Ethiopia. Although Black states that the self-awareness of a society, and hence its ideological component, is its principal unifying element, there is just as little place in his scheme of classification for fascism as for socialism, since the societies where such political systems emerged are so diverse when measured in terms of stages of economic development. Mussolini's Italy is seen as a developmental dictatorship. Hitler's Germany, however, is a "unique case." [31] There, according to Black, because of extraordinary circumstances a leadership inspired by anti-modern conceptions gained control of a state that was already on the threshhold of social integration.

One can object to much in Black's book, and not merely to his curious decision to set the achievement of social integration in Germany at the year of Nazism's triumph, 1933. It is very questionable whether the word "modernization" is really the most comprehensive foundation for an interpretation of fascism.[32] One cannot avoid serious doubts as to whether it is possible in Black's sweeping overview—which does not permit the omission of Mali and Mauritania—to come to grips with any particular historical phenomenon. Still, it must be conceded that in his study one shortcoming is avoided from which mere descriptive historical treatments of fascism as well as model-like theories both suffer: the exaggeration of particular factual matters and relationships on the one hand and, on the other, the obscuring of the frame of reference within which judgements are made.

The question of fascism thus remains a problem. No scholarly congress can resolve it, even though it can bring together those who in the past decade have, in a symptomatic isolation, sought to develop a scholarly frame of reference for dealing with the question of fascism—a frame of reference that might be capable of bringing together, or at least reducing the distance between, many more persons than simply a few dozen experts on fascism.

40

[1] *Fascism in Action. A Documented Study and Analysis of Fascism in Europe.* Prepared at the instance and under the direction of Representative Wright Patman of Texas by Legislative Reference Service of the Library of Congress under the direction of Ernest S. Griffith. 80th Congress, 1st Session, House Document No. 401 (U.S. Government Printing Office, Washington, 1947).

[2] Sigmund Neumann, *Permanent Revolution. Totalitarianism in the Age of International Civil War* (New York, 1942).

[3] Franz Neumann, *Behemoth. The Structure and Practice of National Socialism* (New York, 1942).

[4] Hannah Arendt, *The Origins of Totalitarianism* (New York, 1951).

[5] Carl J. Friedrich and Zbigniew K. Brzezinski, *Totalitarian Dictatorship and Autocracy* (Cambridge, Mass., 1956); Zevedei Barbu, *Democracy and Dictatorship. Their Psychology and Patterns of Life* (New York, 1956); Hans Buchheim, *Totalitäre Herrschaft, Wesen und Merkmale* (Munich, 1962).

[6] Georg Lukacs' *Die Zerstörung der Vernunft* (Berlin, 1954) is an attempt in that direction, but its exclusive focus on Germany makes it more a part of that school of interpretation which seeks the roots of Nazism in peculiarly German tradition.

[7] Henri Lemaître, *Les fascismes dans l'histoire* (Paris, 1959), a work written from a left-Catholic standpoint.

[8] Dante L. Germino, *The Italian Fascist Party in Power. A Study in Totalitarian Rule* (Minneapolis, 1959).

[9] Seymour Martin Lipset, "Der 'Faschismus,' die Linke, die Rechte und die Mitte," in *Kölner Zeitschrift für Soziologie und Sozialpsychologie*, XI (1959), 401–44. An English version forms chapter 5 of Lipset's *Political Man. The Social Bases of Politics* (New York, 1960).

[10] Ralf Dahrendorf, "Demokratie und Sozialstruktur in Deutschland," in *Europäisches Archiv für Soziologie*, I (1960), re-published in Dahrendorf's *Gesellschaft und Freiheit. Zur soziologischen Analyse der Gegenwart* (Munich, 1961).

[11] Ernst Nolte, "Marx und Nietzsche im Sozialismus des jungen Mussolini," in *Historische Zeitschrift*, vol. 191 (1960).

[12] Ernst Nolte, *Der Faschismus von Mussolini zu Hitler. Texte, Bilder und Dokumente* (Munich, 1968), pp. 385–87.

[13] Ernst Nolte, *Die Krise des liberalen Systems und die faschistischen Bewegungen* (Munich, 1968).

[14] Nolte, *Three Faces of Fascism: Action Française, Italian Fascism, National Socialism* (New York, Chicago, San Francisco, 1966), pp. 20–21; (New York and Toronto, 1969), p. 40.

41

[15] *Ibid.*, pp. 421/529.

[16] Ernst Nolte (ed.), *Theorien über den Faschismus* (Cologne and Berlin, 1967), pp. 49–51.

[17] Nolte, *Three Faces*, 454/567 (trans. by ed.).

[18] Eugen Weber, *Varieties of Fascism* (Princeton, 1964), p. 44.

[19] *Ibid.*, p. 87.

[20] *Ibid.*, p. 105.

[21] *Ibid.*, p. 139.

[22] George L. Mosse, "Introduction: The Genesis of Fascism," in *Journal of Contemporary History*, I (1966), 14–26; re-published in the volume *International Fascism, 1920–1945*, ed. by Walter Laqueur and George L. Mosse (New York, 1966).

[23] H. R. Trevor-Roper, "The Phenomenon of Fascism," in *European Fascism* (Studies in Fascism I), ed. by S. J. Woolf (London, 1968), p. 28.

[24] *Ibid.*, p. 24.

[25] *Ibid.*, pp. 36–37.

[26] Johannes Agnoli, "Die bürgerliche Gesellschaft und ihr Staat," in *Das Argument*, 8 (1966), p. 460.

[27] John Weiss, *The Fascist Tradition. Radical Right-Wing Extremism in Modern Europe* (New York, 1967), p. 5.

[28] *Ibid.*, p. 129.

[29] Barrington Moore, Jr., *The Social Origins of Dictatorship and Democracy. Lord and Peasant in the Making of the Modern World* (Boston, 1969), p. 508.

[30] C. E. Black, *The Dynamics of Modernization. A Study in Comparative History* (New York, 1966), p. 146.

[31] *Ibid.*, p. 85.

[32] The concept "modernization" is also fundamental to the second volume of "Studies in Fascism" edited by S. J. Woolf, *The Nature of Fascism* (London, 1968), which came to my attention too late for consideration in this essay. That volume is on the whole a noteworthy attempt to arrive at a definition of the essence of fascism by use of social science categories and models. But the attempt by G. Germani in his contribution to the volume, "Fascism and class" (pp. 65–96), to refine the model offered by A. F. K. Organski in his contribution, "Fascism and Modernization" (pp. 19–41), suffers from the same limitations as Organski's by limiting the analysis almost exclusively to Italian Fascism and Peronism. It is instructive to note how much more successful George L. Mosse's contribution, which employs the traditional methods of intellectual history, is in establishing the common features of European fascism as a whole as well as the differences that distinguish it from communism ("Fascism and the intellectuals," pp. 205–225).

II

SUBSEQUENT
RE-INTERPRETATIONS

In this section four authors present a variety of suggestions and theories about fascism as a generic, multi-national phenomenon. In a study originally prepared as a paper for the annual meeting of the American Historical Association in December 1970 and published here for the first time, William Sheridan Allen, professor of history at the State University of New York at Buffalo, examines what he views as a key factor in the emergence of fascist movements and their success in Germany and Italy. Alan Cassels, professor of history at McMaster University, in a study which first appeared in 1969 and is published here in revised form, offers an explanation for certain conspicuously conflicting attitudes among those who, in the 1930's and 1940's, considered themselves to be fascists. Wolfgang Sauer, professor of history at the University of California at Berkeley, critically examines a number of other works, including Ernst Nolte's, and then offers some stimulating ideas of his own about the causes and nature of fascism. Professor Sauer's study was read as a paper at the annual meeting of the American Historical Association in December 1965 and first published in 1967. The final selection in this section, by the editor of this volume, professor of history at Yale University, was initially prepared as a paper for the annual meeting of the American Historical Association in 1970 and first published in 1972. It appears here in slightly revised form.

3

The Appeal of Fascism and
the Problem of National Disintegration

BY WILLIAM SHERIDAN ALLEN

It is generally agreed that fascism was an effectively attractive political movement only in the period between the World Wars, although elements of its ideology clearly appeared before World War I and were still in circulation a generation after World War II.[1] But as to why fascism became attractive at that point in Europe's history, there is no general agreement or universally accepted theory. Perhaps there should be none—in view of the diversity of the countries involved, the operative factors affecting them, and the variety of movements alleged to be "fascist." At the very least any theory of fascism should involve a complex analysis and eschew mono-causal explanation.[2] What this essay offers is a contribution to such a theory through an examination of one particular element which in no way excludes other factors.

Most of my thesis is synthetic rather than new. It is that one cause for the attractiveness of fascism was national disintegration in an atmosphere of international tension; that fascism appeared when and where it did because World War I drastically exposed the vulnerability of nations suffering from acute disunity; that there was a generic quality to the disunity of Germany and Italy which was produced by their historical development and exacerbated by their attempts to apply traditional remedies; and that therefore the fascist concept of a new form of integration and mass involvement was both seemingly consistent with European traditions and generically similar, at least in Italy and Germany. This much is not exactly original.[3]

The second part of my thesis, however, contains some new thoughts about the process of disintegration: in its most acute form—in Germany—it produced a proliferation of highly self-centered sub-communities, a sort of anti-national social explosion. German Nazism was powerfully affected by this. Spain showed similar traits, although Franco's regime is, for special reasons, not fascist.[4] Italian Fascism lacked the spur of this centrifugal explosion and thus never achieved either the bitterness of the Spanish experience or the daemonic thrust of Nazism.

Such statements imply a general *definition* of fascist movements, which is something scholars have not yet agreed upon. But one can supply a *description* of fascist movements, in the sense of a Weberian "ideal type," especially if we limit ourselves to their characteristics in Germany and Italy during their drive for power.[5] A minimum list of common traits would note that they were movements which opposed the traditional European Left but which, unlike the traditional Right, scorned conservative institutions and reveled in the energy and violence of "revolutionary" methods and goals. (Indeed, they claimed to be uniquely new and tried to reject customary classification.[6]) Unlike traditional parties, they were authoritarian in internal structure and paid allegiance to a single leader who was assigned charismatic attributes. They sought a political dictatorship for their country but demanded more than a monopoly over political decisions; they also wanted to control social organization and even cultural affairs, such as education and mores. They were hyper-nationalistic, insisting that nations must fight a Darwinian struggle for survival. And finally, they were movements supported primarily by the middle classes but which claimed to pursue social unity and promised to integrate all classes and interests within the nation.[7]

This last item is a crucial one, for it puts fascism very much within the framework of European history. Since the French Revolution one grand theme of Europe's development has been the question of how and why nations should be integrated. Historians have emphasized the ideological factors, but there were practical aspects to the question, too. For my thesis it is important to remember that pluralistic integration as it evolved in nineteenth-century Europe (that is, the quest for national unity via a political market in which the separate interests of various elements are presumably reconciled, usually in a parliament) was not a product of Liberalism alone. In addition to mirroring Liberal ideas, pluralistic integration made possible the mobilization of enormous power: it was as much the child of 1793 as of 1789. In other words, pluralistic integration was a response to the objective necessity for mass involvement in the nation, as manifested by France's revolutionary "nation in arms" in contrast to the limited mercenary armies and passive subjects of the old regimes. Absolutism had not involved the masses and therefore it could not survive in competition with systems that did. But when absolutism was chipped away, there was also lost with it a set of institutions which had previously served to resolve divergent interests within the state. Pluralistic integration became the new reconciling mechanism now that the masses had to be involved. Liberal theory *justified* pluralistic integration but the *need* for it arose because mass involvement generated power, and the states of Europe required that power to compete with Napoleonic armies, to cope with the genie let loose by the French Revolution.

The need for and value of mass involvement became apparent only gradually. The specific forms of integration that had emerged in France were by no means universally accepted, although the resultant power of mass armies was: without involvement states lost wars. Broadened involvement of populations in the cause of their states seemed to require and stem from the new integration. Ideological support for this involvement came from nationalism, the concept of the community-of-the-whole: the nation was the "fatherland," the *patrie*, and its citizens were a family.[8] The social concomitants of involvement were the promises of equal opportunity, of at least minimal social justice, and (overriding objective differences in status) of an acceptance of all citizens as full members of the community-of-the-whole, at least in an emotional sense. The practical mechanism for keeping the family harmonious, and therefore committed to the common cause, was broadened suffrage and a national parliament to reconcile conflicting interests, the implication being the existence of an overarching interest in the good of

46

the nation. But the ultimate good of the nation was defined as power in international competition and this power in turn was to be generated by the active involvement of all in the affairs of the nation, especially its wars.

It is important to note, however, that acceptance by dominant elites of the interrelationship between citizen involvement and national integration was often hesitant, spurious, grudging, and power-oriented. Even the supporting concept of nationalism was acknowledged by men like Bismarck only for the power it produced, not for the far-reaching political and social changes it implied. Only rarely did European elites espouse the ideological presuppositions of pluralistic integration—the notion that men might pull together because they were truly participants in a common cause. On the contrary, leaders like Bismarck saw nationalism only as another *force* to be employed in the game of power politics.[9]

The result was that the concepts of involvement and integration were not really accepted as consequentially intertwined or as ends in themselves but as manipulative mechanisms. The roots of British and French power were ill-comprehended. Britain's power derived partly from her slowly developed integration, with the Parliament emerging as an expression as well as a source of this. France, too, despite its exuberant internal quarrels, had an inner solidarity which was not mechanistic but rather historically caused and which was fortified by explicit structural commitments (for example, to the concept of "citizen," a term for which the German language never found an equivalent, at least in all its connotations). Consequently, the efforts toward integration in most of the rest of Europe were specious and ill-based. Dominant elites sought the profits without being willing to make the investments; or even worse, they thought they already had.

Nevertheless the need for involvement and the approach to it through pluralistic integration dominated Europe after the French Revolution. To resist Napoleon Prussia freed its serfs and gave its urban middle classes a measure of self-rule on the local level. Metternich, too, understood the dynamics of the matter but his response was to seek to prevent war, so as to prevent reforms. Even Russia was driven by these imperatives: her defeat in the Crimean

War led to the freeing of the serfs; defeat in the Japanese War to the creation of a national parliament. For Bismarck a national parliament elected by universal manhood suffrage was an adjunct to Prussian universal military training. True, many other factors contributed to the liberalization of nineteenth-century Europe and its degree differed in the various parts of Europe; but a constant impelling element was the recognized dialectical relationship between national power, national involvement, and national integration.[10] By 1914 one can speak of a European tradition in this respect.

World War I served as a massive catalyst to this process for the nations of Europe.[11] That the conflict was won by the Western democracies suggested the superiority of their systems.[12] Conversely, the fates of Russia and Austria-Hungary provided a terrifying warning of the consequences of inadequate integration and involvement. The form assumed by the war itself reinforced the perceived need for involvement while exemplifying new options for integration. On the one hand the extravagant attrition of technological warfare demanded mass armies of total commitment, plus an all-embracing mobilization of the home front. On the other hand the war introduced to each country new methods for achieving this. Authoritarian direction, though mainly based on common consent, replaced political brokerage even in internal affairs. When extended into the economic sphere, such methods blasted the whole Liberal assumption about the efficiency of free markets— economic or political. And when censorship and propaganda were added, the lesson became clear: involvement need not be spontaneous; it could now be manipulated from above. Finally, the war produced an intense feeling of national solidarity in all countries: for most citizens this was felt at least at the outbreak of the hostilities; for the soldiers, in a more sustained fashion through the enforced collectivity of the trenches. But it is important to note that this consisted of an *emotional* unity rather than political consensus, for the latter was especially lacking in Germany and Italy.[13] Furthermore, emotional unity came to Italy not in the enthusiasm of entry into war but in the grim determination to survive the rout at Caporetto.[14] And finally, this emotional unity stood in sharp contrast to the political schisms in Germany and Italy which the war itself intensified and thus made all the more painful.[15]

But to sum up, total war demonstrated the need for integration and involvement as prerequisites for survival; it exemplified concretely how they could be fostered from above without pluralistic mechanisms; it gave at least a fleeting but unforgettable experience to virtually everyone of what national integration felt like. Moreover, for many millions in Germany and especially Italy, this evanescent feeling was the first real experience of national integration.[16]

What followed the war in those two countries was an expansion of the forms of pluralistic integration and a paradoxical failure of this to produce anything approaching unity. This was partly because both countries found themselves in what Eugen Weber calls "a state-of-siege atmosphere." [17] Defeat and unilateral disarmament left Germans with a sense of being preyed upon by hostile neighbors, a conviction reinforced by Polish incursions into Silesia, the French seizure of the Ruhr, the seeming despoliation of reparations, and frequent international humiliation. For Italy the war culminated in what was widely seen as a "mutilated victory," an attitude understandable only in light of the extensively held belief among Italians that they had won the war for the Allies. After all, had not Italy finally defeated her hereditary foe, Austria, and done it, in the end, alone? In contrast to the victories of her unification era, Italy had won without significant foreign aid, but to the exasperation of her nationalists was still treated like a second-rate state.[18]

In both Italy and Germany, therefore, frustration and humiliation led many to seek a new strengthening of the nation. The traditional European formula was applied. Both countries moved, in the wake of war, towards pluralistic integration: in Germany through a revolutionary installation of full parliamentary democracy with proportional representation, touched off by an attempt on the part of traditional elites to go a limited way in the same direction. Italy at last fully democratized her parliamentary government through universal suffrage with proportional representation.[19] Of course it was unlikely that Germany and Italy could achieve overnight the integration that had been acquired over centuries by Britain and France, especially since Germany and Italy, despite all the anguished cries for unity that had been continuously raised by their conservatives, had traditions of opposition to the full logic of integration (primarily because their ruling elites were unwilling to share power).

The result was that instead of tightened integration, each country found that democracy institutionalized divisions and intensified other problems. More time, a broader commitment, and less turbulent conditions might have stabilized the new pluralism, but such favorable circumstances were not available. In an Italy racked by economic crisis, illegal seizures of property, and persistent violence, divergent ideologies polarized the newly potent parties, paralyzed parliament, and precluded effective cabinet government. From the viewpoint of Italian nationalists, the chief problem was the massive upsurge of a socialist movement which had opposed the war, mocked nationalism, and challenged all other social strata. In the 1919 elections the socialists tripled their pre-war representation and constituted an apparently unintegratable third of the nation.[20]

Conditions in Germany were comparable but worse. There was not just runaway inflation but serial economic crises to aggravate social tensions. There were not just threats of revolution but repeated actual attempts by extremists of the left and right. There were not just sporadic violence and vigilantism but widespread assassination and the clash of party armies in the streets. There were not just ineffective cabinets working on a narrow parliamentary basis but a vanishing center and the eventual collapse of the parliamentary system completely, followed by an unstable *de facto* restoration of the previous constitution featuring Hindenburg in the role of substitute *Kaiser*.[21] And as in Italy, the Socialists and Communists were viewed by the entire nationalist spectrum as a massive indigestible minority, not least because of their supposed contribution to Germany's defeat and humiliation. The "stab-in-the-back" legend may have been factually untrue, but for countless upper and middle class Germans it was psychologically valid.

In short, many in both countries felt the world to be very hostile and their nation to be terribly weak. The traditional formula for renewed power—pluralistic integration—only increased internal division and weakness, yet the basic concept of involvement was so deeply ingrained in the culture that it was still widely accepted as a supplier of strength.[22] Therefore both countries were susceptible to arguments for a new integrative system. It would have to be dictatorial to suppress dissension and enforce collaboration upon a large, hostile minority. It could involve the lower classes in the nation by manipulation from above, on the model of the wartime experiments (*i.e.*, through censorship and propaganda, through a general mobilization of society, and through opportunistic plebiscitary politics). And since the goal was national survival, the new integrative system would have to stress spiritual attitudes attuned to the law of the jungle. All this was promised by Fascism and Nazism. They thus seemed to supply logical answers directly correlated with perceived needs and options. Of course in time it would become abundantly clear that the answers were false, that the logic was based upon invalid premises, that the needs derived from an insane system, and that the option of dictatorial integration was both dysfunctional and disastrous. But all this was generally understood only later, after Hitler and Mussolini had led their countries to catastrophe. In the years when they were still making promises, their approach seemed quite logical.

Hitler and Mussolini were important leaders, but their movements succeeded through gaining the favor of the middle class masses and the ruling elites. They won that favor by their basic program.[23] Of course neither had a formal written platform (Nazism's "unalterable" *25 Points* became a joke, while Mussolini boasted about the untheoretical nature of his movement in its early years [24]), but their basic intentions emerged clearly from their speeches and even more so from the style and slogans of their movements. They proposed to exalt national power by building a dictatorially integrated national community on the model of methods and moods familiar from World War I. They also benefitted from being in the right countries at the right time to advance a plausible alternative political approach linked to a major European

51

historical tradition. This is not to say that the triumph of Nazism and Fascism was inevitable; neither was it fortuitous.

II

It may be that the key problem in Germany and Italy was not so much disintegration as it was the flight from disintegration, but it seems impossible to deny that acute disunity was an objective reality in their pre-fascist experiences. The nearly simultaneous arrival of these two countries to a state of ripeness for fascism in this respect derived in part from their own remarkably similar histories. Historians have noted the similarities, but there were differences, too.

Prior to World War I the experience of both countries with pluralistic integration was limited to pseudo-constitutionalism. In Italy the oligarchical suffrage laws, the lack of a party system reflective of the popular will, and the practice of "transformism" (that is, the corruption of politicians) meant that the national parliament failed to provide political brokerage service for society. Italy's Chamber of Deputies represented itself, or at most the interests of regional groupings.[25] In Germany, the Bismarckian constitution denied real power to the national parliament and thus encouraged it to function mainly on behalf of interest groups—religious, economic, or social—instead of deciding national policy. But consider the difference: Italy's problem was essentially amorphousness while Germany's was that of a multiplicity of powerless but well-defined groups. In Italy the exclusion of all but the upper classes from government resulted in the stark distinction between "legal" and "real" Italy.[26] In Germany the participation of all classes produced a complex political struggle involving the representatives of the aristocracy, the bourgeoisie, and the proletariat—and even that description simplifies reality since there were sub-divisions within each class, since deep religious divisions cut across class lines, and since a "mandarinate" of official ideologues persistently attacked the entire idea of interest representation.[27]

Both countries had over a decade's experience with troubled democratization before fascism. But the Giolittan Era, despite the rise of mass ideological parties, the decline of the Liberals, and the plentitude of social disorder, was far less tense than the Weimar Republic in Germany.[28] One reason was the continuity of institutions in Italy (especially the monarchy as a focal symbol), as opposed to the all-questioning shock of defeat and revolution in Germany.

Both Germany and Italy, because of the lateness and superficiality of their political unification, never overcame their inherited regional disunity. Southern Italy had to be conquered at bayonet point in the 1860's in a war against native guerrillas which cost the Italian army more casualties than had the just completed "War of Unification" against Austria. Thereafter, resentment over "Piedmontisation" plus the vast objective differences between northern and southern Italy prevented national identification. And there were lesser regional hostilities, too.[29]

In Germany the Bavarian parliament voted to join the Reich in 1871 by a margin of only two votes and many Bavarians continued to refuse to identify with Germany. The forcible absorption of the Rhineland and of Hanover into Prussia created ongoing resentments while the exclusion of Austrian Germans from the Reich left the question of national unity unresolved. Regional jealousies, threats of secession, sectional parties represented a continuous possibility of fragmentation, though German regionalism lacked the economic and cultural dimensions of its Italian counterpart. Particularism was strong in Germany, but it was never as gross and simple as in Italy. On the other hand, German regionalism was complicated by being linked with religious disunity, too, in some cases.

In both countries the government's struggle with the Catholic Church left permanent scars. In both countries the attempted repression of Socialism in the nineteenth century meant that representatives of the proletariat were never accorded the tolerance they got in France and England.[30] Thus the two strongest mass movements prior to the rise of Fascism and Nazism (i.e., political Catholicism and Marxism) were driven in upon themselves. But both movements were older, more entrenched, and more internally cohesive in Germany than in Italy.

In both countries social division was the main source of na-

53

tional cleavage.[31] The differences derived from disparities in economic development. Italy's major unincorporated element was the peasantry: impoverished, indifferent, and ignored until they became voters for the Catholic Peoples Party after 1904 or soldiers in the First World War.[32] In Germany the highly articulated class division hardened into rigid stratification with a virtual caste at the top and an isolated sub-culture at the bottom.[33] Disunity was severe in both countries, but conditions were more distressing in Germany because disunity was more highly organized.

In fact, almost all the elements of disintegration in Germany were over-organized and had become so even before the First World War. The Weimar Republic, with its superheated pressures, produced out of this refined, multiple fission the explosive phenomenon of community identification: the collapse of virtually all commitment to the community-of-the-whole and a substitution for it of sub-community chauvinism.

III

Of course every complex nation has within it units of primary loyalty which may form tight little communities, whether they are geographic or non-spatial in character.[34] Such special organizations are usually neither exceptional nor a problem for society as a whole. What is rare is when such social entities become so exclusively self-focused that they can neither cooperate with others nor identify with an overriding commonality through ideology, institutions, enlightened self-interest, or some central symbol such as the throne or a flag. When one group acts that way, the nation is concerned. When almost all of them do, the nation is sick, especially when hitherto loose combinations start transcending their original functions and begin acting like communities. Such a sickness is more than simply a weakness in the face of international competition—it is a form of latent civil war. It must not be assumed that such behavior stems from anarchic individualism or the loss of a national focus. On the contrary, we are dealing here with a syndrome which requires anti-individualism, a high degree of group allegiance, and a general rejection of the existing community-of-the-whole.

54

An example of this syndrome may be found in modern Spain, where Catalonians and Basques have acted as regional communities; where the Army and the Church became functional communities; where workers, peasants, and landlords have behaved like social-economic communities.[35] According to Stanley Payne, the problem is not just the separation of Spaniards "into a series of discrete, potentially antagonistic sub-groups" which were so rigid and mutually hostile that Ortega y Gasset called them "water-tight compartments," but also the massive "sub-group conformity" within each.[36] But in the early 1930's the supravening factor in Spain was class division, and civil war was brought on by national bi-polarization into two uneasy sub-group coalitions. What Franco did was not aimed at involving the lower classes. Instead, he tried to ride herd over the Rightist coalition and suppress its common foes and control its inner rifts by traditional authoritarianism.[37] His goal being self-perpetuation, he did not seek national integration—perhaps because of the lack of an external spur: his country was spared by both world wars and has kept to the international backwaters.[38]

Thus it would be a mistake to see the mere existence of discrete sub-communities as invariably predisposing a country towards fascism. Holland provides an even more instructive example. William Shetter has described the "confessional-political blocs into which modern Dutch society is divided and which thoroughly permeate nearly every aspect of contemporary life in the Netherlands." These sub-groups are "such that a person by virtue of his religious, political and other preferences 'belongs' in one and therefore automatically not in any other, the result of which is that the invisible lines existing in any society between 'us' and 'them' tend to be unusually sharply drawn." [39] But there are mitigating factors: the cleavages are ancient and accepted, and they are bridged by the politeness, reserve, and respect for other's views which might be expected in such a small, crowded country. Abetted by a proportional representation election system almost as unworkable as Weimar Germany's, the Dutch have managed to produce convoluted cabinet crises, baroque coalitions, and unstable minority governments. But none of it matters much. Holland is scarcely involved

55

in the tensions of international competition nor does anyone doubt the strength of its national bonds. Ultimately the rigid parliamentary delegations function through a "politics of accommodation," while society survives amongst its own "mutually walled off blocs. . . ." [40]

Germany in the Weimar era had similar problems under different conditions.[41] The sub-communities were more intense and diverse and their rapid proliferation was of recent origin. The behavior of parties, pressure groups, and cultural entities showed an intensification of internal bonds to a point transcending simple goals of association. Association became its own end. German organizations defined themselves with increasing rigidity. They felt themselves competing defensively against all others. Not only did they establish narrow norms for collective behavior, they sought to provide spiritual protection for their members and ego-gratification through the group. One result was the release of tremendous energies, the often noted hyper-activity of Weimar Germany which extended into all spheres: ideological, political, intellectual, cultural, economic, social.

But in this process of collective self-reinforcement, the norms of individual groups tended to supersede values common to society in general. Each group behaving like a community thus saw itself as the proper whole, projected its values as the only true national ones. The major parties, for example, became (in William Ebenstein's words) nascent "potential Germanies." Yet along with this process of community identification went an increasing recognition that it was an unhealthy substitute for a true national community. A major role in this awareness was played by the endemic preachments of intellectuals and *völkisch* theorists about the crucial importance of a mystically bound German community.[42]

But in the real Germany of the Weimar era a national community was impossible precisely because of sub-community behavior: their increasing exclusivity and mutual hostility, their growing inflexibility and narrowness. Individual allegiance to the community-of-the-whole was expressed only when individuals defined it as an extension or reflection of their own sub-community. Emotional patriotism abounded but actual national solidarity was scarce. Ironically, the one political organization consistently willing to sacrifice its interests for the good of the nation was the Social Democratic Party—an organization constantly excoriated by nationalists as a major fomenter of internal divisiveness.

The intellectuals of both the Left and the Right grouped themselves into tight circles around their respective periodicals (especially *Die Weltbühne* and *Die Tat*) disdainfully declining to carry their ideas into practical politics.[43] The Great Coalition broke apart in 1930 over narrowly defined special interests, even though that produced paralysis for the parliamentary system. The democratic parties were unable to coalesce against the Nazi juggernaut. The two working class parties fought against each other beyond the eleventh hour: hostility between Socialists and Communists continued even in the Third Reich's concentration camps. German farmers, facing a structural crisis in agriculture of unprecedented dimensions, maintained three distinct pressure organizations according to the products they marketed, collaborating only in the abortive "Green Front" which lasted less than two years. In short, we see no political cohesion even among the ideologically similar; no joint action even among the socially similar; no economic cooperation even within one clearly defined sector—even though in each instance there were awesome common dangers. Instead each subgroup behaved like a community unto itself. Not even massive external pressure could force these sub-communities to merge with other, similar organizations.[44]

There were several causes for this, most of them circumstantial. One was the unsettled constitutional situation. The Republic was tentative to most Germans; only the Social Democrats defended it to the bitter end (which helped others view the Republic as a partisan institution). This not only signified a fundamental and ideological disagreement over the nature of national integration, but also helped foster sub-communities. With the state form in question, anything seemed possible and everything uncertain. Hence individuals were driven into groups to promote or defend their interests, mostly the latter.

Similar defensive reaction was stimulated from 1918 to 1933 by a steady redistribution of income (at the expense of all but the rich) in a period of general economic scarcity. Each segment fought to keep from slipping backwards against overwhelming and inexplicable economic phenomena such as the inflation and the depression, whose mysterious origins were conducive to mass paranoia. Nor did the so-called stable period (1924–1929) bring surcease, as is often assumed. On the contrary, it produced profound threats: technological unemployment, industrial and commercial concentration, increasingly mortgaged farms.[45] Such "slow crises" drove each interest group into tighter self-integration, lest its people succumb to remote, inexorable forces. The resultant common aggressiveness then jeopardized the brittle social structure inherited from Wilhelmine Germany. Status was threatened, especially amongst the lower middle classes, and this in turn reinforced group defense.

Weimar Germany's constitutional structure also contributed to the formation of political sub-communities. Proportional representation made splinter parties feasible. Any group with one-half of one percent of the vote could win a seat in the national parliament. It has long been noted that proportional representation strengthens the cohesion of party organizations, militates against inter-party compromise, narrows and rigidifies the ideological fronts. Significantly, it was among the middle classes, those most threatened socially, economically, and in their values, that the splinter parties were most numerous. For it was the middle classes who were to form the mass base of Nazism and who were also those most persistently propagandized to abhor separate interests and to seek instead the mystical nationalistic fusion of the *völkisch* community.[46]

Finally, the very idea of "community" was reinforced by Weimar culture.[47] It is not just that Expressionists and the academic establishment fostered the concept, or that Ferdinand Tönnies' book *Community and Society* (published in 1887) suddenly became a runaway best seller in the 1920's,[48] but also that artistic and intellectual communes became faddish. Even before the war, *Die Brücke* used jointly owned paints and brushes.[49] In the twenties the most famous artistic community was the *Bauhaus*, with its own buildings out in the countryside. The newest of the artistic ventures, films, were collective creations.[50] Poets formed groups

58

around themselves;[51] even that reluctant individualist, Bertolt Brecht, insisted on writing as part of an informal collective.[52]

Anti-individualism was in the air. In defiance of semantics the word "socialism" was appropriated by right-wingers.[53] Spengler identified it with the Prussia of Frederick the Great.[54] Möller van den Bruck called for a "German socialism." [55] *Freikorps* terrorists like Erwin Kern and Ernst von Salomon wanted a "true" socialism.[56] "Political soldiers," such as Ernst Röhm, evoked the "socialism of the trenches." [57] Matthias Erzberger, the Catholic Center Party leader, avoided the actual word but called for a "Christian Solidarism" which was essentially guild socialism.[58] Certainly one reason behind the change in name of Hitler's party to "National Socialism" was that it was an attractive term, attuned to current rhetoric.

And it was the traditionally anti-socialist middle classes who swept into Hitler's movement in the largest numbers.[59] In so far as Nazism made one consistent propaganda appeal, it was the promise to create a *Volksgemeinschaft*—a national community. But Nazism had to compete with other political communities in order to absorb them, and it was the necessity of finding a vehicle for fusion, as much as his own inclinations and the convenience of it, that led Hitler and his followers to turn him into a charismatic leader, the mythic *Führer* who stood above ideological, programatic, social, and organizational loyalties.[60] Only thus could the sub-community structure of the Weimar Republic be transcended.

Ironically, the Nazi party itself behaved much like the other sub-communities of the Weimar Republic: it was exclusive, self-obsessed, and derived its dynamism both from the goal of eliminating all competitors and from providing activities and rewards within the bounds of the movement itself. When Hitler came to power the Nazis did destroy competing communities through ruthless subordination (*Gleichschaltung*), all the way down to local bowling clubs—except for the churches and the army.[61] And the Third Reich itself showed the inward norms of what can be called a super-community. It was impervious to the general allegiances of mankind, responding only to the norms and values of a group so

59

fully focused upon itself that it cut itself off completely from the rest of human society.

IV

It will be clear from this analysis of Weimar Germany that the "mass theory" of atomized individuals available for mobilization by elites, which has been advanced as the characteristic of a "pre-totalitarian" society, has no basis in fact. On the contrary, the problem of pre-Hitlerian Germany was not the disappearance of intermediate groups but their increasing tenacity and significance. Individuals did not become manipulable social atoms gathered in an amorphous mass, as argued by Hannah Arendt and William Kornhauser,[62] but rather became involved in social blocs of such rigidity that it took the terrorist *Gleichschaltung* of the Nazi revolution to smash them. If there ever was a "mass society" in Germany it was a product of, not the cause for, the Third Reich.

Nor did the promised "national community" appear, either in Germany or Italy. For all their apparent logic and terrifying consistency, Nazism and Fascism failed utterly to achieve the promises that had won them favor, and the more these regimes seemed to have produced total integration and involvement, the more spectacular was their failure. It now appears that Nazism was unable to win allegiance even with the aid of propaganda and the *Gestapo*. Particularly in the rural villages (which have always been geographic sub-communities) and among the workers of Germany's factories there was no real integration.[63] By and large, external involvement could be compelled in the Third Reich. Yet it is also generally accepted that far from being a monolith, the regime itself was a chaos of squabbling sub-groups whose self-seeking undercut the goals of the *Führer*.[64] The consequence of "total integration" was fantastic inefficiency and stupidity culminating in total disaster.[65] Hitler did not protect his country's international position; he left behind a truncated, divided country whose most extreme nationalists, nowadays, would be delighted to return to the once scorned boundaries of the Weimar Republic.

Mussolini led his country into a suicidal war and also made Italy the virtual vassal of Germany. In his last days he even sold out (to Hitler) Italy's meager gains from the First World War: Trieste and the South Tyrol.[66] The spuriousness of manipulated involvement was revealed by the contrast between the genuine mass enthusiasm for war in August, 1914, and the somber acquiescence of September, 1939.[67]

Effective integration came only in the wake of the Fascist experience. Most Italians refused to fight for Mussolini, but coalesced in the partisan movement against him.[68] Anti-Nazi Germans transcended their political, religious, and social divisions during the Resistance [69] and have since maintained—at least in West Germany—a prosaic but viable community of interest. Of course, Italians and Germans had an ideological "hangover" following their respective experiences, and since World War II both societies have become increasingly homogenized. In fact, their dictators initiated this through the negative contribution of smashing the previous political and societal patterns.[70]

The problem of national disunity now operates within a different atmosphere. The average duration of Italian governments since 1946 has been less than nine months, but—as in Holland—politics lacks passion. In West Germany political life has been decidedly and blessedly dull. Perhaps the reason is that both countries are no longer significant in international competition and have small chance of becoming so no matter how involved their citizens become in the state. They are out of the power game except as dependencies. This is not to claim that there are no internal divisions, but none are like those of the pre-fascist period. Even the glaring division between East and West Germany has produced only ritualistic rhetoric on both sides, plus hesitant diplomacy. No responsible German leader has called for a new "national community."

As suggested in the first section of this essay, fascism appeared to many as an alternative but logical extension of a general European development. German Nazism was that and something more: it can be seen as a form of integration consisting of the triumph of one sub-community over all others in a pathological society. Obviously many other components went into fascism, especially in countries where so-labeled movements made later appear-

61

ances or were engendered by the fashionability of the idea or the apparent successes of the Italian and German regimes. But whatever the ultimate theoretical mix, the role of national disintegration, in its particulars and as part of a broad trend within a traditional context, should not be omitted from consideration.

A final point concerns the question of pathology. I have used the word "logical" to describe the fascist response to the problem of national power through involvement and integration. But the problem exists only within a pathological international context. Fascism seems "logical" only if one has previously accepted the entire system of inter-state competition and even then it is based upon an erroneous comprehension of the nature of national integration. Psychologists have long known that certain forms of madness are highly "logical"—if only you accept the madman's first premise. Fascism was like that. No one expressed it more openly than the Spanish fascist Ernesto Giménez Caballero, who wrote, in 1934:

> We are going to exalt national sentiment with insanity, with paroxysms, with whatever need be. Better a nation of imbeciles than international sanity. [71]

In this sense fascism was a logical extension of a world gone mad. But we should remember that the first madness was that of total war. And as long as international competition remains a determinant in the organization of states, the fascist alternative will remain a potential option. In so far as war has been a driving factor of European development, fascism may be viewed as the nemesis attached to the genius of Western civilization.

I wish to express my appreciation to those colleagues who pointed out to me some of the conceptual deficiencies in the original version of this study, including the editor of this volume; Professor Orville T. Murphy of the State University of New York at Buffalo; Dr. Bedřich Loewenstein, formerly of the Czechoslovak Academy of Sciences; and especially Professor Fritz K. Ringer of Boston University. Naturally they are in no way responsible for the use I have made of their helpful criticisms.

[1] "There was no 'Fascism' anywhere in Europe before the end of the first world war," according to F. L. Carsten, *The Rise of Fascism* (London, 1967), p. 9. On the "era of fascism" see Ernst Nolte, *Three Faces of Fascism: Action Française. Italian Fascism. National Socialism* (New York, 1966), pp. 3–9. On fascism as the inheritor of long-standing conservative concepts, see John Weiss, *The Fascist Tradition. Radical Right-Wing Extremism in Modern Europe* (New York, 1967). On the post-1945 persistence of fascist ideas, see Karl Dietrich Bracher, *The German Dictatorship: The Origins, Structure, and Effects of National Socialism* (New York, 1970), pp. 469–501, and George L. Mosse, *The Crisis of German Ideology: Intellectual Origins of the Third Reich* (New York, 1964), pp. 9–10; on the dimness of their prospects see Carsten, *Rise*, pp. 236–37.

[2] This is not intended to promote the equality of all causative factors, a notion properly excoriated by Arno J. Mayer, *Dynamics of Counterrevolution in Europe* (New York, 1971), pp. 18–19. My own research indicates that fascism in Germany and Italy was essentially an attempt by the middle classes to suppress the political aspirations of their working classes. But that does not explain why Nazism and Fascism were chosen as the instruments for this.

[3] Compare, for example, what Gerhard Ritter said in his article "The Historical Foundations of the Rise of National Socialism," in Maurice Baumont *et al.*, *The Third Reich* (London, 1955), p. 400: ". . . Hitler's mission in history was to accomplish that which the Emperor and his government had been unable to accomplish: to weld the nation into a closed, warlike community. . . ."

[4] Stanley G. Payne, *Falange: A History of Spanish Fascism* (Stanford, 1961), stresses the integrative goals in the ideas of José Antonio Primo de Rivera (pp. 39–40, 133 ff) but quotes him ultimately insisting that the *Falange* was not a fascist movement (p. 78). Richard A. H. Robinson, *The Origins of Franco's Spain: The Right, the Republic, and Revolution, 1931–36* (London, 1970), details the diversity of aims within the pro-Franco coalition (pp. 291 ff).

[5] A list of features is given in Carsten, *Rise*, pp. 230–36.

[6] The need to distinguish precisely between reactionaries, conservatives, and counterrevolutionaries is explained in Mayer, *Dynamics*, pp. 48–55 and *passim*.

[7] For the idea that fascism succeeds only in societies polarized between Left and Right, see John Weiss (ed.), *Nazis and Fascists in Europe, 1918–45* (Chicago, 1969), p. 16.

[8] Eugen Weber, *Varieties of Fascism: Doctrines of Revolution in the Twentieth Century* (New York, 1964), p. 20; George Orwell, "England is a Family," in Louis L. Snyder (ed.), *The Dynamics of Nationalism: Readings in Its Meaning and Development* (New York, 1964), pp. 102–03.

[9] Otto Pflanze, *Bismarck and the Development of Germany. The Period of Unification, 1815–1871* (Princeton, 1963), pp. 122–24. He saw Liberalism in the same way: pp. 111–12.

[10] The germ of these ideas, though in different terms, is in Theodore H. von Laue, *Why Lenin? Why Stalin? A Reappraisal of the Russian Revolution, 1900–1930* (New York, 1964), especially pp. 16, 30–31, and 65 ff.

[11] Carsten, *Rise*, p. 9. The most convenient short summary of the internal effects of World War I is in Gordon A. Craig, *Europe Since 1815* (New York, 1961), pp. 512–18 and 523–24.

[12] Except to those who blamed Germany's defeat on a "stab in the back." But even that theory had a corollary: internal decomposition caused by insufficient national integration, as Hitler stressed in *Mein Kampf*. See Tim Mason, "The Legacy of 1918 for National Socialism," in Anthony Nicholls and Erich Matthias (eds.), *German Democracy and the Triumph of Hitler: Essays in Recent German History* (London, 1971), pp. 215–39.

[13] Ritter, "Foundations," pp. 402–03; Istvan Deak, *Germany's Left-Wing Intellectuals: A Political History of the Weltbühne and Its Circle* (Berkeley, 1968), p. 66, cites illuminating observations by Friedrich Meinecke. Also Albert Krebs, *Tendenzen und Gestalten der NSDAP. Erinnerungen an die Frühzeit der Partei* (Stuttgart, 1959), pp. 46–47. On Italy see Denis Mack Smith, *Italy: A Modern History* (Ann Arbor, 1959), pp. 308, 311; Frederico Chabod, *A History of Italian Fascism* (London, 1963), p. 73.

[14] Christopher Seton-Watson, *Italy from Liberalism to Fascism, 1870–1925* (London, 1967), pp. 482 ff.

[15] Weiss, *Nazis and Fascists*, p. 12; on Germany see Arthur Rosenberg, *Imperial Germany: The Birth of the German Republic, 1871–1918* (Boston, 1964); on Italy see the works cited in the previous two notes plus Arthur James Whyte, *The Evolution of Modern Italy* (New York, 1965).

[16] Smith, *Italy*, p. 312.

[17] Weber, *Varieties*, p. 36.

[18] Gaetano Salvemini, *The Origins of Fascism in Italy* (New York, 1973), pp. 25, 200; also Whyte, *Evolution*, p. 257 and Seton-Watson, *Italy*, pp. 504–05.

[19] Chabod, *Fascism*, pp. 36 ff; Seton-Watson, *Italy*, pp. 547 ff. A detailed correction of the general but erroneous assumption that Italy acquired universal suffrage in 1912 may be found in Salvemini, *Origins*, pp. 60–61, 122, and 225.

[20] Chabod, *Fascism*, pp. 32, 37; Salvemini, *Origins*, p. 155. It can be argued

that supporters of the Catholic Peoples party were also viewed by the upper classes as a threat since some of their leaders organized land seizures by the peasants. See Chabod, *Fascism*, pp. 28–29, and Salvemini, *Origins*, pp. 140–44.

[21] On the Weimar Republic as "controlled anarchy" see Wolfgang Sauer, "Weimar Culture: Experiments in Modernism" in *Social Research*, 39 (Summer, 1972), pp. 254–84, especially pp. 268–70.

[22] For an analysis of Mussolini's speeches showing the reiterated theme that increased Italian power would arise from domestic integration, see Chabod, *Fascism*, p. 72, and Ivone Kirkpatrick, *Mussolini: a Study in Power* (New York, 1964), p. 80.

[23] *Ibid.*, p. 128; Ritter, "Foundations," pp. 403–04; Friedrich Meinecke, *The German Catastrophe* (Boston, 1963), p. 75.

[24] The non-significance of Nazism's "25 Points" is analysed in Hannah Arendt, *The Origins of Totalitarianism* (2nd ed., New York, 1958), p. 324. Mussolini's statement that his movement was based on action, not doctrine, is from his article "The Political and Social Doctrine of Fascism," available in English in George H. Knoles and Rixford K. Snyder, *Readings in Western Civilization* (3rd ed., New York, 1951), pp. 808 ff.

[25] Whyte, *Evolution*, p. 146, and Salvemini, *Origins*, p. 85.

[26] Seton-Watson, *Italy*, pp. 17, 25.

[27] Fritz K. Ringer, *The Decline of the German Mandarins, 1890–1933* (Cambridge, Mass., 1969), shows how the intellectual establishment fostered contempt for interest representation and therefore widened consciousness of internal disharmony. This ideology was so persistent that Ralf Dahrendorf felt obliged to devote a considerable portion of his *Society and Democracy in Germany* (Garden City, N.Y., 1967) to a refutation of it.

[28] Whyte, *Evolution*, pp. 212 ff.

[29] *Ibid.*, pp. 3 f, 140 f, 147 f; Seton-Watson; *Italy*, pp. 26 f; Salvemini, *Origins*, p. 2; H. Stuart Hughes, *The United States and Italy* (rev. ed., New York, 1965), pp. 28 ff.

[30] Seton-Watson, *Italy*, pp. 59, 88 f, 95, 167; Whyte, *Evolution*, pp. 190, 199, 205 ff. Salvemini (*Origins*, pp. 74, 157) argues that the rise of Socialism contributed to Italian national unity and quotes Mussolini to that effect. But the point is not that Italian Socialists favored a unified country (after all, so did their German comrades); rather, that the mere existence of the Socialists aroused resentments, particularly among the nationalists.

[31] Geoffrey Barraclough, "The Social Dimensions of Crisis," *Social Research*, 39 (Summer, 1972), pp. 350 ff.

[32] Whyte, *Evolution*, p. 87; Seton-Watson, *Italy*, pp. 13 ff, 23–25; Salvemini, *Origins*, p. 141.

[33] Guenther Roth, *The Social Democrats in Imperial Germany: A Study in Working Class Isolation and Negative Integration* (Totowa, N.J., 1963).

[34] A working definition was recently given by J. William Fulbright ("In Thrall to Fear," *The New Yorker*, Jan. 8, 1972, p. 59): "The essence of any community—local, national, or international—is some degree of the acceptance of the

principle that the good of the whole must take precedence over the good of the parts." Sociological studies on the function of sub-organizations are summarized by Nicholas Babchuk and John N. Edwards in "Voluntary Associations and the Integration Hypothesis," *Sociological Inquiry*, 35 (number 2, 1965), pp. 149–162. An example of pathological affiliation caused by exclusion from the greater community is discussed by Nicholas Babchuk and Ralph V. Thompson in "The Voluntary Association of Negroes," *American Sociological Review*, 27 (number 5, Oct. 1962), pp. 647–55. I am equally concerned with the intensification of bonds *within* voluntary associations. An example of this is the extravagant sentiment expressed by one of Milton Meyer's respondents (*They Thought They Were Free: The Germans, 1933–45*, Chicago, 1955, p. 90): "The Voluntary Fire Department *über alles!* My life for the Voluntary Fire Department!"

[35] George Hills, *Franco: The Man and His Nation* (New York, 1967), p. 56.

[36] Stanley G. Payne, *Franco's Spain* (New York, 1967), p. 56.

[37] Carsten, *Rise*, pp. 201–04.

[38] Payne, *Franco's Spain*, pp. 76 ff and *passim*.

[39] William Z. Shetter, *The Pillars of Society: Six Centuries of Civilization in the Netherlands* (The Hague, 1971), pp. 6 f.

[40] *Ibid.*, pp. 21, 172. See also Johan Goudsblom, *Dutch Society* (New York, 1967) and Arend Lijphart, *The Politics of Accommodation: Pluralism and Democracy in the Netherlands* (Berkeley, 1968).

[41] The social-economic dimensions of Weimar Germany's problems, as primary causes for the collapse of parliamentary democracy, are stressed by T. W. Mason, "The Primary of Politics—Politics and Economics in National Socialist Germany," newly revised in Henry A. Turner, Jr. (ed.), *Nazism and the Third Reich* (New York, 1972), pp. 178 f.

[42] Mosse, *Crisis*, pp. 2–4, 283–86.

[43] With respect to the *Weltbühne*, mine is a controversial assertion. The case against the *Weltbühne* circle is most fully stated in George L. Mosse's article "Left-Wing Intellectuals in the Weimar Republic" in his *Germans and Jews: The Right, the Left, and the Search for a "Third Force" in Pre-Nazi Germany* (New York, 1970), pp. 171–225; against Tucholsky particularly by Gordon Craig, "Engagement and Neutrality in Weimar Germany," *The Journal of Contemporary History*, 2 (April, 1967), pp. 49–63. Deak, *Left-Wing Intellectuals*, pp. 4–9, 41 f, and 225 ff is more sympathetic to the *Weltbühne*. For a defense of Tucholsky and his colleagues, see Harold L. Poor, *Kurt Tucholsky and the Ordeal of Germany, 1914–1935* (New York, 1968), pp. 83 f, and Fritz K. Ringer, "Mosse's *Germans and Jews*," *The Journal of Modern History*, 44 (Sept., 1972), pp. 392–97.

My position is not that these intellectuals were impractical (the *Weltbühne*'s campaign for a united Left addressed the gravest practical problem of Germany's democratic forces) but that these writers were more interested in talking to each other than to people who might do something (see Mosse, *Germans and Jews*, pp. 193–99, 215). Contrast the behavior of Günter Grass in the 1960's. It is in this way that the *Weltbühne* circle shows the typical group inwardness of a sub-community.

On the *Tat* circle see Walter Struve, *Elites Against Democracy: Leadership Ideals in Bourgeois Political Thought in Germany, 1890–1933* (Princeton, 1973), pp. 353–76, and Klemens von Klemperer, *Germany's New Conservatism: Its History and Dilemma in the Twentieth Century* (Princeton, 1957), pp. 97–100, 129–133, and *passim*. Common to Left and Right intellectuals was the goal of installing themselves as a new national elite, another hallmark of sub-community behavior.

[44] Even the supposedly all-powerful industrialists could not compel fusion among the middle class parties, despite threats to withhold the campaign contributions on which these parties depended. See Henry Ashby Turner, Jr., "Big Business and the Rise of Hitler," *The American Historical Review*, 75 (Oct., 1969), p. 58.

[45] The crucial role of economic factors, especially in the middle period of the Weimar Republic, is stressed in "The Coming of the Nazis," *Times Literary Supplement*, Feb. 1, 1974, pp. 93–96.

[46] Ferdinand A. Hermans, "Proportional Representation and the Breakdown of German Democracy," *Social Research*, 3 (1936), pp. 411–33; Larry Eugene Jones, " 'The Dying Middle': Weimar Germany and the Fragmentation of Bourgeois Politics," *Central European History*, 5 (March, 1972), pp. 23–54.

[47] Peter Gay, *Weimar Culture: The Outsider as Insider* (New York, 1968), pp. 78 f and *passim*.

[48] *Ibid.*, p. 80.

[49] Sheldon Cheney, *The Story of Modern Art* (New York, 1947), p. 397. On other communes see Mosse, *Crisis*, pp. 108–24.

[50] Siegfried Kracauer, *From Caligari to Hitler: A Psychological Study of the German Film* (New York, 1959), p. 5.

[51] Claude David, "Stefan George: Aesthetes or Terrorists?" in Baumont *et al*, *The Third Reich*.

[52] Martin Esslin, *Brecht: The Man and His Work* (New York, 1961), pp. 17, 45 f, 49, and especially 54.

[53] Klemperer, *New Conservatism*, pp. 76–88.

[54] Gay, *Weimar Culture*, p. 85 f.

[55] Roy Pascal, "Revolutionary Conservatism: Moeller van den Bruck," in Baumont *et al*, *The Third Reich*, p. 344 f.

[56] Quoted by Walter Tormin (ed.), *Die Weimarer Republik: Zeitgeschichte in Text und Quellen* (Hanover, 1962), p. 102.

[57] Ernst Röhm, *Die Geschichte eines Hochverräters* (Munich, 1933). Also Robert G. L. Waite, *The Vanguard of Nazism: The Free Corps Movement in Postwar Germany, 1918–1923* (New York, 1959), p. 278.

[58] Klaus Epstein, *Matthias Erzberger and the Dilemma of German Democracy* (Princeton, 1959), pp. 373–77.

[59] On the Nazis as a bourgeois fusion party see Jeremy Noakes, *The Nazi Party in Lower Saxony, 1921–1933* (Oxford, 1971), pp. 246–50.

[60] *Ibid.*, pp. 35–38, 45 f, 48–53, 58 f, 78 f, and 85 f indicate that despite personal differences with him, the leaders of the early Nazi party had no choice but to support Hitler or see their movement break up. The development of the leader cult

as a decision reciprocally reached by Hitler and his followers is stressed in Wolfgang Horn, *Führerideologie und Parteiorganisation in der NSDAP (1919–1933)* (Düsseldorf, 1972), pp. 423–29. The thesis that this was not a practical political move but the consequence of the irrational needs of totalitarian types (a position I do not share) is argued by Dietrich Orlow, *The History of the Nazi Party: 1919–1933* (Pittsburgh, 1969), pp. vii, 1–10, and *passim*. The classic analysis of the pragmatic function of charismatic politics is Joseph Nyomarky, *Charisma and Factionalism in the Nazi Party* (Minneapolis, 1967).

[61] For a description of this see my *The Nazi Seizure of Power: The Experience of a Single German Town, 1930–35* (Chicago, 1965), pp. 209–26.

[62] William Kornhauser, *The Politics of Mass Society* (Glencoe, Ill., 1959) and Arendt, *Origins*, pp. 305–88.

[63] Edward N. Peterson, *The Limits of Hitler's Power* (Princeton, 1969), pp. 404–27. On the factories, see Hans-Gerd Schumann, *Nationalsozialismus und Gewerk-schaftsbewegung: Die Vernichtung der deutschen Gewerkschaften und der Aufbau der "Deut-schen Arbeitsfront"* (Hanover, 1958), pp. 3, 127–30; *Deutschland-Bericht der Sopade* (April, 1935) pp. 22–35; Dietrich Orlow, *The History of the Nazi Party: 1933–1945* (Pittsburgh, 1973), p. 87. I have described other ways in which "totalitarianism" was circumscribed in an article "Objective and Subjective Inhibitants in the German Resistance to Hitler," in Franklin H. Littell and Hubert G. Locke (eds.), *The German Church Struggle and the Holocaust* (Detroit, 1974), pp. 114–123. The entire question of the extent of integration within Nazi Germany is an exceptionally promising field for investigation.

[64] The pioneer study of this is H. R. Trevor-Roper, *The Last Days of Hitler* (3rd ed., New York, 1962). Subsequent studies of individual institutions are too numerous to cite, but all have confirmed this interpretation. Particularly the SS took on sub-community characteristics in the Third Reich.

[65] *Ibid.*, pp. 64 f, 295–99; Mason, "Primacy," pp. 193–96.

[66] F. W. Deakin, *The Six Hundred Days of Mussolini* (rev. ed., New York, 1966).

[67] Popular antagonism toward the war was so strong among Germans in 1939 that Nazi officials feared widespread passive resistance to it. See Orlow, *Nazi Party 1933–45*, pp. 263 ff.

[68] Chabod, *Fascism*, pp. 87, 96, 110.

[69] Hans Mommsen, "Social Views and Constitutional Plans of the Resistance," in Hermann Graml *et al.*, *The German Resistance to Hitler* (Berkeley, 1970), pp. 57–147, especially 90 ff. But even the resisters were obsessed with the idea of "community." See *ibid*, pp. 92–105.

[70] David Schoenbaum, *Hitler's Social Revolution: Class and Status in Nazi Germany 1933–1939* (Garden City, N.Y., 1966), especially pp. 298–301, and Dahrendorf, *Society*. See also Joachim C. Fest, *Hitler* (New York, 1974), pp. 792 ff.

[71] Quoted by Payne, *Falange*, p. 8 and by Hugh Thomas, "Spain," in S. J. Woolf (ed.), *European Fascism* (New York, 1969), p. 286. I use the latter's translation.

4

Janus: The Two Faces of Fascism

BY ALAN CASSELS

The years 1918–1945 are often and justifiably held to comprise a fairly coherent and well-rounded period of modern European history. In the decade or so after World War II the concept of totalitarianism was commonly advanced as the mark of identification, the determinant even, of this epoch.[1] This may have been in some measure a function of the Cold War, for it was undoubtedly convenient on one side of the Iron Curtain to equate Stalinist totalitarianism with that other sort presumably overthrown in 1945.[2] Conversely, the relaxation of the Cold War seems to have given rise to the admission of vital distinctions between communism and fascism, and furthermore to a recognition of fascism itself as perhaps the predominant trait of the years 1918–1945. In turn, this has necessarily stimulated a number of recent enquiries into the nature of fascism.[3] In particular, attention has been directed to the basic question: Was fascism, in fact, a definable entity? Or, on the contrary, were there not a variety of disparate national movements, all employing the word fascism? It is to this problem that this paper is addressed.

Inevitably, in seeking the quintessence of fascism, one is drawn to a consideration of political concepts and social ideas. And immediately one encounters the difficulty that most fascists affected to scorn philosophical constructs. Deeds were deliberately exalted at the expense of theory; doctrine tended to be invented, if at all, in haphazard, opportunistic fashion. However, one may suspect that this emphasis on action for its own sake was mainly a propaganda device to give the fascist movements a vigorous, youthful, devil-may-care appearance. Moreover, fascists had a rough and ready notion of the ideal society at which they aimed, and the charismatic fascist leaders symbolized for their followers at least a generalized set of social and political attitudes. Fascist ideas constituted a vague *Weltanschauung* rather than, as in the case of Marxist-Leninism, an intellectual dialectic. Thus, we are dealing here, not with a precise ideology, but with the loosely formulated aspirations and inchoate impulses which motivated the fascist movements.

Of all forms of fascism the German National Socialist movement, for obvious reasons, has received most intensive study. Within the past few years, after a quarter of a century of scholarship, there appears to have developed something of a consensus on the fundamental nature and purpose of Hitler's regime. Old interpretations of Nazism—as a tool of monopoly capital, or as an embodiment of Prussian militarism, or as a mere expression of Hitler's personal will to power—have been, if not totally discredited, at least severely eroded. In their place has emerged a growing recognition of Nazism as nothing more nor less than a revulsion against the modern world and a total rejection of all its values.[4] Nazism's enemy was the whole complex of assumptions underlying the eighteenth-century Enlightenment and the industrial revolutions of the nineteenth and twentieth centuries.[5] Its ambition was regressive, to fly back to a past age where the complexities of modern life had no place.[6] The specific historical era to which the Nazis aspired to return was not clear. Maybe it was a feudal age; Hitler wrote with reference to the Teutonic knights: "We take up where we broke off six centuries ago." [7] But more likely, this ideal past society was something more primitive, compounded of the Wagnerian operas and ancient Germanic sagas that the *Führer* admired so much. Hitler aptly summarized his own vision in 1937. "The main plank in the National Socialist programme is to abolish the liberal concept of the individual and the Marxian concept of humanity, and to substitute for them the *Volk* community, rooted in the soil and united by the bond of its common blood." [8]

Anti-Semitism was central to this world view. In order to

70

recapture the lost innocence of the past, it was necessary to purge contemporary society of its impurities. And the Jew, in Nazi thought, was not only the symbol but the source of all modern evils. The abuses of capitalism were ascribed to Jewish finance, and the class war and Marxism to Jewish intellectuals.[9] Even Christianity, which Hitler regarded as a perversion, was a Jewish plot: "The heaviest blow that ever struck humanity was the coming of Christianity. Bolshevism is Christianity's illegitimate child. Both are inventions of the Jew." [10] Hence, the destruction of the Jewish race became the Nazi prerequisite for a reversion to an uncorrupt past; "a matter . . . of political hygiene," one Nazi official called it.[11] Hitler was perfectly sincere when he said: "The Jew must clear out of Europe. Otherwise no understanding will be possible between Europeans. It is the Jew who prevents everything." [12]

That Nazism's true nature rested in its primeval and irrational racism is hardly a new contention. It is, for example, implicit in the substance and titles of two early works by the renegade Nazi, Hermann Rauschning: *The Revolution of Nihilism* and *The Voice of Destruction*.[13] But also this view has come to enjoy of late a deservedly expanded currency. This has been due in part to the scholarly attention recently paid to the *völkisch* content of pre-Hitlerian German culture, which offered such fertile ground for Hitler's nihilistic experiment. In this connection, one thinks of G. L. Mosse's *The Crisis of German Ideology*, F. Stern's *The Politics of Cultural Despair*, and P. J. Pulzer's *The Rise of Political Anti-Semitism in Germany and Austria*.[14]

The interpretation of Nazism as a throwback to a barbaric past has been further strengthened, and expressed in more sophisticated fashion than hitherto, by the philosopher-historian, Ernst Nolte, in his *Der Faschismus in seiner Epoche*,[15] translated as *Three Faces of Fascism*. The crux of Nolte's argument is to be found in his use of the concept of transcendence. Transcendence is split into two categories:

Theoretical transcendence may be taken to mean the reaching out of the mind beyond what exists and what can exist toward an absolute whole; in a broader sense this may be applied to all that goes

71

beyond, that releases man from the confines of the everyday world and which, as an "awareness of the horizon," makes it possible for him to experience the world as a whole.

Practical transcendence can be taken to mean the social process, even its early stages, which continually widens human relationships, thereby rendering them in general more subtle and more abstract— the process which disengages the individual from traditional ties and increases the power of the group until it finally assails even the primordial forces of nature and history.[16]

Transcendence would thus appear to be equated with human development and progress. Practical transcendence represents the form that progress, especially Western progress, has taken over the last two centuries. However, as Nolte admits, resistance to this "is more or less common to all conservative movements." The peculiar character of fascism is revealed only in "its struggle against theoretical transcendence." For this constituted not only the denial of past social progress, but also the denial of the intellectual capacity of the human species ever to achieve growth; in short, a denial of even the possibility of progress. In Nolte's summation, this was "the despair of the feudal section of bourgeois society for its traditions, and the bourgeois element's betrayal of its revolution." [17]

Such concepts are of undeniable value in discussing the antiintellectual and anti-modernist National Socialist movement in Germany. And patently Nolte's thesis is conditioned by his acquaintance with the fascist phenomenon in his native Germany. The question remains whether one can apply this construct of antitranscendence, as Nolte tries to do, to fascism at large. Here, it is clearly appropriate to turn to the second most prominent variety of fascism—that of Mussolini's Italy. For Mussolini's regime was always something of an exemplar for international fascism. As the first fascist by a wide margin to gain power, the *Duce* invited imitation. Even in the 1930's when the upsurge of fascism throughout Europe plainly owed much to the physical might of the Third Reich, fascists in search of a foreign model turned at least as often to Fascist Italy as to Nazi Germany.

72

Very broadly speaking, Mussolini's Fascism derived its inspiration from two sources, one for foreign and the other for domestic policy. Abroad, Italian Fascists were enjoined to recreate the glories of ancient Rome. At least one writer has seen in "the idea of Rome" an authentic totalitarian ideology.[18] However, whether this evocation of the past can be equated with Hitler's glorification of primitive, tribal nationalism is very dubious. For one thing, classical Rome was a cosmopolitan ideal, and Mussolini's imperialism lacked the fanatical racism of Nazi Germany.[19] (It was no coincidence that the official introduction of anti-Semitism into Italy in 1938 was met by disapproval and noncompliance on the part of Fascists and non-Fascists alike.[20]) Furthermore, while "the idea of Rome" recalled a concrete historical experience, Nazism's golden age of the past was a mythical, probably prehistoric one. By appealing to a familiar heritage, Mussolini exhorted his Fascists to emulate the deeds of antique Roman heroes; on the other hand, Hitler's use of a legendary past was calculated to induce his followers, not only to do what the distant Teutonic giants had done, but also to be those same tribal heroes, reincarnated in the twentieth century. The Nazi appeal to the past was part of a campaign to transform the very nature of modern man; as such, it was a value-laden concept. By contrast, Fascist Italian patriotism was limited and conventional. Set against the Nazi yardstick, it is difficult to dispute Hannah Arendt's dismissal of Mussolini's regime as "just an ordinary nationalist dictatorship." [21]

When we turn to prescriptions for social action on the home front, an even more significant distinction between the German and Italian forms of fascism is revealed. Mussolini's answer to the problem of the divisiveness of modern, class-ridden society was corporativism, a programme designed to obliterate old regional and class divisions by a reorganization of society along occupational lines. Although the *Duce* was highly successful between the wars in cornering the market in corporative philosophy, this aspect of Fascist Italian activity has often been overlooked.[22] This neglect is no doubt due in part to the belated formulation of corporative doctrine, several years after Mussolini took office. Corporativism in

Fascist Italy thus seemed an effort to apply a veneer of intellectual respectability to an otherwise unprincipled movement—although in fact corporative syndicates within the Fascist party antedated the March on Rome.[23] Perhaps a more important factor in the disregard of Fascist corporativism is the simple truth that corporativism, even when put on paper and on the statute book, was never put into practice. In Mussolini's Italy, and indeed in all other fascist communities where corporativism was purportedly applied, the corporative structure proved to be no more than a cloak for ruthless exploitation of labour and a reservoir of jobs for party hacks.[24] Yet corporativism, however traduced, remained an ideal capable of firing the enthusiasm of a substantial portion of the interwar intelligentsia.[25] Above all, corporativism pointed the direction in which Mussolini wanted to move, only to be thwarted by his own incompetence and the intractability of Italian society.[26] Constituting therefore an innate impulse in Italian fascism, corporativism offers us a guide to that movement's real nature.

Modern corporativism has two ancestors. First, the Catholic church has always regarded society as an organic, corporate whole. And towards the close of the nineteenth century the Vatican, in order to rebut atheistic socialism and its advocacy of the class war, saw fit to refurbish and rebroadcast its traditional corporative ideas. However, Mussolini and most fascist leaders owed their corporativism more to the second source—that of syndicalist socialism. In particular, it was from Georges Sorel that they acquired their fascination with trade unionism and representation by vocation. The point is that both of these traditions, Catholic and socialist, fall squarely into the mainstream of Western thought. Consequently so does corporativism. Not surprisingly, corporativism faces the problems of a modern, industrial age in an eminently rational manner; in theory, it poses a positive and credible solution. It does not propose a retreat to a pre-industrial, rural paradise; rather, in somewhat eclectic fashion, it tries to adapt from the recent past. This was readily admitted in the official statement of Fascist Italian corporativism contained in the 1932 edition of the *Enciclopedia italiana*. Here the authors—Mussolini himself and his erstwhile education minister, Giovanni Gentile—wrote:

74

The Fascist negation of Socialism, Democracy, Liberalism should not, however, be interpreted as implying a desire to drive the world backwards to positions occupied prior to 1789. . . .

Fascism uses in its construction whatever elements in the Liberal, Socialist, or Democratic doctrines still have a living value. . . .

No doctrine has ever been born completely new, completely defined and owing nothing to the past; no doctrine can boast a character of complete originality; it must always derive, if only historically, from the doctrines that have preceded it and develop into further doctrines which will follow. [27]

Thus, Italian Fascism advertised itself as the heir to two centuries of scientific rationalism, and as a modern movement with a progressive social philosophy.[28] It claimed to be, in this sense, a transcendental phenomenon. This, of course, afforded a stark contrast with Nazi Germany. To be sure, corporative ideas were not altogether absent from the Nazi programme; they are discernible as early as 1920 in the famous Twenty-Five Points.[29] But for the Nazis, corporativism was not a modern concept but rather a throwback to a lost world of the medieval guilds. And to Hitler himself, corporativism was mainly a propaganda device to keep certain intellectuals loyal to the movement. Once he gained power, corporativism became of no account; the Nazi Labour Front never approached a genuine corporative experiment, and Nazi economic policy fell into the pragmatic hands of Hjalmar Schacht. More to the point, the ideas and the very names of Nazism's corporative theorists—Gottfried Feder, Walther Darré, Otto Strasser—passed out of circulation after 1933. Unlike Fascist Italy, where at least lip service was always paid to corporative ideals, Nazi Germany dispensed with not only the practice but also the theory of corporativism.[30] This was only natural, not to say inevitable. For it would have been totally inconsistent for the Nazi movement, whose spirit lay in the mythical past, to embrace a socio-economic creed based on a rational appraisal of the modern world.

Let us summarize the contrast drawn so far. On the one hand, Nazism, whose *Führer* had perhaps more scorn for the masses than any other fascist leader, consciously derided man's intelligence and proffered as substitute the cult of primitive feeling. On the other, Italian Fascism, by clinging doctrinally to corporativism, disclosed a residual faith in human reason and in the Enlightenment vision of the perfectibility of man. To simplify drastically, one might term these two sorts of fascism, respectively, backward-looking and forward-looking.[31] Next, a reason for this cleavage within the ranks of international fascism needs to be suggested.

Since the Berlin *Götterdämmerung* of 1945, scholars and publicists have been fascinated by the abnormal fury and extremism of German National Socialism. They have customarily and properly ascribed it to the extraordinary dislocation produced in German life by the technological advances of the period 1871 to 1933. These occurred so swiftly that social patterns and culture were left hopelessly in arrears. In this historical pattern, the failure of the Weimar Republic to produce the expected and urgent social transformation of Germany was shattering. Thus David Schoenbaum writes:

> *What complicated solution in Germany was not a failure to recognize the structural inadequacies of industrial society, but rather a failure to find an alternative social model adequate to correct them. Advancing literacy, urbanization, industrialization, and the development of overseas agriculture all pointed to the liberal society envisaged by the Weimar Convention. But the main currents of social thought since at least the constitution of the Reich pointed away from it.*[32]

And in the same vein the German sociologist, Ralf Dahrendorf:

> *But the parties of the Weimar coalition did not want the social transformation that they needed. . . . Insofar as the Weimar parties had ideas of social reform at all, these were largely directed at the transformation of the authoritarian welfare state into its republican version; but most of them regarded the national question as more important than the social question.*[33]

Now, if the ferocity of Nazism responded to the gulf fixed between the material conditions of German life and the nation's social

76

mores, then presumably a different set of socio-economic factors should have given rise to a different sort of fascism. In other words, the nature of fascism, it might be suggested, was relative to the stage of economic development reached by the national community in which each fascist movement occurred.[34]

By 1933, Germany had experienced a full measure of industrialization, whereupon the Nazis in a fit of destructive rage used the tools of a technological age to attack the very society which industrialism had created.[35] But in 1922 Italy was, by comparison, an industrially underdeveloped country.[36] Perhaps just as important as the material situation was the psychological mood of the Italian nation. Whereas Germans under Weimar felt caught up in the swirl of modernity, articulate Italians after the "mutilated victory" of 1918 perceived their country to be retarded, held back by the brake of the backward South. The ambition of Italian patriots was to emulate the more advanced nations, both nationalistically and economically. The traditional Right in Italy, however, wanted to have its cake and eat it; it wanted modernization but without the attendant evils of liberalism, democracy, and even socialism, which had afflicted the industrializing states of the nineteenth century. This, in effect, is what Mussolini promised to accomplish. To cite the *Enciclopedia italiana* (1932) once more:

> *Fascism is the doctrine best adapted to represent the tendencies and the aspirations of a people, like the people of Italy, who are rising again after many centuries of abasement and foreign servitude. But empire demands discipline, the co-ordination of all forces and a deeply-felt sense of duty and sacrifice: this fact explains many aspects of the practical working of the regime, the character of many forces in the State, and the necessarily severe measures which must be taken against those who would oppose this spontaneous and inevitable movement of Italy in the twentieth century.*[37]

Fascism was supposed to bring Italy into the twentieth century, but without disturbing the privileges of the conservatives. Mussolini's propaganda envisaged an industrialized nation state capable of playing the role of a major European power, while his strident anticommunism guaranteed the status of the traditional upper classes.

77

Corporativism was chosen to fulfil this dual undertaking; corporative theory could be paraded as an up-to-date method of increasing national efficiency, and although inconsistent with absolute *laisser-faire*, it was nonetheless quite compatible with the preservation of capitalism and the *latifondi*.

If this analysis is correct, we have created in embryo two prototypes of fascism. One sprang up in advanced societies, and was nihilistic and backward-looking in the style of Nazism. The other emerged in relatively under-industrialized communities like early twentieth-century Italy, was forward-looking, and promoted itself as an agent of modernization along corporative lines. Now, to apply this hypothesis in a conscientious way to the entire spectrum of fascist movements would be a Herculean task, far beyond the scope of this paper. Therefore, what follows apropos non-German and non-Italian kinds of fascism is of necessity put forward in a most tentative and generalized manner.

Looking first at the less advanced nations, one is confronted by the phenomenon known as clerical-corporative fascism. This is perhaps a misnomer if only because it suggests that the Catholic church played a more active role than, in fact, it did. The church, on balance, was passively tolerant of the fascist movements, and the measure of clerical support fluctuated considerably from one country to another. However, the phrase "clerical-corporative" gives at least a rough indication that in the relatively backward states fascism bore a Mussolinian, rather than a Hitlerian, stamp.[38]

Wherever fascism appeared in the underdeveloped Latin world, for example, it showed a marked resemblance to the corporative variety encountered in Fascist Italy. In Spain, this was predictable, for the Falange, or Spanish fascist party, was shaped by an alliance between Left-wing proponents of national syndicalism and conservative Christian corporativists.[39] For a brief time in 1935–1936 the Falange enjoyed an independent existence under José Antonio Primo de Rivera. Its objective, as described by Stanley Payne, was "to create a nationalist, élitist culture based on modernized Spanish values, harmonizing tradition with the revolutionary demands of the twentieth century." [40] But then the movement was quickly swallowed up in Franco's coalition. Since the

78

eclipse of the Axis in World War II, the Falange has occupied a declining position in Franco's regime. Significantly, however, the one feature of Falangist policy which has been incorporated into Franco's Spain is the institution of Spanish corporativism known as national syndicalism.[41]

Across the frontier in Portugal a strong tradition of corporativism goes back at least as far as the founding of the movement *Integralismo Lusitano* in 1914.[42] It was on this that Antonio Salazar built after establishing his authoritarian rule in 1932. It is, of course, debatable whether Salazar's paternalistic dictatorship should be termed fascist at all. But insofar as Portugal veered towards fascism, it was towards a fascism consciously modelled on Mussolini's Italy. The framework of the "new state" of 1933 was proudly proclaimed "the first Corporative constitution in the world." [43] A "second corporative drive" was announced in 1956 as part of a programme to update Portugal's economy. Salazar's corporative regime has been authoritatively summed up as "an 'industrializing' and 'modernizing' dictatorship." [44]

A third version of Latin corporative fascism occurred in Argentina between 1946 and 1955. Here, corporative ideas took the title of *Justicialismo*, which Juan Perón liked to describe as the Third Position, a compromise between individualism and collectivism. *Justicialismo* served Perón as a somewhat imprecise "national doctrine," ideally suited to hold together the heterogeneous coalition of social forces on which his power rested. Nevertheless, like Fascist Italian corporativism, Argentinian *Justicialismo* held out the prospect of reform and progress in a recognizably fascist style.[45]

All of these Latin examples of fascism or quasi-fascism were nationalistic; occasionally they were moved by memories of historic imperial splendor; there were traces of anti-Semitism. But in no case was any of these movements inspired by a racial vision of the past, nor did any seek a refuge in mythology as did Nazi Germany.[46]

Austria, as constituted after 1918, was another under-industrialized country, but here Pan-Germanism was a rampant force. All fascist groups were therefore bound to indulge in racist nationalism more or less. In this context, it is perhaps remarkable to what

79

extent Austrian fascism conformed to the corporative pattern we have traced for economically retarded areas. Of course, the Austrian Nazi party, from 1925 a mere appendage of Hitler's movement,[47] must be ruled out as representative of Austrian fascism. Instead, the most indigenous Austrian fascist movement was undoubtedly that of the *Heimwehr*. During the 1920's the *Heimwehr* accumulated about it a good deal of corporative doctrine. Its chief theoretician was Othmar Spann whose ideal was a *Ständestaat*, a state based on professional representation. The *Heimwehr*'s corporativism was elevated into a sort of party platform by the Korneuburg Oath of 1930. In March 1934 the *Heimwehr* joined with the clerical corporativists in Dollfuss' Fatherland Front; and in May Chancellor Dollfuss declared Austria a Christian corporative state.[48] The *Heimwehr* remained loyal to Mussolini, who supplied the movement liberally with funds and arms, and Dollfuss and his successor, Schuschnigg, remained true to the corporative version of fascism. All of which goes some way towards explaining why by 1938 Austria's corporative fascists had been outflanked by the extreme racist, Berlin-dominated Austrian Nazis.[49]

It is not until one turns to Eastern Europe that the correspondence of under-industrialized community and the corporative style of fascism is seriously disturbed. Hungary and Rumania were certainly backwards in economic terms, and both produced native fascist movements. In Hungary fascism was represented by the regime of General Gömbös from 1932 to 1936 and also by Ferenc Szálasi's Arrow Cross organization; their Rumanian counterpart consisted of the series of brotherhoods founded by C. Z. Codreanu, culminating in the Legion of the Archangel Michael and its political arm, the Iron Guard. These groups did not eschew corporativism. Gömbös was an avowed imitator of Mussolini and all his works; Szálasi, put into power in Budapest in 1944 by the Nazis, talked of "national capitalism," by which he implied a kind of corporativism. In Rumania the Iron Guard became the political home of Mihail Manoilescu, one of the foremost corporative theorists of the 1930's.[50] However, there was one overriding factor in the Danubian situation which prevented these movements from developing in the corporative direction taken by the fascisms of

80

other backward countries. This was the intensity of racial feeling in the area, which in the interwar period expressed itself in a fierce anti-Semitism. Rumanian anti-Semitism had been deep-seated for generations, while in Hungary the prejudice stemmed largely from the Béla Kun episode of 1919. In both countries, in fact, the Jew was equated with bolshevism and, as in Nazi Germany, Hungarian and Rumanian fascist movements preoccupied themselves with the purging of the national society of these alien elements. In the process their objective became, not to build a rationally conceived corporative state of the future, but to re-create some racially pure society out of the legendary past. Thus, Gömbös and Szálasi dreamed and spoke of a "Carpathian-Danubian Great Fatherland," conceived in terms of mythical "Turanianism" or "Hungarism." [51] Even more firmly rooted in an imaginary past was Codreanu's "mystic nationalism." [52] Writes the Rumanian Zevedei Barbu:

> For example, Cordreanu identified himself with the "people," an idealized community which he never defined save in vague and abstract terms such as "unity," "purity," "Christianity." It was an unhistorical entity including all Rumanians who had existed in the past and would exist in the future. [53]

The elemental nature of this vision was symbolized by the bag of Rumanian soil which each member of the Iron Guard was expected to wear about his neck. [54] The similarity to the primeval, tribal nationalism of the Nazis is striking.

Danubian fascists resembled the Nazis in some respects because of the common factor of racial thinking. But if the identity of Nazism was in reality determined by the stage of economic development attained by Germany, then it is to the advanced states of Western Europe—France, Belgium, and Great Britain—that one must turn for a genuine parallel. [55]

The French scene is complicated by the fact that, although fascism undoubtedly existed in France, it never coalesced into a single movement or doctrine. Of the so-called leagues of the 1930's, some were unmistakably fascist, but none succeeded in providing the nucleus for an integrated fascist front. For this reason fascism in France remained "a mood, an anti-conformist spirit," or in the

81

best-known metaphor, "a fever," which infected much of the traditional Right and a substantial portion of the Center too.[56] This meant that French fascism was conditioned, not so much by outright fascist groups, as by others on the far Right which displayed fascist inclinations. Certainly the most prominent of these was the *Action Française*,[57] which can at best be called proto-fascist.

If one takes the *Action Française* and the dictums of its archpriest, Charles Maurras, to be symptomatic of the French fascist fever, then it becomes clear how alike were the fascisms on both banks of the Rhine.[58] From its appropriate beginning in the Dreyfus Affair the *Action Française* was a dedicated foe of the whole French Revolutionary tradition. The corruption of French life began in 1789; particularly resented were Jacobin centralization and the Revolution's egalitarianism which provided opportunities for the Jews. Maurras did not originate but he elaborated skillfully on the notion of two Frances—one, the *pays légal;* the other the *pays réel.* In the latter, which existed before 1789, some indeterminate Latin and Catholic culture reigned supreme.[59] So once more we come across the hankering after a vague, romanticized past characteristic of Nazi Germany. Maurras' *pays réel* was the equivalent of Hitler's *Volksgemeinschaft.*

Although in eclipse during the 1930's, the *Action Française* came to the fore again after the fall of the Third Republic in 1940. Maurrassian ideas infused the National Revolution of Vichy France. Anti-Semitism was legalized. The Vichy intellectuals derided the vice of modern French rationalism.[60] Such corporative doctrines as were espoused drew inspiration, not from modern syndicalist socialism, but from medieval communalism. Marshal Pétain recalled the French people to the ancient verities of earth and fatherland.[61] The over-all regressive tendency of Vichy has been well summed up by René Rémond:

> *Although the needs of the moment required the regime to make use of all the nation's resources, the theme of a return to the land was in tune with the basic direction of the agrarian feelings and thought that went to make up the traditionalist organicism. It was the ancient rural society that emerged from the depths of the past.*[62]

82

By 1944 the Maurrassians themselves had been replaced by the thoroughgoing collaborationists with the Nazi occupation forces. But the change was more one of degree than of kind; to execute the National Revolution, it was found necessary to employ Nazi political methods.[63] The dream of the *Action Française*, of the Vichy government, and of most Frenchmen stricken with the fascist fever was to return to a blissful, racially pure, pre-industrial age. The difference with the German National Socialists lay not in purpose, but in a certain reluctance to use brutal means to achieve the goal.

Belgium, another fairly industrialized nation, also produced fascist groups whose vision was directed to the past rather than the future. For instance, Jean Degrelle came to fascism through Maurras' *Action Française*, and significantly his Rexist party's newspaper was called *Pays réel*.[64] The Rexist movement was short on programme and philosophy, little more in fact than an emotional reaction against the modern world.[65] An idealized "popular community" was set against "the concept of the individual which forms the erroneous philosophical foundation of the present regime and which was born of the catastrophic ideologies of the seventeenth and eighteenth centuries."[66] Other Walloon fascists aspired to a re-creation of the sixteenth-century union of Holland, Flanders, and Luxemburg. Flemish fascists propounded union with their racial kin in Holland and even Germany.[67] In short, all rejected the twentieth century; all betrayed a longing for nationalism of an ancestral, tribal sort.

But, of course, Great Britain is the touchstone of the technologically developed nations of Western Europe. If fascism in advanced communities did indeed take on the form of a complete and nihilist rejection of modernity, then this should certainly have been evident in industrialized Britain. In Sir Oswald Mosley British fascism possessed certainly the most intellectually able of all the fascist leaders, and one who imposed his unmistakable personal stamp on the movement. On the surface, Mosley was far from an emotional admirer of bygone times. His first book, written in conjunction with John Strachey in 1925, bore the title *Revolution by Reason*. His answer to the Great Depression was couched in rational, progressive terms, and consisted of a mixture of corporativism and

83

what would later be called Keynesian economics. And his speeches were punctuated with pleas for a "modern" approach.[68] True, he was prone to speak of the British "race," and to attract people like A.K. Chesterton, the novelist's brother, who "saw Mosley as the man who would remove the stain of industrialism from England's green and pleasant land." [69] However, nothing really foretold the drastic change that Mosley and his British Union of Fascists underwent in 1934. In the space of a year or so the intellectual concentration on concrete economic problems gave way to an irrational and rabid anti-Semitism, which was accompanied by the deliberate use of violence. The most likely explanation for this shift is that it was a strategy designed to transform the B.U.F. into a mass movement. Hitherto, Mosley and his adherents had been regarded as a useful ginger group on the flank of the conventional political parties. It was only with the adoption of anti-Semitism that the B.U.F. was able to poll close to twenty per cent in some working-class districts (although at no time did it represent a power in national politics).[70] In response to his new racist orientation, Mosley's speeches grew more demagogic, and rang with increasing references to English "stock," "soil," "heritage" [71]—words redolent of all those fascists enraptured by *völkisch* and other tribal myths.

Oddly, Mosley himself did not seem to recognize the enormity of the change wrought in himself and British fascism after 1934. He has always protested—sincerely in all probability—that his movement was never anti-Semitic.[72] It was rather as though he stumbled into racism accidentally. Which is to say that in 1933 or 1934 Mosley came to the subconscious realization that for a fascist movement in industrial Britain to expand, it would have to capitalize on resentment against the current environment by turning its back on the modern world and all its philosophical assumptions. The token of Mosley's conversion was his embrace of the anti-Enlightenment forces of racism and violence. Thus, it is possible to see in the British experience too the congruence of advanced economic development with fascism of a regressive variety.

Thomas Mann wrote of fascism in 1938 that it was "a disease of the times which is at home everywhere and from which no country is free." [73] Fascism at large was a reaction against the liberal pluralism and Marxian dogma of an age of materialism. But if the generic cause of the fascist movements was uniform, the results varied. Where the perplexities of an industrialized community became overwhelming, fascism responded in an anti-transcendental, atavistic fashion. It propounded a radical reordering of society, and its logical conclusion was a totalitarian regime. In practice, this occurred in Nazi Germany alone. In neither Great Britain nor Belgium did the fascists come close to winning power, and in France the Vichy regime was more fascist-oriented than genuinely fascist. In industrial Western Europe fascism only promised and hinted at the primitive barbarism that Hitler actually realized. On the other hand, we have several examples of fascism in practice in less advanced societies. There, fascist movements remained mostly within a modern, rationalist framework; and perhaps because of this partial attachment to traditional values, they were able to cooperate with traditional conservatives. Thus, the Spanish Falange became a part of Franco's coalition of monarchists, aristocrats, clerics, and military nationalists. The Austrian *Heimwehr* in its heyday was directed by Prince Starhemberg, scion of the old Austrian nobility. The Iron Guard shared power briefly in Rumania with the non-fascist General Antonescu. Hungarian fascists relied on the favor of Admiral Horthy, the regent and true representative of the Magyar "historic classes." Even in Fascist Italy, Mussolini never succeeded in displacing the twin pillars of the establishment—the monarchy and the church; at best he neutralized them by co-operation.

In summary, then, the division of fascist movements according to socio-economic environment reflects on another question often asked of fascism: Was it a revolutionary or a conservative phenomenon? In industrial states fascism was racist, backward-looking, and tended to reject the power structure which emerged from the nineteenth century. Fascism here achieved a species of radicalism, although whether of the Left or Right would be hard to say. But in under-industrialized nations, by assuming a more transcendental, forward-looking stance, fascism remained relatively conventional and tied to establishment forces. This kind of fascism inevitably took on the appearance of an agent of traditional conservatism.

The hypothesis that fascism wore two faces has been advanced here as a working model to facilitate investigation. Our comprehension of the years 1918–1945 still requires further analysis of the most vital component of his epoch of fascism—or fascisms.

¹ The best known examples are probably H. Arendt, *The Origins of Totalitarianism* (1st ed.; New York, 1951), and C. Friedrich (ed.), *Totalitarianism* (Cambridge, Mass., 1954).

² L. K. Adler and T. G. Patterson, "Red Fascism: The Merger of Nazi Germany and Soviet Russia in the American Image of Totalitarianism, 1930's–1950's," *The American Historical Review*, LXXV (1970), 1046–64.

³ See, for instance, G. Allardyce (ed.), *The Place of Fascism in European History* (Englewood Cliffs, N.J., 1971); F. L. Carsten, *The Rise of Fascism* (London, 1967); N. Green (ed.) *Fascism: An Anthology* (New York, 1968); W. Laqueur and G. L. Mosse (eds.), "International Fascism, 1920–1945," *Journal of Contemporary History*, I (1966); E. Nolte, *Three Faces of Fascism: Action Française, Italian Fascism, National Socialism*, trans. L. Vennewitz (New York, 1966); E. Weber, *Varieties of Fascism* (Princeton, N.J., 1964); J. Weiss, *The Fascist Tradition* (New York, 1967); S. J. Woolf (ed.), *European Fascism* (London, 1968), and the same editor's *The Nature of Fascism* (London, 1968). On regional fascism, see C. Delzell (ed.), *Mediterranean Fascism* (New York, 1970); R. H. Kedward, *Fascism in Western Europe* (London, 1969); P. Sugar (ed.), *Native Fascism in the Successor States* (Santa Barbara, Calif., 1971).

⁴ For an early indication of this emergent consensus, see the very useful bibliographical article by A. G. Whiteside, "The Nature and Origins of National Socialism," *Journal of Central European Affairs*, XVII (1957–58), 48–73.

⁵ "The ideas [of Nazism] . . . amounted to a rejection of the enlightenment of the eighteenth century on the political plane and the industrialization of the nineteenth century on the economic plane" (A. J. Nicholls, "Germany," in Woolf, *European Fascism*, p. 67).

⁶ "Millions of Germans had not got over their longing for a return to the primitive racial community of the folk which would rid them at one blow of all perplexities afflicting the modern world: capitalism, communism, liberalism, democracy, plutocracy, newspapers, elections, big-city life—the whole complex rigmarole of contemporary urban civilization" (G. Lichtheim, *The Concept of Ideology* [New York, 1967], p. 229).

⁷ A. Hitler, *Mein Kampf*, trans. R. Manheim (Boston, 1943), p. 654. R. Koehl, "Feudal Aspects of National Socialism," *American Political Science Review*, LIV (1960), 921–933, draws a parallel between the social ideas and party structure of Nazism and certain feudal concepts of medieval Europe.

⁸ Quoted in Weiss, *Tradition*, p. 9.

⁹ "The Jewish train of thought in all this is clear. The Bolshevization of Germany—that is, the extermination of the national folkish intelligentsia to make possible the sweating of the German working class under the yoke of Jewish world fi-

nance—is conceived only as a preliminary to the further extension of this Jewish tendency of world conquest (Hitler, *Mein Kampf*, p. 623).

[10] *Hitler's Table Talk, 1941–1944*, trans. N. Cameron and R. H. Stevens (London, 1953), p. 7.

[11] Quoted in Weiss, *Tradition*, p. 108. On anti-Semitic persecution as an act of social purification, see N. Cohn, *Warrant for Genocide* (London, 1967), pp. 261–262.

[12] *Hitler's Table Talk*, p. 235.

[13] (New York, 1939) and (New York, 1940).

[14] (New York, 1964), (Berkeley, Calif., 1961), and (New York, 1964).

[15] (Munich, 1963).

[16] Nolte, *Three Faces of Fascism*, p. 433.

[17] *Ibid.*, p. 453. G. L. Mosse in his review article of *Three Faces of Fascism* in the *Journal of the History of Ideas*, XXVII (1966), 621–625, points out quite correctly that while Nazism rejected bourgeois transcendence, it substituted its own species of transcendence based on race.

[18] D. Germino, *The Italian Fascist Party in Power* (Minneapolis, 1959), pp. 136–139. It is now fairly well established that Mussolini failed in his ambition to establish a genuine totalitarian regime; this is the conclusion reached by A. Aquarone, *L'organizzazione dello Stato totalitario* (Turin, 1965). Cf. A. Cassels, *Fascist Italy* (New York, 1968), pp. 69–72.

[19] Weiss, *Tradition*, p. 114, contends that Mussolini's invasion of Ethiopia was racially motivated. But as much could be said of all European examples of the "new imperialism," and the concept of racism is thereby expanded and diluted almost to the point of uselessness.

[20] The most comprehensive work on anti-Semitism within Italy is R. De Felice, *Storia degli ebrei italiani sotto il Fascismo* (Turin, 1961).

[21] Arendt, *Origins*, p. 256. Even Nolte, *Three Faces of Fascism*, p. 370, is constrained to admit this distinction: "The swastika did not, like the lictor's bundle, recall a remote but nevertheless still tangible historical era: as an ancient and prehistoric symbol it was supposed to proclaim the future victory of 'Aryan man.'" Cf. Koehl, *American Political Science Review*, LIV, 921: "Behind the [Nazi] talk of a 'New Order' lurked the ghost of an empire long dead. But Mussolini's imagery was based upon a centralized, legalistic Roman Empire. Hitler's propaganda spoke of a second thousand-year Reich. Not the short-lived Bismarckian creation, but the fabled medieval empire of Ottonians and Hohenstaufens gleamed in the back of Hitler's mind. Indeed, to Nazi theorists, the Roman tradition as well as all modern state bureaucracy was anathema."

[22] For example, in the index of Nolte's extensive *Three Faces of Fascism* there are only three brief entries under "Corporatism"; the index to I. Kirkpatrick, *Mussolini: Study of a Demagogue* (London, 1964), the most comprehensive biography of the *Duce* in English, reveals also a scant three references under "The Corporative State."

[23] H. Finer, *Mussolini's Italy* (London, 1935), pp. 492–497.

[24] A good recent exposé of the gulf between word and deed in Fascist Italy is

D. Mack Smith, *Italy: A Modern History* (Ann Arbor, Mich., 1959), pp. 389–435, *passim*.

²⁵ Recent studies which assay a proper evaluation of the role of corporativism in Italian Fascist ideology are M. Ledeen, *The Fascist International* (New York, 1972); E. R. Tannenbaum, *The Fascist Experience: Italian Society and Culture, 1922–1945* (New York, 1972). On the attraction of Fascist corporativism outside Italy, see J. P. Diggins, *Mussolini and Fascism: The View from America* (Princeton, N.J., 1972).

²⁶ See, for instance, Mussolini's remark after his fall in 1943: "The greatest tragedy of my life came when I no longer had the strength to repel the embrace of the false Corporativists, who were in reality acting as agents of capitalism. They wished to embrace the Corporative system only in order to destroy it" (quoted in Weiss, *Tradition*, p. 91). Mussolini's standard self-apology constitutes his *Memoirs, 1942–1943*, ed. R. Klibansky, trans. F. Lobb (London, 1949), esp. Appendix III, pp. 231–243.

²⁷ "The Social and Political Doctrine of Fascism," *International Conciliation*, No. 306 (Jan. 1935), pp. 12–13.

²⁸ R. Sarti, "Fascist Modernization in Italy," *The American Historical Review*, LXXV (1970), 1029–45.

²⁹ "We demand . . . the formation of Diets and vocational Chambers for the purpose of executing the general laws promulgated by the Reich (cited in *The Speeches of Adolf Hitler, 1922–1939*, ed. N. H. Baynes [London, 1942], I, 102).

³⁰ H. Holborn, "Origins and Political Character of Nazi Ideology," *Political Science Quarterly*, LXXIX (1964), 548–549, writes of Hitler after his accession to office: "He quickly stopped the activities of the party in favor of artisans, small businessmen, and the like, and before very long gave up the attempt at building a corporative state. What came into being is probably best called a 'command economy,' a term coined by Franz L. Neumann. . . . Italian fascism, too, was of no significance for the growth of Nazi ideology. . . . The adoption of corporativism by Italian fascism found some imitation among National Socialists, but it did not become official policy after 1933." Cf. Nicholls in Woolf, *European Fascism*, pp. 63–64, 77–80, and Weiss, *Tradition*, pp. 103–104.

³¹ Weber, *Varieties*, p. 16, expresses something of this notion in terms of the contradictory expectations of fascism's mass following, "some envisaging a return to a sort of Jeffersonian golden age, while others wanted to forge ahead, through revolution, to a new collectivist social order."

³² *Hitler's Social Revolution* (New York, 1966), p. 14.

³³ *Society and Democracy in Germany* (New York, 1967), p. 398.

³⁴ A. F. K. Organski, *The Stages of Political Development* (New York, 1965), chaps. 1, 5, 6 *passim*, distinguishes between the "syncratic" fascism of newly industrializing communities and the totalitarian National Socialism ("the politics of national welfare") of industrialized Germany. Cf. W. Sauer, "National Socialism: Totalitarianism or Fascism?" *The American Historical Review*, LXXIII (1967), 415–422.

³⁵ ". . . the problem of an arrested bourgeois-industrial society, convinced by its guilt-feelings and its impotence of its own superfluousness, and prepared to

89

destroy itself with the means of the very bourgeois-industrial society it aimed to destroy" (Schoenbaum, *Revolution*, p. 300.

[36] Organski, *Stages*, pp. 9–13, 122–125, 134–135; Sauer, *The American Historical Review*, LXXIII, 419, 421. The best appraisal in English of Italy's economic conditions in the first quarter of the twentieth century is to be found in S. B. Clough, *The Economic History of Modern Italy* (New York, 1964), chaps. 3–6.

[37] *International Conciliation*, No. 306, p. 16. The equation of corporativism with modern industrial rationalization was made most explicitly by Mussolini's Minister of Justice, Alfredo Rocco (E. R. Tannenbaum, "The Goals of Italian Fascism," *The American Historical Review*, LXXIV (1969), 1195–1199).

[38] H. R. Trevor-Roper, "The Phenomenon of Fascism," in Woolf, *European Fascism*, pp. 18–38, divides fascism into two categories, "dynamic" and "clerical conservative." But then, inexplicably, he proceeds to put Mussolini's Italy into the same camp as Nazi Germany, offering both as examples of dynamic fascism.

[39] Hence, the lengthy title of Juntas de Ofensiva Nacional Sindicalista (JONS), which fused with the Falange in 1934; see S. G. Payne, *Falange: A History of Spanish Fascism* (Stanford, Calif., 1961), pp. 10–48, *passim*.

[40] *Franco's Spain* (New York, 1967), p. 96.

[41] "Something very similar to national syndicalism was the only device that could be used to harness the Spanish working class after the outbreak of the war in 1936. This was the indispensable contribution of *falangismo* to the Franco regime. To be sure, the syndical system was organized entirely as the government saw fit, but it was vital nevertheless" (Payne, *Falange*, p. 267).

[42] H. Martins, "Portugal," in Woolf, *European Fascism*, pp. 302–312.

[43] *Ibid.*, p. 315.

[44] *Ibid.*, p. 332.

[45] A. P. Whitaker, *Argentina* (Englewood Cliffs, N.J., 1964), pp. 132–134.

[46] In the beginning *Integralismo Lusitano* was quite racist and backward-looking, but had lost these traits by the 1930's (Martins, in Woolf, *European Fascism*, pp. 308–312). José Antonio Primo de Rivera had hopes for a revival of Spanish imperialism, but he was more immediately concerned with the task of curbing Catalan and Basque separatism (Payne, *Falange*, pp. 80–81). Perón's nationalism was to a great extent anti-Americanism, and an important reason for his fall was that he deserted the cause and struck a deal with Standard Oil of California (Whitaker, *Argentina*, pp. 145–150). On the limited anti-Semitism of Spanish and Argentinian fascists, see Payne, *Falange*, p. 126, and Whitaker, *Argentina*, p. 13.

[47] A. G. Whiteside, "Austria," in *The European Right*, ed. H. Rogger and E. Weber (Berkeley, Calif., 1965), p. 333.

[48] *Ibid.*, pp. 334–344. Cf. L. Jedlicka, "The Austrian Heimwehr," *Journal of Contemporary History*, I (1966), 127–144, who stresses the Christian orientation of Dollfuss' experiment, and also K. R. Stadler, "Austria," in Woolf, *European Fascism*, pp. 88–110.

[49] Whiteside in Rogger and Weber, *The European Right*, pp. 344–362.

[50] For good over-all descriptions of Hungarian and Rumanian fascism, see

NOTES / CASSELS

N. M. Nagy-Talavera, *Green Shirts and Others* (Stanford, 1970). See also I. Deák, "Hungary," in Rogger and Weber, *The European Right*, pp. 364–405, and E. Weber, "Romania," *ibid.*, pp. 512–573.

⁵¹ Deák in Rogger and Weber, *The European Right*, pp. 377–378, 388–395. Carsten, *Rise*, pp. 175–176, makes an explicit comparison between these "queer tribal patterns" in Hungary and German *völkisch* ideas.

⁵² E. Weber, "The Men of the Archangel," *Journal of Contemporary History*, I (1966), 105, refers to Codreanu's "mystic nationalism, the only reality of which was a ferocious anti-Semitism."

⁵³ "Rumania," in Woolf, *European Fascism*, p. 163.

⁵⁴ *Ibid.*, p. 157.

⁵⁵ The argument which follows naturally denies the assertion that "the German crisis was *sui generis*" made by, among others, Mosse, *Crisis*, p. 315.

⁵⁶ Robert Brasillach is generally held to have given currency to the notion of a fascist fever (E. Weber, *Action Française* (Stanford, Calif., 1962), p. 514, and the same author's "France," in Rogger and Weber, *The European Right*, p. 108). Also on the intangibility of French fascism, see R. Girardet, "Notes sur l'Esprit d'un Fascisme français," *Revue Française de Science Politique*, V (1955), 529–546, and R. J. Soucy, "The Nature of Fascism in France," *Journal of Contemporary History*, I (1966), 27–30. On the adoption of fascist tenets by French non-fascists, see R. Rémond, *The Right Wing in France*, trans. J. M. Laux (Philadelphia, 1966), pp. 273–299.

⁵⁷ On the enormous influence of the Action Française in French conservative circles, see Rémond, *Right Wing*, pp. 233, 245–253, and Weber, *Action Française*, pp. 517–522.

⁵⁸ Nolte has been criticized for placing the Action Française in the same category as National Socialism and Italian Fascism; see the reviews of *Der Faschismus in seiner Epoche* by F. Stern, *The Journal of Modern History*, XXXVI (1964), 225–227, and by E. Weber, *The American Historical Review*, LXIX (1964), 741–743; see also Sauer's comments, *ibid.*, LXXIII, 414–415. For my part, I can accept Nolte's explanation for the inclusion of Action Française in a study of antitranscendental phenomena. As this paper has already demonstrated, I differ with Nolte over his equation of Mussolini's Fascism with Hitler's Nazism.

⁵⁹ Nolte, *Three Faces of Fascism*, pp. 100–141; Rémond, *Right Wing*, pp. 234–245; Weber, *Action Française*, pp. 522–534.

⁶⁰ See, for example, P. Drieu La Rochelle, *Notes pour Comprendre le Siècle* (Paris, 1944), p. 50: "France was destroyed by the rationalism to which her genius had been reduced. Today, rationalism is dead and buried. We can only rejoice at its demise. The destruction of the monster that had been gnawing away at the very soul of France was the *sine qua non* of her revival." Another such intellectual was Gustave Thibon; Rémond, *Right Wing*, p. 314, writes: "The slogan Work, Family, Country, sums up this program, and its substitution for the Republican triptych has a symbolic value. Against abstract principles which generate dissension, the National Revolution was pleased to oppose concrete and elementary realities which form the warp and woof of existence. It reproved so-called sterile and corrosive in-

91

tellectualism; it preached a return to actuality—this was the title of a book by Gustave Thibon."

[61] R. Aron, *The Vichy Regime*, trans. H. Hare (New York, 1958), pp. 150–156; P. Farmer, *Vichy—Political Dilemma* (New York, 1955), pp. 223–256, *passim*.

[62] Rémond, *Right Wing*, p. 315.

[63] S. Hoffmann, "Quelques Aspects du Régime de Vichy," *Revue Française de Science Politique*, VI (1956), 46–69.

[64] Weber, *Varieties*, pp. 125–126.

[65] Rexist policy was summed up in the phrase anti-*pourris; pourris* signified both corrupt parliamentary politicians and the brooms with which they were to be swept away (J. Stengers, "Belgium," in Rogger and Weber, *The European Right*, pp. 157–163).

[66] J. Denis, *Bases Doctrinales de Rex* (Brussels, 1936), pp. 9–10.

[67] Weber, *Varieties*, p. 122. The *Dietschland* ideal—a Dutch-speaking union of Flanders and Holland—was advanced by Van Severen's *Verdinaso* fascist movement, until Van Severen embraced the objective of a *Dietsche Rijk*—recreation of the old union of Holland, Belgium, and Luxemburg. Whereupon the *Dietschland* programme became largely the property of the Flemish *Vlaamsch National Verbond* (Stengers, in Rogger and Weber, *The European Right*, pp. 150–156).

[68] C. Cross, *The Fascists in Britain* (London, 1961), pp. 23–24, 38–40, 44–45, 73–74; O. Mosley, *The Greater Britain* (London, 1932), pp. 149–160. Mosley retains his belief in a modified form of corporative economics; see his *My Life* (London, 1968), pp. 332–334, 361–362. A. Skidelsky, "Great Britain," in Woolf, *European Fascism*, p. 233, attributes Mosley's economic ideas to his acquaintance with the "interventionist state" of World War I.

[69] Cross, *Fascists in Britain*, p. 79. B.U.F. funds came to a considerable extent from individual donations by members of "the minor landed gentry" who seemed to believe that fascism was the way back to a rural Merrie England (*ibid.*, p. 90). On Mosley's latent racism, see J. R. Jones, "England," in Rogger and Weber, *The European Right*, p. 65.

[70] Cross, *Fascists in Britain*, pp. 119–168, *passim*.

[71] See, for instance, his speech in favour of appeasement in 1939: "They shall not die but they shall live to breathe the good English air, to love the fair English countryside, to see above them the English sky, to feel beneath their feet the English soil. This heritage of England, by our struggle and our sacrifice, we shall give to our children. And, with that sacred gift, we tell them that they come from that stock of men who went out from this small island in frail craft across the storm-tossed seas to take in their brave hands the greatest Empire that man has ever seen" (*ibid.*, pp. 189–190).

[72] Mosley, *My Life*, pp. 336–347.

[73] Quoted in Nolte, *Three Faces of Fascism*, p. 7.

5

National Socialism:
Totalitarianism or Fascism?

BY WOLFGANG SAUER

It is only two decades since National Socialism has left the scene, and yet the literature dealing with it is already immense. The fifty-year rule, never much respected by historians, has been quickly ignored in the face of so provoking a subject. This was all the more easy since, in this case, no Cerberus guarded the gates of the archives. Never before in the history of historiography did the documentary record of events become accessible to historians so quickly and comprehensively. One of the thought-provoking effects of this state of affairs is that historians suddenly have begun to wonder whether this surfeit of documents may not be, as one of them put it in a recent review, "a source of confusion rather than clarification." [1]

One way to avoid confusion is to define clearly the concepts and theories used in interpreting Nazism and to evaluate them in terms of the available evidence. Such an enterprise may seem all the more urgent since well-established concepts have become questionable in recent years. The following discussion attempts to clarify the problem. It first surveys past efforts of interpretation, then reviews present studies in this field, and, finally, develops some suggestions for further interpretive analyses.

The study of Nazism has so far traversed three periods with the two turning points being the outbreak of the Second World War and the start of the cold war. [2] In the first period, prior to 1939, scholars tended to explain National Socialism in terms of fascism. Adolf Hitler seemed merely a German variant of Benito Mussolini, and both appeared, during the Great Depression and the popular front, to be but varieties of the agony of capitalism. Many writers were strongly influenced by socialist thought and, what is more, by socialist hopes. They sensed a profound revolutionary change in their time and interpreted it in terms of Marx's prophecies of the coming of the classless society. From this point of view, the rise of fascism in many parts of Europe appeared as a desperate last effort of monopoly capitalists to reassert their control over the masses against the tide of socialism, using the stick of terror and the carrot of pseudo-socialism. Fascism, in this view, was understood as a mere manipulation by big business. The outstanding example of this approach was Franz L. Neumann's *Behemoth* with its emphasis on social and economic analysis.[3]

Historiography proper started with the Second World War. Under the impact of the war situation and in view of a growing awareness among social scientists of the differences between Nazism and other forms of fascism, authors tended to interpret the former as a Germanism, that is, some particularly German form of social disease. Studies focused, consequently, on the historical roots of Nazism and analyzed them especially in terms of intellectual history. The tendency of scholars in this field to stress logical sequences in historical developments may have contributed to the well-known deterministic interpretation of German history. A. J. P. Taylor's *Course of German History* [4] is characteristic of this determinism, though Taylor did not emphasize intellectual history. German responses after 1945 varied from the apologetic tone of Gerhard Ritter to the searching analysis of Friedrich Meinecke and the universal view of Ludwig Dehio.[5]

In the third period, starting with the cold war, the prevalent interpretation was that of totalitarianism. Nazism now appeared as but one form of a more general disease of modern society similar to Communism. Socialist hopes had yielded to deep pessimism in light of such staggering and embarrassing experiences as World War II, the rule of Stalinism in Russia and in Eastern Europe, and the rise of mass society, automation, and managerial bureaucracy in the West. Instead of the end of capitalism, the end of civilization seemed to loom ahead. Characteristic is the change in the attitude of Neumann who referred, in the early 1950's, to Sigmund Freud's idea that "conflicts deepen with the process of civilization, for . . . the increasing technical progress which in itself ought to make possible a greater measure of instinct gratification, fails to do so." [6] What was true of former Marxists was no less true of conservatives. To writers such as Hannah Arendt, Carl Joachim Friedrich, and Jacob L. Talmon,[7] totalitarianism appeared more or less a kind of suicide of civilization, a dialectical reversal by which progress turned against itself. Their studies stressed the omnipotence and the monolithic structure of totalitarian regimes and analyzed them in terms of the relationships between ideology and terror and between elites and masses.

It should be noted, however, that this survey deals with shifts in emphasis among interpretations and not with the replacement of one interpretation by another. Actually, the theories of fascism, Germanism, and totalitarianism coexisted to a degree from the outset.[8] In addition, a fourth interpretation that has emerged since the war defines Nazism as but a modern variant of classical tyranny. Held mainly by British historians, this view rejects the thesis advanced by Friedrich and others that totalitarian dictatorship is an entirely new phenomenon, unprecedented in history; the British school stresses, instead, historical continuity. In this regard it approaches the thesis of Dehio who interpreted Nazism as the last link in a long chain of European struggles for hegemony. The case of tyranny has been most powerfully argued by Alan Bullock in his biography of Hitler, but similar views have been held both by Hugh Trevor-Roper, who compared what he called Hitler's court to the late Roman monarchy, and by Taylor, who recently argued that Hitler was but a traditional statesman.[9] The discontinuity thesis has been rejected, interestingly enough, also for Communism. Karl Wittfogel, for example, has maintained that a continuity runs from Oriental despotism to modern Communist totalitarianism in Russia and China.[10]

These historicist interpretations in terms of classical tyranny or Oriental despotism have so far been what might be called a minority opinion. Yet they should be noted the more carefully since

95

the totalitarianism approach has generally begun to lose ground since the end of the 1950's. Khrushchev's anti-Stalinist and coexistence policies, the conflict between Russian and Chinese Communism, and a growing awareness in the West that industrial society might eventually produce mass prosperity rather than deadly conflict—all these developments militated against the apocalyptic visions of the totalitarianism theory. In addition, scholars had meanwhile begun to penetrate the mountains of documentary material and had gained a closer view of the historical realities of the Third Reich. These realities proved to be quite different from the monolithic image of totalitarianism. If we compare, for example, the view of Nazi rule as it emerges from Friedrich's studies to that which appears in Robert Koehl's article on "Feudal Aspects of National Socialism," [11] we might wonder whether the two authors are talking about the same subject.

An unfortunate effect of using the totalitarianism approach is the emergence of a striking imbalance in covering the field of Nazi history. While we have an abundance of studies on the Nazi terror system, on military and war history, and on the history of the resistance, we know little or nothing about the problems of Nazi domestic politics and social history after 1934. The feuds within and between the bureaucracy and the party, the organization and social composition of the party and most of its affiliated organizations, the Nazi economic policy, particularly the Four-Year Plan, the effects of this policy and of the war on German society, and the attitude of various social groups, particularly of the workers, toward the Nazi government are subjects of major importance that are neglected to a surprising degree by studies of Nazism.[12] Even in the case of Nazi ideology, we know more about its roots and about its propaganda system [13] than about its structure and its functional role in the social system.

Such evidence seems clearly to suggest that a revision of the existing conceptual framework is needed. To be sure, the totalitarianism theory cannot be dismissed entirely. Modern dictatorships have undoubtedly developed new characteristics, and totalitarianism is certainly one of them. It is, however, hardly as important as the totalitarianism theory has maintained. The theory of Germanism has been abandoned already as a possible alternative; William Shirer's attempt to revive it was a popular rather than a scholarly success.[14] The question as to why Nazism rose just in Germany certainly remains, but scholars seem generally to agree that the understanding of the problem needs a wider horizon than a mere national perspective can provide.

Recent writings even show a tendency to conceive the responsibility for the Nazi atrocities in a broader way than before. This problem has caused three of the most passionate debates in recent years: the controversies over Arendt's comment on Adolf Eichmann, over Rolf Hochhuth's criticism of Pope Pius XII, and over Taylor's new *coup de main* on the established thesis regarding the origins of the Second World War.[15] Historiography has gained from these debates mainly by the stimulation they provided. Books like Raul Hilberg's *The Destruction of the European Jews* and Ernst-Wolfgang Böckenförde's critical article on German Catholicism in 1933 [16] had dealt even earlier with similar problems. Taylor's book, however, raises a major historiographical problem that deserves brief discussion here.

Taylor's thesis is professedly an attempt to anticipate a revision of historical opinion, which he believes will eventually occur as it did after World War I. But the idea of revision arose after 1918 from original research rather than from a consideration of what future historians might say. Taylor's results are not, however, too convincing in terms of research. His thesis seems to be, therefore, but an attempt to escape a condition that is at least uncommon, if not unprecedented, in historiography. In Nazism, the historian faces a phenomenon that leaves him no way but rejection, whatever his individual position. There is literally no voice worth considering that disagrees on this matter, and it is probably not accidental that Taylor felt the stress of the situation most strongly.[17] Does not such fundamental rejection imply a fundamental lack of understanding? And if we do not understand, how can we write history? The term "understanding" has, certainly, an ambivalent meaning; we can reject and still "understand." And yet, our intellectual, and psychological, capacities reach, in the case of Nazism, a border undreamed of by Wilhelm Dilthey. We can work out explanatory theories, but, if we face the facts directly, all explanations appear weak.

Thus, the attempt to write the history of Nazism confronts the historian with an apparently unsolvable dilemma and raises the question of what historical understanding and historical objectivity may mean in the face of Nazism. One of the merits of the totalitarianism theory was that it took care of this condition; from this point of view, one might be tempted to define it as a scholarly formulation of our lack of understanding.

Is there a better way to conceal our weakness? Among the established concepts one remains: fascism. To be sure, the theory of fascism has also suffered severely from both the politics of and the historical studies on Nazism. This concerned, however, the Marxist-Leninist interpretation of fascism, and it may be worthwhile to ask if this interpretation is the only possible one. Attempts have indeed been made recently to repair the damaged tool for use. Some outstanding examples are Seymour Lipset's *Political Man*, which contains a comprehensive study of fascism on the basis of election analyses; the article by Iring Fetscher in which the author explicitly aims at a refutation of the Marxist concept of fascism; Eugen Weber's works on the *Action Française* and the European Right; and Ernst Nolte's volume *Three Faces of Fascism*. Mention must also be made in this context of Arthur Schweitzer's *Big Business in the Third Reich* in which the author attempts, unsuccessfully, I believe, to fuse elements of Max Weber's and Marxist theories.[18] These works constitute, as a whole and despite differences in approach and position, the first serious attempt to develop a workable, non-Marxist concept of fascism. Their results are less conclusive regarding the relationship between fascism and totalitarianism; this issue needs further clarification. A shift in emphasis toward an interpretation in terms of fascism is, nevertheless, unmistakable. In this context it is notable that works like William S. Allen's study of Nazi rule in a northern German town, Schweitzer's study, and Alan S. Milward's brilliant book on *The German Economy at War* [19] show a disposition of historians to turn to the neglected topics of Nazi history. In the case of Schweitzer the turn is obviously related to the fascism approach; his book continues the earlier analysis of Neumann. Allen and Milward, by contrast, seem to have chosen their subjects without major theoretical considerations.[20] But whatever the reasons for this turn, the tendency expressed in all of these works seems to be the most characteristic development in recent studies of Nazism.

Leaving aside the mainly empirical studies of Allen and Milward, we may ask what image of fascism emerges from these works. A summary is naturally difficult in view of the differences in individual positions, and yet there are two closely related points of agreement. First, the authors agree that fascism is not, as the Marxist interpretation holds, merely a manipulation by monopoly capitalists: it is a mass movement with a character and aim of its own, indicating a major crisis in liberal democracy and capitalism. Whether or not this crisis is temporary remains controversial. Second, it is now established beyond doubt that the lower middle classes, both rural and urban, were at least one of the major social components of fascist movements.

There are also many divergences and discrepancies, however. Some confusion exists regarding the distinction between fascist movements and fascist regimes. Fetscher's analysis shows that fascist movements can ally, in view of their basic opportunism, with a wide variety of other groups; Schweitzer has exemplified this in the case of Nazism.[21] Consequently, there may be a marked difference between the original, relatively homogeneous fascist movements prior to the seizure of power and what emerges as fascist regimes after that event. This leads to the equally important problem of the relationships between fascist movements and their allies. For example, Lipset's interesting definition of fascism as the extremism of the liberal Center, in contrast to Right-wing extremism and Left-wing extremism (Communism), does not sufficiently explain why fascist regimes were frequently built on alliances with conservatives while alliances with Communists never materialized. Which social groups, then, were likely to become allies of fascist movements, and what functional role did these alliances play in the structure of the individual fascist regimes?

Other questions concern the social composition and the revolutionary aims of the movements. On the first question, most authors limit their analysis to the lower middle class and the problems of its definition. This is, indeed, an important issue since the concept of the lower middle class still needs clarification, both in itself and in relation to the varieties of fascist supporters. Historical evidence shows that support of fascism may not be confined to the classical elements of the lower middle class (*Mittelstand*—peasants, artisans, small businessmen, and so forth), but may extend to a wide variety of groups in the large field between the workers on the one hand and big business, the aristocracy, and the top levels of bureaucracy on the other. This evidence agrees, interestingly enough, with Leo Baeck's statement that it was among the workers, the aristocracy, and the upper strata of the civil servants that the Jews found strongest support against persecution in Germany.[22]

Important as such an analysis is, however, it is still incomplete; it neglects the military element as a major social component of fascist movements. The military is apparently still not a category for social analysts. Among the authors quoted, only Fetscher recognizes its importance to fascism. It may even be said that a distinct interest group was formed within the fascist mixture by what might be called the military desperadoes, veterans of the First World War and the postwar struggles, who had not been reintegrated into either the civilian society or the armed forces. In an age of mass armies they were a sizable minority. Having become primitive warriors in four years and more of struggles, they sought to return into the arms of the mother army and to reform it according to their own model. Their conflict with society was, hence, not mainly economic, though this factor certainly was not absent. The main conflict was that between militarism and pacifism. In a time when the League of Nations appealed to the widespread warweariness and the rising pacifism of the masses, the military desperadoes fought, not only for their own survival, but for the survival of soldiery in general.

The desperadoes were, thus, natural participants in the fascist revolution, but they did not merge entirely in the movement. Both in Italy and Germany the social differentiation was reflected in varying degrees in organizational differentiations between the party and the militia or the *Sturmabteilung* (SA), respectively. This indicates that the conflict over militarism re-emerged in varied form within the fascist movements. What was a conflict of principles in the relationship between the military desperadoes and society was a conflict of preferences in the fascist movements. The lower-middle-class members regarded the military desperadoes as a weapon to force their way into government; the military desperadoes hoped that the lower-middle-class members would provide the mass basis without which they could not expect to rule.

After the seizure of power the smoldering conflict within the fascist movements had to be resolved if the fascist regimes were to last. In Germany the conflict was terminated by Hitler when, in June 1934, he crushed the Röhm "revolt" which was, as I should like to maintain against Hermann Mau and others, predominantly a movement of the military desperadoes.[23] To be sure, the SA contained in its rank and file large parts of the lower-middle-class Nazi supporters, but Ernst Röhm had ousted their representative in the leadership of the SA, Chief of Staff Otto Wagener, immediately after he assumed office in 1931.[24] Röhm was, and always remained, the leader of the military desperadoes, and he defended their interests in 1934. He may have received some lower-middle-class support, so that his opposition might appear, consequently, as an embryonic revolt of the movement against Hitler's alliance with big business and the army. Yet Röhm's opposition was aimed as much against the Nazi party as against Hitler, and his victory would invariably have led to a conflict with, and possibly a defeat of, the lower-middle-class forces. They were not better off with Hitler, however; the party won against Röhm, but lost against Hitler (and, *nota bene*, Heinrich Himmler and Hjalmar Schacht). Hitler's victory prevented the pending conflict within the movement from breaking through the facade of the *Volksgemeinschaft* (folk community), and rearmament "resolved" the conflict by securing occupations both for all types of business and for the desperadoes. It may be added that basically the same situation existed in Italy, though things were somewhat different, and above all, less radical, there. One wonders whether Mussolini's imperialist adventure in Abyssinia did not play a role equivalent to Hitler's crushing of the Röhm revolt.[25]

The control fascist regimes achieved over the dynamism of their movements creates doubts concerning the revolutionary character of fascist movements. There is virtual agreement among scholars that fascist movements contained, contrary to the Marxist thesis, a true revolutionary potential. This seems to conflict, however, with the noted opportunism of these movements. Rudolf Heberle's well-known study on the Schleswig-Holstein peasants, recently republished in its unabridged German form,[26] first revealed this point, and Lipset has now been able to generalize Heberle's results. A look at the fascist regimes in operation, moreover, would show that, whatever the revolutionary potential of the movements, the revolutionary results were meager.

How can this problem be resolved? May an answer be found by setting fascism in a wider historical framework? This is the way Nolte approaches his subject, but his answer is suggestive rather than conclusive. He advances the thesis that fascism was a revolt against the universal process of secularization, democratization, and international integration in the modern era. When this process reached its critical stage in the period of the two world wars, those elements in the culture that were doomed to perish revolted, according to Nolte, with increasing radicalism and decreasing rationality, or, in national terms, from the French *Action Française* through Italian Fascism to German National Socialism. On the last, most radical stage, fascism turned, Nolte argues, into a resistance against what he calls the "transcendence." He does not succeed, however, in clarifying this point sufficiently.

Nolte's thesis is not new in terms of facts. Its originality lies in assigning a metaphysical dimension to the fascist revolt and definitely attaching this revolt to a historical period. Fascism, Nolte suggests, is dead. This is, on the one hand, a more optimistic variation of the totalitarianism analysis: on the other hand, he tries to ascribe a historical meaning to fascism, which would provide a starting point for historical understanding. Much of this remains abstract and vague, however—mere *Ideengeschichte* (history of ideas).

102

If the modernization process was universal, was fascist revolt also universal? If so, why does Nolte deal only with France, Italy, and Germany? If not, why did the fascist revolt occur only in these (and some other) countries? And what was the cause for differentiation? Why was this revolt most radical in Germany? Or, to put the question in a sociological rather than a national form, which social groups provided the mass basis of fascism, and why were just these groups anti-modernist in their orientation? And, finally, what exactly does "transcendence" mean, and by which concrete means did the fascist resistance against it manifest itself?

Nolte's neglect of these questions can be attributed primarily to his method, which he calls "phenomenological" and which he conceives as an attempt to return to G.W.F. Hegel's integration of philosophy and history.[27] This attempt is, however, problematical. Hegel's striking success in synthesizing philosophy and history depended on his dialectical "logic"; Nolte's method is not dialectical. Nor does Nolte develop an alternative. He has not succeeded, therefore, in invalidating Leopold von Ranke's argument against Hegel that philosophy in itself does not produce a method for the analysis and organization of empirical facts. Philosophy alone was, indeed, not sufficient for Nolte; his phenomenological method turns out, under scrutiny, to be essentially Dilthey's good, old method of empathy, supplemented by some fragmentary social-scientific concepts formed *ad hoc* to satisfy immediate needs.

To be sure, Nolte makes this method operative by confining his study mainly to an interpretation of the ideas of the fascist leaders—Charles Maurras, Mussolini, Hitler—and he achieves much in this way, especially with regard to psychological and ideological analysis. Such a biographical approach is too narrow, however, to support Nolte's generalizations. What is true of the fascist leaders is not necessarily true of the masses of their followers. Their attitudes and motivation can be recognized only by a social analysis that includes economic factors. Nolte would perhaps respond to such a suggestion with as much contempt as he shows for the use of the concept of industrialization.[28] What does his concept of "practical transcendence" mean, however, if not that economic factors have adopted in modern societies a significance that transcends their "materialistic" meaning? And if this is true, how can we expect to gain meaningful results about modern societies without taking these factors into account? Nolte's method, in fact, seems to conflict heavily with his concept of "practical transcendence."

This must raise some doubts about the origin of Nolte's thesis of fascism as an anti-modernist revolt. Indeed, he seems to have obtained his thesis, not through his biographical analyses, but rather through an analysis of Maurras's ideas. Nolte's decision, not too plausible at first glance, to raise the *Action Française* to a prominent position in the history of the origins of fascism, has, actually, methodological rather than historical reasons. The *Action Française* is important to Nolte because Maurras succeeded in building an intellectual bridge between the counterrevolutionary tradition and fascism, thereby establishing a unified concept of anti-modernism that Nolte found apparently suggestive as an analytical concept for his own study. His chapter on the *Action Française* is, thus, actually a part of his methodological introduction.

The conclusion that Nolte arrived at his thesis in a methodologically irregular way does not necessarily imply that the thesis is wrong. It does imply, however, that he has not proven his case. Fascism and counterrevolution are actually different social phenomena, the latter being the earlier position of a part of what has been defined here as the allies of fascism. Fascism had its own independent antecedents: pseudo-revolutionaries like Father Jahn and the anti-Semites of the 1880's and 1890's (as examples in Germany).[29] To be sure, counterrevolution showed a combination of revolutionary and reactionary elements similar to fascism, but it was a revolution from above while fascism is a revolution from below. The discussion of Maurras by Nolte explains, therefore, the possibility of the fascist-conservative alliance, but it does not explain fascism. Nor does Nolte provide a satisfying answer to the question of the origins of fascism, especially in the German case. Nolte's chapters on pre-1914 Germany and Austria are in fact among the weakest in his book, though this is owing partly to Nolte's general weakness in historical knowledge.

These criticisms do not, however, detract from the value of

the book, which is a major step forward in the study of fascism. If verified, Nolte's hypothesis can offer, for example, an explanation for the fascist tendencies in the military; its metaphysical implications might, in addition, open a way to understand certain aspects in the relationship between the churches and fascism. Nolte might indeed have achieved his aim of developing a comprehensive theory of fascism had it not been for his mistaken conception of the relationship of philosophy and history and his refusal to consider the socio-economic aspects of the problem.

The task is, then, to provide the non-Marxist theory of fascism with a socio-economic dimension; more precisely, the task is to bring the earlier attempts of this kind up to date. Some contributors to the discussion in the 1930's have already laid important foundations for a socio-economic theory of fascism.[30] We have only to adjust these foundations to today's advanced stage of practical experience, historical research, and theoretical thought. With regard to theory the most important recent contribution probably comes from economic historians who have worked out, on the basis of the experiences of both the Great Depression and the underdeveloped countries, a non-Marxist concept of economic development that is highly suggestive to the analysis of fascism.

The attempt to use this concept for the interpretation of fascism poses, of course, certain problems. The Marxist trap of economic determinism is but a minor difficulty. Apart from the fact that the difference between causes and conditions in social developments has meanwhile become sufficiently familiar to social scientists, it must also be stressed that the main purpose in using, here, an economic theory for a historical analysis is merely a heuristic one. In addition, the "theory of economic growth" is, in the last analysis, not strictly an economic theory. It is rather a historical synthesis of the process of industrialization on the basis of a socio-economic analysis. Consequently, it already implies that the relationship between social and economic factors is a reversible one. In applying this theory to the interpretation of fascism, we merely shift the perspective without abandoning reversibility.

A more important problem arises because we have to face, as

105

usual, several conflicting formulations of that theory. Only those formulations that focus on continental European conditions, however, are useful to the analysis of fascism. This reduces the number of alternatives to two: the models of Alexander Gerschenkron and W.W. Rostow.[31] If we analyze the results of these two theories with regard to the social context of industrialization, we find that they are complementary. Gerschenkron's theory of "relative backwardness" provides a model of historical differentiation missing in Rostow's "stage" theory, and the latter offers a model for periodization not developed by Gerschenkron.

The critical problem is the development of a model for the advanced period of the industrialization process. Gerschenkron's model of relative backwardness cannot be directly extended to it since it deals with the starting conditions, while Rostow's definition as a stage of "high mass consumption" is still unsatisfactory.[32] Rostow hits, certainly, the essential point: that industry, if it exceeds a certain limit of growth, must turn to mass production. He is also aware that private mass consumption is not the only possible response. Rostow's idea, however, that societies on the stage of mass production have a choice between high mass consumption and national political expansion (or, between private mass consumption and mass consumption by the state), does not entirely agree with the historical evidence. There is certainly an element of choice in the situation; yet it may be that there are also constraints working against a choice. They may be owing to the consequences of relative backwardness, or to differential national developments and resulting international tensions and crises such as war. Rostow neglects the impact of national economic growth on international relations and vice versa; this seems to be, in fact, the major weakness of his theory. If we analyze twentieth-century history from this point of view, we do indeed find a period of world crises (World War I, the Great Depression, World War II) spreading between Rostow's stages of industrial maturity and high mass consumption.

In terms of a theory of economic growth revised in this way, fascism can be defined as a revolt of those who lost—directly or indirectly, temporarily or permanently—by industrialization. Fascism is a revolt of the *déclassés*. The workers and industrialists do not fall under this definition; it applies mainly to most of the lower middle class as defined above. They indeed suffered, or feared they would suffer, from industrialization—peasants who opposed the urbanizing aspects of industrialism; small businessmen and those engaged in the traditional crafts and trades that opposed mechanization or concentration; white-collar workers (at least as long as they felt the loss of economic independence); lower levels of the professions, especially the teaching profession, which opposed changing social values; and so forth. Also the military joins here, with opposition against the industrialization of war, which tended to destroy traditional modes of warfare and which by its increasing destructiveness intensified pacifism and antimilitarism. On the other hand, groups like the aristocracy, the large landlords, the higher bureaucrats, and so on, who lost also by industrialization, generally did not turn to fascism. In exact distinction, then, fascist movements represented the reaction of the lower-class losers, while the upper-class losers tended to react in a nonfascist way, but were potential allies of fascist regimes.

Such an analysis seems to be a way of explaining the intriguing paradox of a revolutionary mass movement whose goals were antirevolutionary in the classical sense. As a movement of losers, it turned against technological progress and economic growth; it tried to stop or even to reverse the trend toward industrialization and to return to the earlier, "natural" ways of life. In this respect the movement was reactionary, but, as a movement of the lower classes, its means were necessarily revolutionary. In defining fascism as a revolt of losers, we can also understand better both fascist atavism and fascist opportunism. Since the process of industrialization as a whole is irresistible, the existence of civilization is inextricably bound to it. Fascist revolt against industrialization must, therefore, eventually turn against civilization too. This was most evident in Germany, where Nazism developed into full-fledged neobarbarism, but it is also true of the other fascist movements, though for various reasons neobarbarism remained, there, more or less underdeveloped. Such a definition of fascism as a neobarbaric revolt against civilization seems to describe in more

107

concrete terms what Nolte calls the resistance against the "tran-scendence."

The same condition led to fascist opportunism. Since fascists acted, as losers, essentially from a position of weakness, they were compelled, in spite of their tendency toward violence, to compro-mise with their environment, even with their industrial enemy. This accounts for the contradiction that fascist regimes often fos-tered industrialization and yet insisted, ultimately, upon setting the clock back. The dialectic that resulted from this condition led even-tually to a point at which the movement assumed suicidal propor-tions. Industrialization was sought in order to destroy industrial so-ciety, but since there was no alternative to industrial society, the fascist regime must eventually destroy itself. This was the situation of Nazism. The Nazis built an industrial machinery to murder the Jews, but once in operation the machine would have had to con-tinue and would have ruined, indirectly at least, first the remnants of civilized society and then the fascist regime. Industrialization of mass murder was, thus, the only logical answer Nazism had to the problems of industrial society.

The analysis of fascism in terms of economic growth also offers a way to define more precisely the fallacy in the Marxist-Leninist concept of fascism. The fallacy lies in that Marxism blurs the distinction between early commercial and late industrial capi-talism. Fascism indicated a conflict within capitalism, between tra-ditional forms of commercialism and the modern form of indus-trialism. The fact that the former had survived in the twentieth century only on the lower levels of the middle classes accounted for the social locus of fascism. It is true, therefore, that fascism was capitalist by nature; it is not true that it was industrial. It is also true that fascist regimes often were manipulated in varying ways and degrees, but the share of industrialists in manipulation was rather small. Fetscher shows convincingly that the share was in-deed larger in industrially underdeveloped Italy than it was in in-dustrially advanced Germany.

On the other hand, the difference between fascism and Bol-shevism appears, in light of this analysis, more fundamental than the totalitarianism analysis would admit. Neither V.I. Lenin nor

Joseph Stalin wished to turn the clock back; they not merely wished to move ahead, but they wished to jump ahead. The Bolshevik revolution had many elements of a development revolution not unlike those now under way in the underdeveloped countries. One of the striking differences between the two systems appears in the role of the leaders. The social and political order of Bolshevism is relatively independent from the leadership; it is, so to speak, more objective. Fascist regimes, by contrast, are almost identical with their leaders; no fascist regime has so far survived its leader. This is why Bullock's interpretation of Hitler in terms of traditional tyranny has some bearing. The limits of this approach would become evident, I believe, if scholars could be persuaded to balance their interest in Hitler's secret utterances and political and military scheming by also stressing his role as a public speaker. The Nazi mass rallies with their immediate, ecstatic communication between leader and followers were, indeed, what might be called a momentary materialization of the Nazi utopia, at least so far as the "Nordic race" was concerned.[33]

Finally, it is plain from an analysis in terms of economic growth that the degree of radicalization must somehow be related to the degree of industrialization. The more highly industrialized a society, the more violent the reaction of the losers. Thus Germany stood at the top, Italy lagged behind, and Spain and others were at the bottom. In Germany, fascism gained sufficient momentum to oust its allies. By the dismissal of Schacht, Werner von Blomberg, Werner von Fritsch, and Konstantin von Neurath in 1937–1938, the Nazis assumed control over the economy, the army, and the diplomacy, those exact three positions that their conservative allies of January 30, 1933, had deemed it most important to maintain.[34] In Italy a fairly stable balance was sustained between the movement and its various allies until the latter, relying on the monarchy and assisted by Fascism's defeat in war, finally ousted the Fascists. In Spain, the borderline case, the allies assumed control from the outset and never abandoned it. Similar observations can be made with the many cases of pre-, proto-, and pseudo-fascist regimes in Central, Eastern, and Southeastern Europe.

The thesis of the parallel growth of industrialization and fascist radicalization seems to conflict, however, with the evidence of some highly industrialized societies such as France and England where fascist opposition never gained much momentum. The problem can be solved only by adding a broader historical analysis involving the specific national, social, and cultural traditions that industrialization encountered in individual societies. It is perhaps not accidental that the industrialization process ran relatively smoothly in West European nations whose political rise concurred with the rise of modern civilization since the late Middle Ages. Fascist opposition, by contrast, was strongest in the Mediterranean and Central European regions where the premodern traditions of the ancient Roman and the medieval German and Turkish Empires persisted. The religious division between Protestantism and Catholicism may also have some relevance: one remembers both Max Weber's thesis on the correlation of Protestantism and capitalism and the recent controversy on the attitude of Pope Pius XII toward Fascism and Nazism. In other words, fascism emerged where preindustrial traditions were both strongest and most alien to industrialism and, hence, where the rise of the latter caused a major break with the past and substantial losses to the nonindustrial classes.

This definition is still incomplete, however, since it does not tell why fascism emerged rather simultaneously throughout Europe though the countries affected were on different levels of economic growth. We face here the question of the "epoch" of fascism, raised but not answered by Nolte. The general conditions of fascism as defined above existed, after all, earlier. In Germany, for example, lower-middle-class opposition against industrialization had already emerged in the mid-nineteenth century and accompanied economic growth in varying degrees through all its stages.[35] Why did it not turn into fascism prior to 1914, though it did so on parallel stages of growth in Italy and Spain after the First World War? At this point the importance of the military element for the analysis of fascism becomes apparent again: Only after total war had militarized European societies and had created large military interests were the conditions required for fascism complete.[36] The First World War

110

had tremendously strengthened industrialization in technical terms, but it had diverted it from production to destruction. After the war the victorious nations of the West managed, on the whole, to stabilize industrial society and to return to production, but the defeated nations and those industrially underdeveloped found it extremely difficult to follow the same course. When they met with economic crises, many of them abandoned whatever advance they had made toward democracy and turned to fascism.

This breakdown occurred roughly along the social and cultural lines defined above. If we examine the geographical distribution of fascist regimes in Europe between the two world wars, we find that they emerged mainly in three areas: the Mediterranean coast; the regions of Central, Eastern, and Southeastern Europe; and Germany. In the first area, the original and highly developed Mediterranean urban and commercial civilization that reached back to antiquity faced destruction by the invasion of industrialism as released or accelerated by World War I. Defeat, either imagined as in the case of Italy or real as in the case of Spain at the hands of Abd-el-Krim at Anual in 1921, played an additional role. In the second area, an old feudal civilization struggled with the problems arising out of a sudden liberation from Habsburg or tsarist dominations as well as from competition with both Western industrialism and Eastern Bolshevism. Both regions were predominantly Catholic. In the third area, a technologically fully developed industrial society clashed violently with the stubborn resistance of surviving remnants of preindustrial forms of society over who was to pay for defeat and economic crises. Catholicism played, here, a dual and partly contradictory role. On the one hand, it seems to have influenced indirectly Nazism as such top Nazi leaders as Hitler, Himmler, and Goebbels were Catholic by origin, and the Vatican was quick to compromise with the Hitler regime. On the other hand, the vast majority of the Catholic population was relatively immune to Nazi temptations. Significantly enough, Protestantism also split, though along somewhat different lines.

These differentiations suggest a division into three subtypes of fascism: the Mediterranean as the "original" one; the various and

111

not too long-lived regimes in Central, Eastern, and Southeastern Europe as a mixed, or not full-fledged, variation; and German Nazism as a special form.

The "epoch" of fascism starts, thus, with the aftermath of the First World War, but when does it end? Eugen Weber and Lipset agree with many scholars who believe that there is no epoch of fascism, that fascism is a general condition of modern society contingent upon crises in liberal democracy.[37] This is certainly indisputable as far as fascist attitudes and movements are concerned; it is quite another problem, however, whether fascist regimes will emerge again. This emergence seems unlikely for two reasons. First, the socio-economic development in the highly industrialized societies of the West generally rules out the re-emergence of the historical condition of fascism—a disarrangement of society in which the rise of large masses of *déclassés* coincides with the rise of a sizable group of military desperadoes. There are no longer economic losers of industrialization, at least not on a mass scale, and Charles de Gaulle's victory over the rebellious French military shows that military desperadoes alone will not get very far.[38] In addition, the horrible experience of neobarbarism puts a heavy burden on all attempts at imitation. If the success of fascism under modern, Western conditions is unlikely, there remain, theoretically, the underdeveloped countries as possible breeding grounds of fascism. Yet it is doubtful whether opposition against industrialization will assume there the form of fascism since these countries lack the specific traditions of the ancient and medieval civilizations that conditioned the antimodernist revolt in Europe. The second reason working against fascist regimes is, thus, that fascism is inseparable from its Central and South European conditions; it is, in fact, one of the products of the dialectical movement of European civilization.

[1] Walter Laqueur, "Nazism and the Nazis: On the Difficulties of Discovering the Whole Truth," *Encounter*, XXII (Apr. 1964), 41.

[2] For an earlier bibliographical survey, see Andrew G. Whiteside, "The Nature and Origins of National Socialism," *Journal of Central European Affairs*, XVII (No. 1, 1957–58), 48–73.

[3] Franz L. Neumann, *Behemoth: The Structure and Practice of National Socialism* (2d ed., New York, 1944).

[4] A. J. P. Taylor, *The Course of German History* (London, 1945; 2d ed., New York, 1962).

[5] Gerhard Ritter, *Europa und die deutsche Frage* (Munich, 1948), *Das deutsche Problem: Grundfragen deutschen Staatslebens gestern und heute* (new rev. ed., Munich, 1962); Friedrich Meinecke, *Die deutsche Katastrophe* (Wiesbaden, 1946), tr. as *The German Catastrophe* (Boston, 1963); Ludwig Dehio, *Gleichgewicht und Hegemonie* (Krefeld, 1948), tr. as *The Precarious Balance* (New York, 1965).

[6] Franz L. Neumann, *The Democratic and the Authoritarian State* (Glencoe, Ill., 1957), 273.

[7] Hannah Arendt, *The Origins of Totalitarianism* (2d, enlarged ed., Cleveland, 1958); Carl J. Friedrich and Zbigniew K. Brzezinski, *Totalitarian Dictatorship and Autocracy* (Cambridge, Mass., 1956); Jacob L. Talmon, *The Origins of Totalitarian Democracy* (London, 1952).

[8] The shifts in emphasis can clearly be observed if one rearranges the works quoted in Whiteside, "Nature and Origins of National Socialism," according to date of publication.

[9] Alan Bullock, *Hitler: A Study in Tyranny* (rev. ed., New York, 1960); Hugh R. Trevor-Roper, *The Last Days of Hitler* (London, 1947); A. J. P. Taylor, *The Origins of the Second World War* (London, 1961).

[10] Karl A. Wittfogel, *Oriental Despotism: A Comparative Study of Total Power* (New Haven, Conn., 1957).

[11] Robert Koehl, "Feudal Aspects of National Socialism," *American Political Science Review*, LIV (Dec. 1960), 921–33.

[12] For some recent studies indicating a change, see note 19, below. One of the neglected topics is the story of rescuers of Jews. Research in this field has recently been organized by Rabbi Harold M. Schulweis in the Institute for the Righteous Acts, Oakland, California. For an earlier attempt, see Kurt R. Grossmann, *Die unbesungenen Helden: Menschen in Deutschlands dunkelsten Tagen* (Berlin, 1957).

[13] The most recent contributions are Zbynek A. B. Zeman, *Nazi Propaganda* (Oxford, England, 1964), and Ernest K. Bramsted, *Goebbels and National Socialist*

113

Propaganda, 1925–1945 (East Lansing, Mich., 1965). Hajo Holborn, "Origins and Political Character of Nazi Ideology," *Political Science Quarterly*, LXXIX (Dec. 1964), 542–54, gives valuable suggestions for a comprehensive analysis. Specifically, the press is treated by Oron J. Hale, *The Captive Press in the Third Reich* (Princeton, N.J., 1964).

[14] William L. Shirer, *The Rise and Fall of the Third Reich* (New York, 1960).

[15] Hannah Arendt, *Eichmann in Jerusalem: A Report on the Banality of Evil* (New York, 1963); Rolf Hochhuth, *Der Stellvertreter* (Hamburg, 1963) tr. as *The Deputy* (New York, 1964); Taylor, *Origins of the Second World War*.

[16] Raul Hilberg, *The Destruction of the European Jews* (Chicago, 1961); Ernst-Wolfgang Böckenförde, "Der deutsche Katholizismus im Jahre 1933," *Hochland*, LIII (No. 3, 1961), 215–39.

[17] For a historiographical analysis of Taylor's work, see Edward B. Segel, "A. J. P. Taylor and History," *Review of Politics*, XXVI (Oct. 1964), 531–46.

[18] Seymour M. Lipset, *Political Man* (New York, 1960), Chap. V; Iring Fetscher, "Faschismus und Nationalsozialismus: Zur Kritik des sowjetmarxistischen Faschismusbegriffs," *Politische Vierteljahrschrift*, III (Mar. 1962), 42–63; an English translation of Fetscher's article, in slightly revised form, appears as a chapter in his book *Marx and Marxism* (New York, 1971), 274–301; Eugen Weber, *Action Française* (Stanford, Calif., 1962); *The European Right: A Historical Profile*, ed. Hans Rogger and Eugen Weber (Berkeley, Calif., 1964); Eugen Weber, *Varieties of Fascism* (Princeton, N.J., 1964); Ernst Nolte, *Der Faschismus in seiner Epoche* (Munich, 1963), tr. as *Three Faces of Fascism* (New York, 1966 and 1969); Arthur Schweitzer, *Big Business in the Third Reich* (Bloomington, Ind., 1964).

[19] William S. Allen, *The Nazi Seizure of Power: The Experience of a Single German Town, 1930–1935* (Chicago, 1965); Alan S. Milward, *The German Economy at War* (London, 1965). Since the completion of this article in May 1966, further studies have been published confirming this trend and covering many of the hitherto neglected subjects.

[20] Allen tends, in fact, to use the totalitarianism concept, but his results disprove largely his thesis that Nazi rule led to an "atomization" of society. (See e.g., Allen, *Nazi Seizure of Power*, 278.)

[21] Schweitzer, *Big Business*, distinguishes two periods in the Nazi rule: "partial Fascism" with alliances between fascism and other groups until 1936 and "full Fascism" after this date. The thesis is basically correct, though Schweitzer is too rigid on serveral points. (Cf. Carl Landauer's criticism, *Journal of Economic History*, XXV [1965], 293–95.)

[22] *Das Dritte Reich und die Juden*, ed. Leon Poliakov and Josef Wulf (Berlin, 1955), 439.

[23] Hermann Mau, "Die 'zweite Revolution'—der 30. Juni 1934," *Vierteljahrshefte für Zeitgeschichte*, I (Apr. 1953), 121. Cf. my analysis of the SA and the Röhm crisis in Karl Dietrich Bracher et al., *Die Nationalsozialistische Machtergreifung: Studien zur Errichtung des totalitären Herrschaftssystems in Deutschland* (2d ed., Cologne,

1962), 829–966. In the present article, I have tried to supplement the political analysis of my earlier study by adding a social dimension.

[24] Cf. Bracher et al., *Nationalsozialistische Machtergreifung*, 882–83.

[25] See Gaetano Salvemini, *Under the Axe of Fascism* (New York, 1936), 391. Salvemini's suggestion of a comparison between Mussolini's Abyssinian war and Hitler's Röhm purge has so far not been taken up by historians.

[26] Rudolf Heberle, *Landbevölkerung und Nationalsozialismus: Eine soziologische Untersuchung der politischen Willensbildung in Schleswig-Holstein 1918 bis 1932* (Stuttgart, 1963), tr. as *From Democracy to Nazism: A Regional Case Study on Political Parties in Germany* (Baton Rouge, La., 1945).

[27] Nolte, *Three Faces* (New York, 1966), 429–30; (New York, 1969), 537–38; *Der Faschismus in seiner Epoche*, 516–17.

[28] Nolte, *Three Faces* (New York, 1966), 451; (New York, 1969), 563–64; *Der Faschismus in seiner Epoche*, 541.

[29] The German anti-Semitic movement around 1900 has attracted, understandably enough, much attention in recent years. It is important to note, however, that it was only a part of a broader trend that extended to France (the Dreyfus affair, Edouard Drumont) and Austria (Karl Lueger and the Christian-Social party). As a whole, it has not yet been sufficiently investigated; Nolte (*Three Faces of Fascism*) and Weber (*Action Française*) focus on France while Peter G. J. Pulzer, *The Rise of Political Anti-Semitism in Germany and Austria* (New York, 1964), disregards France.

[30] Harold D. Lasswell, "The Psychology of Hitlerism," *Political Quarterly* (No. 4, 1933), 373–84; David J. Saposs, "The Role of the Middle Class in Social Development: Fascism, Populism, Communism, Socialism," in *Economic Essays in Honor of Wesley Clair Mitchell, Presented to Him by His Former Students on the Occasion of His 60th Birthday* (New York, 1935); Talcott Parsons, "Some Sociological Aspects of the Fascist Movement," (1941), reprinted in Talcott Parsons, *Essays in Sociological Theory* (Glencoe, Ill., 1954).

[31] Alexander Gerschenkron, *Economic Backwardness in Historical Perspective* (Cambridge, Mass., 1962), esp. 1–51, 353–64; W. W. Rostow, *The Stages of Economic Growth* (Cambridge, Eng., 1959); *The Economics of Take-off into Sustained Growth*, ed. id. (London, 1963). Cf. the review by Henry Rosovsky, "The Take-off into Sustained Controversy," *Journal of Economic History*, XXV (1965), 271–75.

[32] Rosovsky, "The Take-off," 274–75, proposes to replace the concept of "stage" by that of the "long swing." This might, however, deprive the concept of growth of its meaning and would necessitate, therefore, a decision on whether the idea of growth should be abandoned altogether or whether the idea of swing must be adjusted to that of growth. In the latter case, the concept of stage might prove indispensable as a complement.

[33] This is one of the reasons why the lack of a collection of Hitler's speeches, as complete as technically possible, is one of the most serious obstacles to a successful study of Nazism. Such a collection is indispensable not only for a biography of Hitler (how can we expect to understand a man whose political career was built to

115

such an extent on success as a public speaker if we have no means to analyze him in this role?), but still more for the analysis of the Nazi ideology. Only if we approach the Nazi ideology through a dynamic analysis will we be able to solve the methodological dilemma of dealing rationally with Nazi irrationalism and with whether the Nazi ideology had substance or was merely a tactical function. To this effect we must follow the course of Hitler's thought and its response to the successive political changes, and this can be done only by following him through his speeches.

[34] The focus of present studies on the spectacular Blomberg-Fritsch affair has blurred the comprehensive character and the importance of the change in 1937–1938.

[35] Already Marx observed the antimodernist attitude of the petty bourgeoisie, though he partly misinterpreted it. The anti-Semitic movement at the end of the century was indicative of the growing radicalization of lower-middle-class opposition. (See Hans Rosenberg, *Grosse Depression und Bismarckzeit* [Berlin, 1966]; for France, see André Siegfried, *Tableau politique de la France de l'ouest sous la troisième république* [Paris, 1913], 413; cf. Lipset, *Political Man*, 131–32.)

[36] The *Vaterlandspartei*, organized in 1917 by military and agrarian groups (Alfred von Tirpitz; Wolfgang Kapp) in Germany to support imperialist warfare, was, significantly enough, the first prefascist mass movement. The foundation of the Nazi party later followed the same pattern: Hitler acted originally as an agent of the Munich headquarters of the *Reichswehr*. In addition, Anton Drexler, the founder of the first nucleus of the Nazi party, was a member of the *Vaterlandspartei*. Both the *Reichswehr* officers in Munich and Drexler aimed at overcoming what they felt was the major shortcoming of the *Vaterlandspartei*: it had no appeal to the workers. (Among recent accounts, see Georg Franz-Willing, *Die Hitlerbewegung* [Hamburg, 1962], I.)

[37] Weber, *Varieties of Fascism*, 3; Lipset, *Political Man*, Chap. V.

[38] It would be different in case of large-scale war which might, of course, drastically change present social conditions.

116

6

Fascism and Modernization

BY HENRY A. TURNER, JR.

As conspicuous as the revival of interest in fascism during the past decade is the lack of agreement about it. Close to a decade of scholarly discussion has yielded nothing even approaching a consensus on the essential characteristics of fascism as a generic phenomenon, its causes, or even which movements and regimes properly deserve the label. Indeed, there are almost as many differing theories about fascism as there are treatments of the subject.[1] To complicate matters further, the discussion has spawned a luxuriant cluster of epiphenomena, variously designated as proto-fascist, quasi-fascist, semi-fascist, fascistic, fascoid, and fascistoid. There remains, however, a continuing awareness of the need to come to grips conceptually with what are undeniably some of the most important and perplexing political phenomena of the recent past. Until now, the most common approach has been to employ concepts and categories that have been developed to deal with other political phenomena. These efforts have produced a wide variety of conflicting and sometimes self-contradictory formulations such as "radical rightists," "reactionary revolutionaries," and "revolutionary conservatives." It may be that the correct formula has simply not yet been found. But another possibility is that these conventional concepts and categories are wholly inadequate for getting at the essence of fascism. It may be, in other words, that what is needed is a new frame of reference altogether.

Such a frame of reference may possibly be provided by the theory of modernization, which, in general outlines at least, has

117

gained wide acceptance among social scientists. According to this theory, the one underlying development of recent history is the displacement of traditional societies by an unprecedentedly thorough and rapid process of change, basically similar everywhere, involving industrialization, urbanization, secularization and rationalization. If there is validity to this analysis, an examination of the relationship of fascism to the process of modernization seems long overdue. Thus far, none of the theorists of modernization have explored this problem with any degree of thoroughness. Moreover, there is sharp disagreement among those who have taken a stand on the subject. Some have characterized the Italian Fascist and German National Socialist regimes as agents of modernization.[2] Others have looked upon them as examples of breakdowns of that process or as attempts at "de-modernization."[3] What follows here is not an attempt to resolve the problem. Rather, it is an effort to stimulate further analysis by posing certain questions that may be germane, by suggesting some possible solutions, and by exploring their implications for the study of fascism as a generic phenomenon.

Initially, the focus of this inquiry will be on Italian Fascism and German National Socialism. These were the two movements that originally gave rise to the notion that there was a generic phenomenon that could and should be called fascism. Today they remain its only universally accepted paradigmatic manifestations. To include other putative fascisms at the outset would be to repeat an error that mars much of the existing literature, where one encounters numerous studies of fascism based on the assumption that it encompassed a sizeable number of cases. By a circular process, such studies almost always arrive at definitions of fascism tailored to accommodate all the cases included.[4] But since authors have differed widely on the cases to be included, and since the legitimacy of virtually all putative fascisms other than those of Italy and Germany has been challenged, this inquiry will begin with an examination of the relationship of these two paradigmatic cases to modernization. Then, the implications for other movements and regimes also alleged to be fascist will be considered.

Italian Fascism and German National Socialism will be treated here as autonomous political phenomena, not as mere

118

agents or tools of privileged conservative or reactionary forces. In Soviet-bloc countries, where the investigation of fascism has yet to benefit fully from de-Stalinization, scholarship still remains for the most part fettered by the Comintern's 1933 definition of fascism as "the openly terroristic dictatorship of the most reactionary, most chauvinistic and most imperialistic elements of finance capital." [5] As a result, little light has been cast on the subject by publications produced there. In non-Communist societies, too, fascism continues to be viewed in some quarters as only a front for other forces or, as one much-acclaimed recent study puts it, "an attempt to make reaction and conservatism popular and plebeian." [6] Since this viewpoint has been effectively refuted elsewhere, it will not be accorded further consideration here.[7] Instead, Italian Fascism and Nazism will be regarded as political forces in their own right, whose leadership cadres had goals of their own. The central question here will be what those leadership cadres wanted to do with their societies, in particular, whether they wanted to continue with the process of modernization or whether they sought to oppose or even undo it. The emphasis, that is, will be on goals rather than, as with most theories of totalitarianism, on methods.

I

Although many writers have attributed anti-modernist attitudes to the Nazis, the relationship of Nazism to the process of modernization as a whole has yet to be fully examined. Rejection of the deleterious social and psychological effects of that process has, after all, been no monopoly of the Nazis. Even many proponents of modern change have decried the moral relativism, the anonymity, and the alienation that have accompanied it. Defenders of modernization have regarded these as regrettable by-products of progress; most critics of that process have considered them as grounds for slowing down or halting change. The Nazis drew much more far-reaching conclusions. In their eyes, modern industrial society was wholly and unavoidably incompatible with what they held to be the only true wellspring of social life: the folk culture. Just as their diagnosis was more drastic, so was their remedy. Whereas other opponents of modernization sought merely to slow down or halt

119

that process or, at the most, to turn the clock back to what were seen as happier or sounder times in the recent past, the Nazi leaders were bent on nothing less than a fundamental transformation of existing social reality. Recognition of this has led some to describe the Nazis as "revolutionaries." This seems inappropriate, however, in view of the progressive, forward-looking connotations that have become attached, rightly or wrongly, to the word "revolution." While most visionary revolutionaries of modern times have looked to the future, to a new world, the Nazis sought their models in the past. They looked, to be sure, not to the historic past, but rather to a mythic and eclectic version of the past. What they proposed was an escape from the modern world by means of a desperate backward leap toward a romanticized vision of the harmony, community, simplicity, and order of a world long lost. Their thinking thus seems best characterized as a utopian form of anti-modernism—utopian in the double sense of being a visionary panacea and being unrealizable.

There was, of course, no formal or official Nazi utopia. What is referred to here are the kinds of schemes and the sorts of precepts found in the writings and utterances of the leadership cadre of National Socialism. While virtually all the Nazi leaders sought precepts for the future in the past, there was little agreement on exactly what those precepts should be, beyond a general commitment to restore to the German people an ethnic purity that was imagined to have existed in the past. At least two major strands of Nazi utopianism can be identified. One was represented by the Party's so-called "left wing." Its adherents looked for precepts to the late Middle Ages and early modern times. They believed the cure for the ills of modern industrial society lay in a revival, in revised form, of manorial and corporate relationships, in the reconstruction of an elaborate web of responsibilities and restrictions. Although they referred to their anti-capitalist outlook as "socialism," it had little connection with the mainstream of modern socialist thought. They aimed not at the conquest and further development of modern industry under new auspices, but sought instead to halt its growth and, in some cases, even to dismantle it, at least partially. Most of their aims were not calculated to serve the interests of the industrial working class but were designed instead to rescue the *Mittelstand*, the old middle class of tradesmen, artisans, and small entrepreneurs.[8] Clearly, the Nazi "left wing" belongs in the venerable tradition of backward-looking, regressive anti-capitalism, not in the tradition of modern socialism.

Regardless of how anachronistic their goals were in the light of demographic realities, the "left-wing" Nazis at least proposed concrete economic and social remedies for economic and social problems. The same cannot be said of the other principal variant of Nazi utopianism, that embodied by men such as Hitler, Himmler, Darré, and Rosenberg. Their utopias were far more archaic and eclectic, as well as much further removed from reality. For their precepts they looked to the early Middle Ages, but also to pre-Christian, even pre-civilized, times.[9] As remedies for the problems of the industrial heartland of Europe in the twentieth century they prescribed a revival of the cults of soil and sword. They strove, that is, to free the bulk of the German people from the grip of industrial society and return them to the simple agrarian life. Moreover, they strove to rededicate the German people to martial values: to the proposition that war is not merely an acceptable means for the pursuit of political aims, but a positive and essential good in and of itself; that heroism on the battlefield is a necessary and enobling aspect of life. These Nazis, particularly Hitler, were indifferent to legislative and institutional adjustments of the sort proposed by the "left wing" of the Party. They sought instead to transcend existing reality at one blow and substitute for it a radically different social order. And, of course, it was they, or perhaps more accurately, it was Hitler who triumphed and shaped the vicious and calamitous history of the Third Reich.[10]

In terms of socio-economic issues, the "left wing" Nazis have usually been—mistakenly—regarded as the radical component of the Party. It is true that their schemes for a re-ordering of Germany's economic life alarmed many bankers and industrialists at the time. But it was Hitler and his henchmen who, in the long run, were bent upon changes of an incalculably more radical sort. This has been obscured by the widespread readiness to accept the peacetime years of Nazi rule as an accurate expression of the regime's as-

121

pirations. Since little in the way of fundamental economic or social changes was effected in the pre-war Third Reich, most observers have concluded that there was no serious intention to seek such changes. There are strong indications, however, that for the decisive leadership group of the regime, most particularly Hitler himself, the peacetime years were only a preparatory phase, a staging ground so to speak, for a far-reaching transformation of German society to be effected in the wake of a Nazi military triumph. In this connection, Hitler's war aims are of key importance. It is now abundantly clear that he was in no sense, as Marxist-Leninists still insist, a mere tool of the "monopoly capitalists," who launched the Second World War to enable German big business to indulge its allegedly insatiable appetite for plunder and exploitation at the expense of the human and natural resources of other countries. Instead, from all indications Hitler was very much his own master. Moreover, his central and overriding war aim throughout was to conquer *Lebensraum*, arable soil in eastern Europe.[11] As has been widely recognized, this *Raumpolitik* had an economic rationale, if a highly impractical one: it was designed to end Germany's dependence on imported foodstuffs and raw materials, thereby eliminating the need to produce industrial goods for export and achieving economic autarky for Germany. What has not been sufficiently noted is the extent to which the pursuit of *Lebensraum* was intended by Hitler and his henchmen to serve a socio-ethical purpose as well. By reducing Germany's need for industry and thus for industrial workers, and by providing fertile soil upon which these displaced workers and others could be resettled, the acquisition of *Lebensraum* was expected to open the way to a vast new wave of German eastward colonization comparable to that of the Middle Ages, making possible a significant degree of de-urbanization and de-industrialization. Millions of Germans were to be freed from enslavement to those factories that would no longer be needed to produce export goods required to pay for imported foodstuffs. They were to be liberated from the corrupting, debilitating industrial cities, which, in the opinion of the Nazi leaders, had come to threaten the very survival of the folk.[12] Resettled on the land in the

122

East, these colonists were expected to revert to the simple, pure folkways of their ancestors, becoming once more a sturdy yeomanry and an inexhaustible reservoir of warriors for future wars.[13] With racial purity thus supplemented by cultural purity, German society would at last be restored to health.

Although these Nazi schemes were unrivalled in their ruthless audacity, the same hostility to modern industrial society that gave rise to them can be found in others. Numerous precursors to the utopian anti-modernism of the Nazis have been identified in late nineteenth- and early twentieth-century Germany.[14] Moreover, the growing body of scholarship on what has been described as "cultural fascism" indicates that the same general sort of tendencies were apparently present all across Europe, particularly in artistic and literary circles.[15] It is customary to explain these tendencies in terms of the nefarious effects of such intellectual influences as romanticism, social darwinism, and the writings of Nietzsche. But cannot the popularity of such attitudes perhaps be more adequately explained as the expression of a genuine crisis of popular culture, taking that term in its deepest and broadest sense? After all, the late nineteenth and early twentieth centuries marked, for most of western and central Europe, the great watershed of modernization, when the changes wrought by that process began to affect the life of the populace at large in a direct fashion. It was then that the old and settled patterns of life were first disrupted and displaced on a large scale. Only then, for example, did society's center of gravity shift from the countryside to the city; with unprecedented rapidity, millions were torn loose from the customary patterns of agrarian life and thrust into an alien, anonymous urban world. In that same process, venerable cultural values were subjected to widespread challenge and discreditation. Traditional religion, in particular, lost ground rapidly; secularism, previously reserved almost exclusively for the privileged and educated, became a mass phenomenon for the first time. Many of those thus torn loose from their cultural and societal roots found a new secular point of reference in the socialist movement. But others remained uprooted and adrift in a threatening, brutal industrial world for

123

which they were ill prepared. It seems scarcely surprising that some of the latter proved to be susceptible to movements vehemently hostile to that world.

This crisis of popular culture was still further heightened by the First World War, during which the impact of modernization challenged even the ancient and deep-seated cluster of values based on martial valor. Rooted in mankind's prehistoric past, the heroic ideal remained into modern times a far more fundamental part of the popular culture of Europe than is generally recognized; even Christianity, despite its antithetical ethical code, made little headway against the martial code, having chosen many centuries earlier to effect an accommodation in order to gain influence over the holders of power in the warrior societies of Europe. Pacifism, or at least opposition to international conflict, was a growing force by the early twentieth century, buttressed by the rejection of war by the socialist parties. But the enthusiastic response of the masses to the outbreak of fighting in 1914 revealed that pacifist convictions were still limited largely to a thin stratum of intellectuals. However, what pacifist agitation had failed to accomplish was achieved to a remarkable degree by the war itself. For the first time, the impact of industrialization on warfare became massively manifest, and the anonymous and methodical slaughter made possible by modern weapons evoked a wide-spread revulsion against traditional martial values. Belief in individual heroism, in combat as a contest of strength and willpower that pitted man against man, was rendered absurd in the eyes of millions through the dominance of the battlefield by the machine gun, long-range artillery, and poison gas. Those who recognized this had made the first step toward emancipation from one of the most retrograde components of traditional culture. But others, for reasons still not fully explained, emerged from the carnage of the war with their faith in martial values still intact.[16] For them, denunciations of war and the heroic ideal amounted to an infuriating desecration of a lofty and noble code. In Italy and Germany this resentment was further heightened by frustration and shame over the outcome of the war and the peace settlement; this may help to account for the fanaticism of those ad-

124

herents of Italian Fascism and National Socialism that have aptly been labeled "military desperadoes." [17]

II

The crucial problem for the purposes of this inquiry is whether, if German National Socialism can accurately be characterized as an expression of utopian anti-modernism, the same was true of Italian Fascism. Was there a kinship between the Nazi drive for *Lebensraum* and the Fascists' quest for a revived Roman Empire, astraddle the Mediterranean? [18] Was a similar desire to effect a return to the soil behind Mussolini's pledge to "ruralize" Italy, "even if it costs billions and takes half a century"? [19] Were the Fascists, like the Nazis, as committed to the martial ideal as would seem to be indicated by Mussolini's famous formulation: "War is to man what maternity is to a woman"? [20] Or, alternatively, does Mussolini's propagation of the doctrine of "productivism" indicate that he was in reality a modernizer, bent upon propelling Italy into the forefront of the new age by accelerating the process of modernization? [21] These questions remain unresolved. Only a few writers have confronted them thus far, and their answers differ, often diametrically. Some have viewed the Fascists, like the Nazis, as extreme opponents of the modern industrial world; [22] others have portrayed them as at least would-be modernizers. [23]

Since the problem of Italian Fascism's relationship to modernization has only recently begun to be considered, it is to be hoped that further inquiries will yield a clarification. Those who undertake such inquiries would do well, however, to keep in mind certain essential distinctions that must be made with regard to Nazism and modernization. The German case would seem to indicate, for example, that a positive attitude toward the products of modern industry should not necessarily be equated with approval of the larger process of modernization. Despite his denunciations of the "materialism" of modern society, Hitler relished speeding through the countryside in his powerful Mercedes-Benz convertible or descending dramatically out of the clouds in a chartered airplane. Neither he nor his associates displayed any inclination to

125

dispense with indoor plumbing or central heating. Most were, in fact, fascinated by technology and, despite their hostility to industrial society, stood in awe of German industry. It is revealing, however, that this awe derived not from a recognition by the Nazi leaders of industry's potential for improving the nation's standard of living. It resulted instead from their realization that industry was a source of immense power that could be harnessed for the pursuit of their own anti-modern utopias.[24] Moreover, the Nazis accorded to the products of industry, such as automobiles, airplanes, tanks, and other modern weapons, a curious sort of autonomy, viewing them largely in isolation from the social, economic, and political concomitants of the processes that made them possible. In other words, the Nazis wanted to have the products of industry but without industrial society. Something of this same tendency to attribute an autonomous existence to the material products of industrial society seems to have characterized the Italian futurist movement, to which Mussolini was for a time apparently favorably inclined.[25] It would be interesting to learn whether, and to what extent, he and other Fascist leaders subscribed to similar attitudes.

On the basis of the German experience, it also seems dangerous to assume that even the implementation of what appear objectively to be modernizing policies is proof that a regime is committed to modernization. Once the Nazis came to power, they generally allowed most of the manifestations of modernization they had excoriated while they were an opposition movement to continue with little interference, at least during the peacetime years. Despite continuing rhetoric to the contrary, industry grew still bigger in the Third Reich, German cities became still larger, the flight from the land persisted, and women continued to be drawn into the labor force.[26] This seeming paradox has puzzled a good many observers, but there is a simple explanation. How, after all, was it possible to obtain vast stretches of *Lebensraum* for the purpose of an extensive de-industrialization and de-urbanization of Germany in the mid-twentieth century other than by conquest? And how was such conquest possible except by resort to a vast industrial war machine? The Nazis, that is, practiced modernization out of necessity in order to pursue their fundamentally anti-modern aims.[27]

126

For them, modernizing policies were not ends in themselves but mere means to a very different goal which, once realized, would render them largely unnecessary. Might there have been something of this behind the apparent modernizing measures of the Fascist regime in Italy as well? Could those policies also have been only means toward a similarly backward-looking utopian goal in the form of the oft-proclaimed revival of the Roman Empire? Might not such policies have been designed only to ready Italy for the warfare which Mussolini and other Fascists, like the Nazis, so lavishly praised as an intrinsic and elevating aspect of human culture?

It is, of course, conceivable that Mussolini and his associates were simply political opportunists who were indifferent to modernization, or that Italian Fascism was a mixed case, containing both modernist and anti-modernist elements and following no clear line or a vacillating one. It is also conceivable that Fascism may have undergone a transformation after the achievement of power, possibly through a shift in strength in favor of a pro-modernist faction. Like all governing groups in twentieth-century Europe, the Fascists had to cope with rising material and social aspirations awakened in the populace by earlier stages of modernization—aspirations that were especially acute in Italy because of that country's severe demographic and economic problems. As elsewhere, there were undoubtedly strong incentives in Fascist Italy for at least an accommodation with modernization. The Nazi leadership successfully withstood such temptations, doggedly pursuing its anti-modern utopian schemes into a suicidal war against hopeless odds. In the course of their much longer reigns, on the other hand, such rulers as Franco in Spain and Salazar in Portugal were to allow their nonutopian forms of anti-modernism to be considerably eroded by modernizing measures. Is it possible that the same could have been true of the Italian Fascists? Or might the ultimate plunge into war at the side of Nazi Germany indicate that they had never abandoned a pursuit of utopian precepts derived from a vision of Italy's past, but had instead only been temporarily deterred by Italy's weakness and vulnerability?

If it should prove that the Italian Fascists, like the Nazis, did in fact represent a particularly extreme form of anti-modernism, the next task would be to explain why this became the focus of potent political movements in Italy and Germany, whereas in most of Europe it remained a diffuse set of attitudes held by a few intellectuals or, at most, the rallying point for hapless splinter parties. With regard to causal factors of a socio-economic nature, the theory of modernization may be able to provide a conceptual framework more satisfactory than the Marxist doctrine of "monopoly" or "late" capitalism, which posits a basic identity between all capitalist societies, including those in which no alleged fascist movement has assumed importance. One finds a number of suggestive parallel features if one looks at the shape and pace of modernization in Italy and Germany (omitting from the comparison the backward South of Italy) that seem to distinguish their experiences from those of other major European nations. In both countries, the process of change began relatively late and proceeded rapidly but unevenly. Certain sectors of the two economies and certain regions of the two countries were transformed swiftly, rapidly displacing or disadvantaging large numbers of people involved in older modes of production and distribution. On the other hand, some sectors and regions were only partially affected, leaving intact sizeable vested interests which feared further changes and were hostile to those that had already taken place. In both countries, in short, the shape and pace of modernization may have been such as to produce especially large reservoirs of hostility toward that process. Conversely, similar factors may help to explain the failure of utopian anti-modernism to assume political importance in other European countries. May not modernization in Britain have been too long-established, too thoroughgoing, and too far-advanced to allow such a widespread reaction in the twentieth century? And may not France have escaped for the opposite reason, because modernization had proceeded with comparative slowness there in the late nineteenth and early twentieth centuries, thus leaving French society less affected by rapid transformations and disruptions of the sort experienced in Germany and northern Italy? [28]

It is inadequate, however, to seek an explanation for the existence of widespread anti-modernist sentiments solely in material terms. Many middle-class Germans who cast their ballots for the Nazis cannot be classified, either economically or socially, as "losers" in the process of modernization. Nevertheless, their political behavior may not necessarily have been unrelated to modernization, for there are strong indications that they perceived in a negative light those processes of change from which, by any objective measure, they themselves derived material and even social benefits.[29] A number of historians have provided illuminating studies of certain aspects of Germany's cultural, social, and political heritage that contributed to this negative response.[30] Unfortunately, the theorists of modernization have accorded little attention to what might be termed a subjective, or "soft," side of that process. Yet it may well be that people's perceptions of the changes wrought by modernization are just as important in determining political responses as is modernization's "hard" side of objective social and economic effects.

This is not to imply that everyone who joined the Nazi or Italian Fascist parties, voted for them, or supported their regimes harbored utopian anti-modernist views, even if it should prove that such an outlook did predominate among their leaders. Presumably, hostility toward the manifestations of modernization can be as vague and inchoate a sentiment as any other, so that even those followers who may have been anti-modernists might not necessarily have been adherents of the utopian variety. Moreover, given the limitations of human perception and the capacity of humans for self-delusion, as well as the calculated efforts of the Nazi and Fascist leaders to make their movements appealing to as many people as possible by toning down their views before certain kinds of audiences, it seems quite possible that some of their followers may not have been anti-modernists at all. Certainly both movements garnered considerable support because of their adroit exploitation of intensely emotional issues that had little direct connection with underlying processes of technological and societal change, such as the lost war in the case of Germany, and the allegedly lost peace in that of Italy, as well as the economic crises in both countries. The two movements, that is, became significant political forces as a consequence of their tactical success in mobilizing coalitions of malcon-

129

tents; by no means all, or even most, of these malcontents necessarily subscribed to, or were even aware of, the full implications of the ideological predilections of the leadership cadres.

The acquisition of power by the Nazis and Italian Fascists also cannot be attributed to acceptance of utopian anti-modernism by the bulk of the citizenry, since both movements came to power as minority groups, although the Nazis were far stronger in 1933 than the Fascists had been in 1922. Still, it might be worthwhile to consider the extent to which their successes can be explained in terms of the exploitation, by extreme anti-modernist forces, of a stalemate between rival groups of modernizers. Both the Fascists and the Nazis gained power by taking advantage of political opportunities that arose when the parliamentary machinery of the two countries became paralyzed, in large measure as a consequence of a deadlock between those who wanted to continue modernizing under the untrammeled auspices of private enterprise and those who wished to move in the direction of a greater degree of state control. In Germany as in Italy this deadlock accorded decisive political importance to groups that might be described as conservative and reactionary anti-modernists, those who wished to slow down the process of change or to turn the clock back somewhat, but not to impose a utopian remedy. These groups, badly underestimating the Nazis and the Fascists, entered into what they mistakenly assumed would be partnerships with them; instead, they installed them in power. In both cases, this crucial if short-lived alliance of anti-modernist forces was facilitated by the catalytic effect of the threat represented by the presence of utopian modernizers—in Germany in the form of the Communists, in Italy in the form of the Communists and the militant elements of the Socialist Party.

III

If it should prove that both Italian Fascism and Nazism represented, at least insofar as their leadership cadres were concerned, political manifestations of utopian anti-modernism, there would be a working definition of paradigmatic fascism in terms of fundamental socio-economic issues to replace the now discredited

130

"agent theory" of the Marxist-Leninists. And that definition would provide a criterion that could be employed to evaluate the numerous other movements and regimes also alleged to be fascist. Since the existing literature on these other putative fascisms has seldom been addressed to fundamental socio-economic issues, no attempt can be made here to apply that criterion in a comprehensive fashion. But in some cases, such as the Norwegian *Nasjonal Samling* led by Vidkun Quisling, and the early Spanish *Falange*, previous studies clearly suggest extreme anti-modernist tendencies.[31] On the other hand, certain purported fascists seem to have been quite free of such tendencies. Jacques Doriot, Oswald Mosley, and the Juan Perón of the 1940's and 1950's, for example, can hardly be characterized as anti-modernists of any sort, much less utopian anti-modernists. Indeed, all three were, at least in terms of their aspirations, enthusiastically in favor of modernization.[32] How, then, can one explain their affinity with Fascist Italy and/or Nazi Germany? The answer may lie in an error of perception, but an understandable one. Doriot, Mosley, and Perón looked to Italian Fascism and Nazism for precepts only *after* those movements had come to power. And, as noted above, both the Nazis and the Fascists implemented many modernizing policies after attaining power, even if, as in the German case and possibly that of Italy, only as a means to anti-modernist ends. Is it not possible that Doriot, Mosley, and Perón saw the Nazis and Fascists merely as dynamic, effective, non-socialist authoritarian modernizers? If so, how many other alleged fascists of the 1930's and 1940's, in Europe and elsewhere, were also only would-be modernizers who fell victim to the same error of perception? [33]

A good many widely-held beliefs about who was a fascist and who was not might thus be overturned if utopian anti-modernism should prove to be a central and common characteristic of the Italian and German movements. The implications for traditional thinking about fascism as a generic phenomenon would, however, be far more dire if, as also seems possible, such a definition were inapplicable to Italy. For if Italian Fascism should, upon closer examination, turn out to have been predominantly pro-modernist,

131

then the two paradigmatic manifestations of fascism would stand opposed to one another on what many now hold to be the fundamental issues of modern times.[34] One, that is, would have been committed to furthering the process of modernization by repressive, authoritarian methods, the other to employing similar methods but as a means of reversing that same process through a fanatical and ultimately suicidal pursuit of an unattainable, archaic utopia. If this should indeed be the case, there would be grounds for arguing that, in terms of underlying socio-economic issues, Italian Fascism and Nazism do not belong in the same category at all. And if the paradigms of fascism are revealed as fundamentally different, what basis is there any longer for a generic concept? It should not be forgotten that the generic category in political analysis is at bottom metaphoric, a borrowing from biology. Nor should it be forgotten that biologists have abandoned or revised their application of the term genus wherever they have recognized that what had previously been regarded as constituent species were in actuality set apart by basic differences.

Even if one does not choose to look at the problem in terms of the theory of modernization, there are still other grounds for asking whether fascism is a valid or useful generic concept. Anyone who reads many studies of fascism as a multi-national problem cannot but be struck by the frequency with which writers who begin by assuming they are dealing with a unitary phenomenon end up with several more-or-less discrete sub-categories.[35] Regardless of whose criteria are applied, it seems very difficult to keep fascism from fragmenting. In spite of this, there has been a general reluctance to consider what must be regarded as a definite possibility: namely, that fascism as a generic concept has no validity and is without value for serious analytical purposes. Generic terms in the social sciences are in no way sacrosanct in and of themselves. They are constructs designed to facilitate communication and analysis. Their use always involves the sacrifice of a certain amount of accuracy, since even the best never fit perfectly all the individual cases to which they are applied. But so long as they provide illumination by adding perspective and revealing larger patterns, that sacrifice is worthwhile. When, however, a generic term begins to confuse and confound rather than clarify, then its use ceases to be justified. It is time to consider whether that is not the case with fascism.

The generic term fascism is in origin neither analytical nor descriptive. It was coined not in the serenity of the scholar's study but in the heat of political battle.[36] Its principal authors were Marxist opponents of the Italian and German movements, which they mistook for twin agents of "finance capital." Since Italian Fascism was initially the more important, they employed its name, transforming it into a generic label. In the absence of any other designation for what appeared to many contemporaries to be a multi-national phenomenon, it quickly gained general acceptance, even by many of those against whom it had been originally directed. Invoked by countless politicians and hardened into print by the mass media, it was uncritically adopted by scholars. In many respects, it is a typical product of our garrulous and hasty age, which assigns generic labels to social phenomena even before they have assumed full shape. Yet from the vantage point of today, it seems quite conceivable that it was from the outset a construct based on merely superficial similarities, such as common organizational forms and tactical styles, common political enmities, and common international interests. These may have seemed to many contemporaries adequate grounds for generalization, but they may also have obscured far more fundamental differences.

In the light of these unresolved questions, it seems unwise to continue with studies of fascism that start with the assumption that there must have been such a generic phenomenon. It seems more appropriate to consider carefully whether some or even all of the movements and regimes alleged to have been fascist may not be classified more meaningfully in some other way. One possibly illuminating criterion, though by no means the only one, is the relationship of these putative fascisms to the process of modernization. For if the essence of what has hitherto been described as fascism should be found to lie in an extreme revolt against the modern industrial world and an attempt to recapture a distant, mythic past, it should be kept in mind that there is no guarantee that such movements may not arise again. It would be indeed unfortunate if, in our vigilance against a rebirth of the familiar forms of what has been thought of as fascism, we should be led to overlook the emergence of new varieties of utopian anti-modernism quite different in appearance from earlier ones.

¹ By far the most ambitious and impressive attempt to arrive at a definition of fascism is Ernst Nolte's *Three Faces of Fascism* (New York, Chicago, San Francisco 1966); (New York and Toronto 1969); originally published in German as *Der Faschismus in seiner Epoche* (Munich 1963). This article owes much to Nolte's work. Yet three volumes of scholarly essays on the subject published since the appearance of Nolte's book reveal that there is still little in the way of agreement among the experts: Walter Laqueur and George L. Mosse, eds., *International Fascism, 1920–1945* (New York 1966), also published as vol. 1, no. 1 of *Journal of Contemporary History*, 1966; S. J. Woolf, ed., *European Fascism* (London 1968); S. J. Woolf, ed., *The Nature of Fascism* (London 1968; New York 1969). Similarly diverse views can be found in the following: F. L. Carsten, *The Rise of Fascism* (Berkeley 1967); H. R. Kedward, *Fascism in Western Europe 1900–45* (London 1969); Arno J. Mayer, *Dynamics of Counterrevolution in Europe* (New York 1971); Hans Rogger and Eugen Weber, eds., *The European Right. A Historical Profile* (Berkeley 1966); Peter Sugar, ed., *Native Fascism in the Successor States, 1918–1945* (Santa Barbara 1971); John Weiss, *The Fascist Tradition* (New York 1967). Despite their titles, two recent volumes by A. James Gregor contribute nothing to the analysis of fascism as a generic phenomenon. Instead of offering a theory about fascism, Gregor revives, in watered-down form, the familiar and discredited theory of totalitarianism. Focusing almost solely on Italian Fascism, and arbitrarily relegating Nazism to the periphery of his considerations (often excluding it altogether), Gregor depicts fascism as nothing more than a form of national developmental dictatorship, essentially similar to Soviet and Chinese Communism; as well as to authoritarian regimes throughout the so-called third world: Gregor, *The Ideology of Fascism* (New York 1969); idem., *The Fascist Persuasion in Radical Politics* (Princeton 1974).

² David Apter, *The Politics of Modernization* (Chicago 1965); C. E. Black, *The Dynamics of Modernization* (New York 1966); A. F. K. Organski, *The Stages of Political Development* (New York 1965). Black does note, however, that the Nazi leaders were "inspired by antimodern conceptions," *Dynamics*, 165.

³ S. N. Eisenstadt, "Breakdowns of Modernization," *Economic Development and Cultural Change*, XII (July 1964), 345–67; S. N. Eisenstadt, *Modernization: Protest and Change* (Englewood Cliffs 1966), 132–35, 160; J. P. Nettl and Roland Robertson, *International Systems and the Modernization of Societies* (New York 1968), 48.

⁴ This practice has been analyzed by George Macklin Wilson in an article rejecting application of the term fascism to Japan: "A New Look at the Problem of 'Japanese Fascism'," *Comparative Studies in Society and History*, X (July 1968), 407 (republished in this volume). For an example, see Seymour Martin Lipset, *Political Man* (New York 1960), 131–76.

135

⁵ John M. Cammett, "Communist Theories of Fascism, 1920–1935," *Science and Society*, XXXI (Spring 1967), 155.

⁶ Barrington Moore, Jr., *Social Origins of Dictatorship and Democracy* (Boston 1966), 447. As a study of fascism, Moore's book labors under a considerable handicap as a consequence of his virtual exclusion of the paradigmatic Italian and German cases, which are alluded to, but never thoroughly analyzed.

⁷ See Iring Fetscher, "Faschismus und Nationalsozialismus," *Politische Vierteljahrsschrift*, III (March 1962), 42–63, translated as a chapter in the author's *Marx and Marxism* (New York 1971), 274–301; Roland Sarti, *Fascism and the Industrial Leadership in Italy, 1919–1940* (Berkeley 1971); H. A. Turner, Jr., "Big Business and the Rise of Hitler," *The American Historical Review*, LXXV (October 1969), 56–70. For an arresting independent Marxist challenge to the orthodox view, see T. W. Mason, "The primacy of politics—Politics and economics in National Socialist Germany," in Woolf, ed., *The Nature of Fascism* (n. 1), 165–95. The articles by Mason and Turner also appear, in revised form in *Nazism and the Third Reich*, ed. by H. A. Turner, Jr. (New York 1972).

⁸ The basic studies of the Nazi "left wing" are Reinhard Kühnl, *Die nationalsozialistische Linke 1925–1930* (Meisenheim am Glan, 1966) and Max Herschel Kele, *Nazis and Workers* (Chapel Hill 1972). See also the treatment in Dietrich Orlow, *The History of the Nazi Party: 1919–1933* (Pittsburgh 1969).

⁹ On the affinity of the Nazi leadership for medieval institutional patterns, see the suggestive article by Robert Koehl, "Feudal Aspects of National Socialism," *The American Political Science Review*, LIV (December 1960), 921–33 (reprinted in Turner, ed., *Nazism and the Third Reich*; cf. n. 7, above). On the utopian tendencies of Nazism, see also Norman Cohn, *Warrant for Genocide* (New York 1966), 169 ff.

¹⁰ There are indications, however, that elements of the "left wing" survived what have usually been regarded as its conclusive defeats and persisted in influential positions until the end of the Third Reich; see Alan Milward, "French Labour and the German Economy, 1942–1945: An Essay on the Nature of the Fascist New Order," *Economic History Review*, XXIII (August 1970), 336–51.

¹¹ On the remarkable consistency of Hitler's foreign policy views and actions from 1924 on, see Eberhard Jäckel, *Hitlers Weltanschauung* (Tübingen 1969), 29–57, now translated as *Hitler's Weltanschauung: A Blueprint for Power* (Middletown, Connecticut 1972), 27–46. The chapter in question also appeared in Turner (ed.), *Nazism and the Third Reich*; cf. n. 7, above.

¹² Hitler's scorn for modern industrial cities has not received the attention it deserves. In his unpublished book of 1928 he described them as "abscesses on the body of the folk (*Volkskörper*), in which all vices, bad habits and sicknesses seem to unite. They are above all hotbeds of miscegenation and bastardization. . . ." See Gerhard L. Weinberg, ed., *Hitlers Zweites Buch* (Stuttgart 1961), 61 f. On the antiurban component in Nazi ideology, see Klaus Bergmann, *Agrarromantik und Grossstadtfeindschaft* (Meisenheim am Glan, 1970). Surprisingly, Bergmann maintains in his conclusions—yet without proof—that Hitler did not entirely subscribe to the rural utopianism of the movement (355). In another study it has been argued that

Hitler's enthusiastic participation in the planning for post-war Berlin is proof that he was not anti-urban: Barbara Miller Lane, *Architecture and Politics in Germany, 1918–1945* (Cambridge, Mass., 1968), 189. However, Albert Speer reports in his memoir—*Erinnerungen* (Berlin, 1969), 92 f.; *Inside the Third Reich* (New York, 1970), 79—that Hitler was exclusively interested in the intimidatingly imposing government quarter of his future capital. When the discussion turned to projects designed to make Berlin a more liveable place for its millions of inhabitants, the *Führer* lost interest. The idea of a return to the soil was not limited to the Nazis, having marked as well the thinking of some leading members of Heinrich Brüning's cabinet; see Henning Köhler, "Arbeitsbeschaffung, Siedlung und Reparationen in der Schlussphase der Regierung Brüning," *Vierteljahrshefte für Zeitgeschichte*, XVII (1969), 287–295. For these men, however, resettlement programs were more a practical emergency measure in a grinding economic crisis than a utopian goal. They also showed no signs of considering conquest of additional land, limiting themselves to comparatively modest resettlement schemes within Germany's existing boundaries.

[13] For the importance accorded to this project in the Third Reich, see Robert Koehl, *RKFDV: German Resettlement and Population Policy, 1939–1945* (Cambridge, Mass. 1957). For Hitler's wartime views on German colonization in the East, see Norman Cameron and R. H. Stevens, trans., *Hitler's Secret Conversations, 1941–1944* (New York 1953), *passim*. On Himmler's ideas, see Josef Ackermann, *Heinrich Himmler als Ideologe* (Göttingen 1970).

[14] See George L. Mosse, *The Crisis of German Ideology* (New York 1964) and Fritz Stern, *The Politics of Cultural Despair* (Berkeley 1961).

[15] See, for examples, John R. Harrison, *The Reactionaries* (New York 1967); Alistair Hamilton, *The Appeal of Fascism* (New York 1971); Robert Soucy, "Romanticism and Realism in the Fascism of Drieu la Rochelle," *Journal of the History of Ideas*, XXXI (January–March 1970), 69–90; William R. Tucker, "Politics and Aesthetics: The Fascism of Robert Brasillach," *The Western Political Quarterly*, XV (December 1962), 605–17; William R. Tucker, "Fascism and Individualism: The Political Thought of Pierre Drieu la Rochelle," *Journal of Politics*, XXVII (February 1965), 153–77; Renee Winegarten, "The Fascist Mentality—Drieu la Rochelle," *The Wiener Library Bulletin*, XII (Winter 1967/68), 37–43 (republished in this volume); Renee Winegarten, "The Temptations of Cultural Fascism," *ibid.*, XIII (Winter 1968/69), 34–40.

[16] For a suggestive attempt at an answer, see James H. McRandle, *The Track of the Wolf* (Evanston 1965), 51–79.

[17] Wolfgang Sauer, "National Socialism: Totalitarianism or Fascism?," *The American Historical Review*, LXXIII (December 1967), 411 (republished in this volume).

[18] In *Mussolini's Early Diplomacy* (Princeton 1970), Alan Cassels attributes the Fascist regime's drive for territorial expansion on the eastern shores of the Mediterranean and in East Africa to a desire for "national glory and living space for Italy's surplus population. . . ." (391). Cassels characterizes this policy as an arrogation of the "Crispian tradition," but it would be worthwhile to examine whether the Fas-

137

cists' motives may not have more closely resembled those of the Nazis than those of the liberal imperialists of the late nineteenth century.

[19] Quoted in Carl T. Schmidt, *The Plough and the Sword* (New York 1938), 43.

[20] Max Gallo, *L'Italie de Mussolini* (Verviers, 1964), 243.

[21] On Fascist "productivism", see Sarti (n. 7), 22 ff.; also Charles S. Maier, "Between Taylorism and Technocracy: European ideologies and the vision of industrial productivity in the 1920s," *Journal of Contemporary History*, V (No. 2 1970), 40–45.

[22] Nolte (n. 1); Sauer (n. 17). Italian scholars have, virtually without exception, dealt with Fascism as an isolated, national problem, ignoring all except Marxist theories of fascism as a generic phenomenon. A recent departure from this approach may be found in Renzo De Felice's *Le interpretazione del fascismo* (Bari 1969).

[23] Sarti (n. 7); also Sarti's article, "Fascist Modernization in Italy: Traditional or Revolutionary?" in *The American Historical Review*, LXXV (April 1970), 1029–1045; Alan Cassels, "Janus: The Two Faces of Fascism," The Canadian Historical Association, *Historical Papers* (1969), 165–84 (republished in this volume); A. James Gregor, *The Ideology of Fascism* (New York 1969); Edward R. Tannenbaum, "The Goals of Italian Fascism," *The American Historical Review*, LXXIV (April 1969), 1183–1204.

[24] In his memoir (n. 12), Albert Speer relates that Hitler objected to industry on the grounds that it gave rise to Communism and bred an intelligentsia, something the *Führer* regarded as undesirable (*Erinnerungen* 322; *Inside*, 309). Yet Speer records that upon his appointment as Munitions Minister in 1942 Hitler advised him to circumvent the bureaucracy whenever possible and deal directly with industry, since that was where the best brains were (*Erinnerungen*, 218; *Inside*, 202). According to Speer, Hitler abandoned his original plan to de-industrialize the occupied territories of the East only when he came to realize the necessity of utilizing industrial installations there on behalf of the German war effort (*Erinnerungen*, 322; *Inside*, 309).

[25] See James Joll's essay on Filippo Tommaso Marinetti and Fascism in his *Three Intellectuals in Politics* (New York 1965), 133–84.

[26] For the best analysis, see David Schoenbaum, *Hitler's Social Revolution* (New York 1966).

[27] *Ibid.*, 288.

[28] For comparative data on the rate of change, see Surendra J. Patel, "Rates of Industrial Growth in the Last Century, 1860–1958," *Economic Development and Cultural Change*, IX (April 1961), 316–30. On the obstacles to change in France, see John E. Sawyer, "Strains in the Social Structure of Modern France," in E. M. Earle (ed.), *Modern France* (Princeton 1951).

[29] See the illuminating analysis of middle-class political behavior in a small German town in William Sheridan Allen, *The Nazi Seizure of Power* (Chicago 1965).

[30] See Mosse (n. 14) and Stern (n. 14); also Herman Lebovics, *Social Conserva-*

138

tism and the Middle Classes in Germany (Princeton 1969); Klemens von Klemperer, *Germany's New Conservatism* (Princeton 1957).

[31] On Quisling, see Paul M. Hayes, "Quisling's Political Ideas," in Laqueur and Mosse, eds. (n. 1), 145–57; also T. K. Derry, "Norway," in Woolf, ed., *European Fascism* (n. 1), 217–30. On the *Falange*, see Bernd Nellesen, *Die verbotene Revolution* (Hamburg 1963) and Stanley Payne, *Falange* (Stanford 1961); such tendencies seem to have been most evident in the JONS faction led by Onésimo Redondo y Ortega and Ramiro Ledesma Ramos.

[32] On Mosley, see R. J. A. Skidelsky, "Great Britain," in Woolf, ed., *European Fascism* (n. 1), 231–61. On Doriot, see Gilbert D. Allerdyce, "The Political Transformation of Jacques Doriot," in Laqueur and Mosse (n. 1), 56–74; also Dieter Wolf, *Die Doriot-Bewegung* (Stuttgart 1967). On Perón, see George I. Blanksten, *Peron's Argentina* (Chicago 1953) and Tomas Fillol, *Social Factors in Economic Development: The Argentine Case* (Cambridge, Mass. 1961).

[33] According to the findings of a recently published study, this seems to have been the case in the 1930's with the Chinese Kuomintang Party's blue-shirt movement, which proclaimed itself "fascist." One leader of this movement said during an interview in 1969: "Fascism is now thought to be backward (*lo-hou*). But then it seemed to be a very progressive means of resurrecting the nation." See Lloyd E. Eastman, "Fascism in Kuomintang China: The Blue Shirts," in *The China Quarterly*, No. 49 (January–March, 1972), p. 3.

[34] This has been argued by Alan Cassels, who has suggested that in backward countries, such as Italy, fascism was a forward-looking agent of modernization while in advanced countries, such as Germany, it was backward-looking and nihilistically regressive (n. 23). However, Cassels encounters difficulties in applying this thesis to the putative fascisms of eastern Europe. In addition, as suggested above, the cases of Mosley and Doriot seem to contradict his formula.

[35] See, for examples, George L. Mosse, "Introduction: The Genesis of Fascism," in Laqueur and Mosse (n. 1); Sauer, (n. 17); Hugh Trevor-Roper, "The Phenomenon of Fascism," in Woolf, ed., *European Fascism* (n. 1); Eugen Weber, *Varieties of Fascism* (Princeton 1964).

[36] On the history of the term itself, see Ernst Nolte, ed., *Theorien über den Faschismus* (Cologne 1967); Wolfgang Schieder, "Faschismus," in C. D. Kernig, ed., *Sowjetsystem und demokratische Gesellschaft*, vol. 2 (Freiburg, Basel, Vienna 1968), 438–77; now available in English translation: C. D. Kernig, ed., *Marxism, Communism and Western Society. A Comparative Encyclopedia*, vol. 3 (New York 1972), 282–302.

III

FOUR CASE STUDIES

This final section consists of studies of particular instances of purported fascisms. Stanley G. Payne, professor of history at the University of Wisconsin at Madison, in a study which first appeared in 1973 and is published here in revised form, addresses himself to the controversial question of what individuals and groups in Spain can be properly regarded as fascist. Hans Rogger, professor of history at the University of California at Los Angeles, assesses critically the contention that fascism actually first appeared in tsarist Russia and offers some thoughtful observations on the necessary prerequisites for the appearance of fascist movements. Professor Rogger's study was first published in 1964. The perplexing problem of whether there was fascism in Japan is subjected to searching analysis by George Macklin Wilson, associate dean for international programs at Indiana University, in a study that appeared initially in 1968. Finally, Renee Winegarten, British literary critic, examines in a study first published in 1968 the ideas and personality of one of the most articulate self-proclaimed fascist intellectuals of France.

141

7

Spanish Fascism in
Comparative Perspective

BY STANLEY G. PAYNE

The term "fascism" remains one of the most loosely defined in the political lexicon. It is frequently used in a vague generic sense to refer to any sort of more-or-less right-wing organization or government that is authoritarian in aim or structure. Twentieth-century dictatorial régimes can be divided into two general categories: those of the Communist left and those of the anti-Communist right. There now exists considerable diversity even among Communist states, but the degree of difference between the numerous anti-Communist authoritarian régimes that have existed since 1922 is much greater. The term fascism can be applied to the entire broad genus only at the cost of depriving it of any specific content.

The only absolutely clear and uncontestable use of the term can be made with regard to Mussolini's régime in Italy between 1922 and 1943. However, a score of other radical nationalist movements emerged in Europe during that period bearing certain notable ideological and structural similarities to Italian fascism. During the 1930s they claimed to have mastered the direction of history. This has led many historical commentators to conclude that at the very least fascism was a generic phenomenon that could logically be defined as embracing a whole range of European parties and movements during the 1930s and early 1940s.

Scholarly study of fascism as a generic phenomenon made little headway during those years and then languished altogether after 1945. Political scientists have little interest in political history, whereas historians resist conceptualization and broad comparative analysis. Their attention was for long focused on the history of Nazi Germany, while the spread of Stalinism and growth of the Cold War stimulated the formation of the "unitotalitarian theory," whose most eloquent champion was Hannah Arendt.[1] This approach has since been generally discredited, as the great differences between several variants of totalitarian régimes, whether Communist or Nazi, have become clearer.

The study of fascism as a general historical phenomenon only began to receive direct attention in the 1960s, thanks to the pioneering efforts of Eugen Weber [2] and, at greater length, Ernst Nolte.[3] During the past decade the literature attempting to analyze generic fascism has increased greatly in Germany,[4] Italy,[5] France,[6] England,[7] and the United States.[8] This has added greatly to our knowledge and understanding of fascist, Nazi and radical nationalist movements in Europe during the 1930s and early 1940s, but has achieved little toward a scholarly consensus on the exact definition, significance and usage of the concept "fascism." At a session of the meeting of the American Historical Association in December 1970, devoted to the problem, there were strong suggestions that the whole attempt to arrive at a common definition and explanation of the varieties of what was presumed to be fascism was futile and might as well be given up. After a decade of analysis, the "unifascist" concept seems to be going the way of "unitotalitarianism."

Even if one accepts the proposition that the only political entity to which the term "fascist" can be exactly applied is the Italian régime of Mussolini, there remains the problem of how exactly to define the structure and ideology of Italian Fascism.

When Mussolini came to power he lacked a clear-cut ideology and one was only developed *ex post facto*, with the aid of right-wing Nationalist ideologues such as Alfredo Rocco and idealist philosophers such as Giovanni Gentile. The codification of a Fascist ideology occurred between 1925 and 1930, concurrent with the development of the Fascist state system, not preceding it. The dominant characteristics of Italian Fascist doctrine may be briefly summarized as:

143

1. Exaltation of hypernationalism
2. Preaching of national "mission" and "empire"
3. Espousal of radical tactics and aims, including positive evaluation of the use and significance of violence, and the positing of the goal of "national revolution"
4. Doctrine of élitism
5. Rationale of the totalitarian state, based on the single party and principles of leadership and hierarchy
6. Corporatist doctrine of national class and economic integration
7. Goal of economic development; some emphasis on productionism and modernization
8. Exaltation of youth
9. Philosophical vitalism, stressing emotion and the function of myth or idealism
10. Cultural goal of the "new man"
11. Nominal aim of incorporating the major aspects of the national cultural and spiritual tradition in a new synthesis.

This typology of doctrinal/structural characteristics is more precise and in some respects distinct from Nolte's specification of a hypothetical "fascist minimum." The latter notion is based on the supposition that Fascist and Nazi-type movements are so nearly similar that it is not worth while to distinguish between them. Hence Nolte's "fascist minimum" is designed as the simplest typology that can include both Fascism and Nazism as distinct from other political movements. It has often been observed that fascist-type movements could be more easily defined by what they were against rather than what they were for. Consequently Nolte's six-point postulation begins with three negations—anti-Marxism, anti-liberalism and anticonservatism—to which are added three other characteristics: the leadership principle, a "party-army" and the aim of totalitarianism.[9]

This typology of the "fascist minimum" is reasonably successful in isolating the qualities that Nazism and Fascism had in common and that set them off from other political movements.

144

Yet, as Nolte would admit, it is grossly inadequate as a full typology of either movement and blurs over the major differences between them. It ignores the traditionalist dimension in "mature" Fascism, approximating it to Nazi radicalism, and cannot deal with the normativeness of racism for Nazism when contrasted with the originally almost philosemitic character of Fascism.[10] Other prime differential characteristics of Nazism that cannot be assimilated into a "unifascist" concept include the fixation on militarism and aggression as a primary goal, the genuine lack of seriously codified culture and ideology, and the radical insistence on approximating, rather than merely postulating, totalitarianism.

When these fundamental differences are taken into account, it would appear that greater clarity can be achieved by distinguishing between four different types of rightist authoritarian movements and/or régimes: a) Fascism; b) Nazism; c) ideologically flexible or uncodified syncretic systems; and d) reactionary monarchist movements.

In the political lexicon that I employ, "fascist" refers to those political groups whose doctrines and aims were basically very similar to those of the mature Italian Fascist party and reveal no major discrepancies or contradictions to them. Such organizations include Falange Espanola and to a less clear extent most of the other West European parties of authoritarian revolutionary nationalism: Doriot's Parti Populaire Français, the Austrian Heimwehr, Degrelle's Rexists, and several other movements in France and the Low Countries.[11]

Nazism was obviously less fit for imitation than Fascism because of its grounding in racism and its thoroughly irrational war-and-*Lebensraum* approach to politics. The only other notable political variant in Europe that could easily be compared to the Nazi type was the "Szeged" sector of radical Hungarianism in the 1930s. Smaller North European movements such as the Danish National Socialists, the Latvian Thunder Cross, and Quisling's little band were clearly based on the Nazi model but altogether lacked significance. The Finnish Lapua movement had some of the same characteristics, with a mystical racism and heavy stress on direct territorial expansion involving large-scale militarist irrendentism. Under

145

Nazi occupation or hegemony, fascist movements tended more and more to take on radical Nazi characteristics, the most obvious examples being the main Western fascist leaders, Mussolini, Doriot, and Degrelle.[12]

The category of "ideologically flexible or uncodified syncretic systems" is admittedly vague. It includes regimes ranging from the conservative Catholic type of Dollfuss' Austria, Salazar's Portugal, and Smetona's Lithuania through the Balkan régimes of Antonescu and Metaxas to the major Hispanic military-based régimes and on down to primitive Caribbean dictatorships. Each of these régimes has had distinct historical-structural characteristics and the entire group may be broken down into subtypes if one so desires. What distinguishes such régimes from those of fascism or Nazism is their lack of unified ideology together with the absence of fully-elaborated authoritarian state structure. At least one of these—the Spanish Franquist state—harbored a major fascist component during its early years and has also achieved the most precise and developed structure. Yet the régime's ultimate rejection of ideology and normative fascism—due in large measure, though not entirely, to the change in the international power context after 1942—has given it a distinct complexion that could not at all be assimilated into the Italian typology.

Writing on the basis of his "unifascist" theory, Ernst Nolte has labelled the period 1930–45 the "fascist era" in European history, but so broad a characterization has recently and deservedly come under criticism. In most European countries, Fascist- or Nazi-type movements played a negligible role and had comparatively little chance to seize power. In Europe as a whole, the several variants of "antifascism" altogether enjoyed greater basic political strength. Rather than a "fascist era," there was a ten-year period of German Nazi hegemony in Europe based above all on military power.

If the period was not truly a "fascist era" in terms of the overall preponderance of political commitment, there was nonetheless in the years immediately after 1933 a notable "fascist vertigo" that strongly affected diverse elements of the centre and right. That is, across a significant minority of the political spectrum,

146

there was manifested a growing intoxication with rather vague notions of approximating the radical nationalist authoritarianism established in Germany or Italy. The popular support gained by Nazi- or Fascist-type movements varied considerably. The Nazis garnered 37.4 percent of the vote at their high-water mark in 1932, and the Arrow Cross movement registered approximately 20 percent in the Hungarian elections of 1939. In 1936 the several fascistic parties in Belgium altogether collected nearly 20 per cent of the vote. In their major electoral showing, the Italian Fascists themselves won approximately 15 per cent of the national vote in 1921 [13]—presumably their "natural" share. The French fascistoid parties were considerably weaker; the largest of them, Doriot's PPF, was apparently not supported by more than about 2 per cent of the French electorate.[14] Even that figure was rather high when compared with Spain. In the final elections of 1936, the Falange got only 44,000 ballots—about 0.7 per cent of the national vote. On that basis one might conclude that direct fascism had less popular appeal in Spain than in any other large country of continental Europe outside Russia, with the possible exception of Poland. So long as anything approaching normal political conditions prevailed in Spain—equivalent to those of Italy in 1921 or Germany in 1932—Falangism proved an irrelevant force.

Compared with other countries, how is the absolute insignificance of Spanish fascism prior to the absolute collapse of the Spanish polity to be explained? Obviously many factors must be considered, but the two problems that demand greatest attention are the remarkable weakness of Spanish nationalism and the character and extent of political alternatives. When contrasted with Italy, Spain is found to have had little in the way of a prefascist culture, and this was of course partly due to the fact that Spain had so little in the way of any sort of modern nationalist agitation. Prefascist culture in Italy was composed of three strains: one was the radical nationalism of the Associazione Nazionalista Italiana and of irredentist and colonialist elements; the second was the complex of neoidealist doctrines and irrationalism that was predominant among many litterateurs and philosophers and that also influenced

147

radical politics on both the left and right; the third was the sharp downgrading of parliament by some of the most prestigious elements of the intelligentsia.

None of these factors obtained in Spain. Regenerationist politics of the early twentieth century failed to promote a new and modern form of Spanish nationalism. Spain's complete lack of involvement in major power rivalries and the complete absence of any sort of foreign menace after 1898 obviously had much to do with this. There was no irredentist problem, and the issue of Gibraltar could not serve as a substitute. Moreover, there were also internal factors discouraging the development of active modern nationalism. One was a greater climate of cultural pessimism about modernization than in any other European country save perhaps Portugal. Another was the slowness of the development of any major internal challenge to social and political identity, and this was of course related to the comparatively slow rates of social and structural change prior to the First World War.

Equally significant was Spain's peculiar structure of reverse regional roles in the nineteenth and early twentieth centuries. The civically dominant regions did not coincide with those that led the way in economic and cultural modernization. By contrast, the regional balance in Italy was "normal"; that is, the modernizing and industrializing regions of the north also provided the country's civic leadership. Milan was not merely the industrial centre of Italy, it was the centre of Italian nationalism in 1910, the focus of military interventionism in 1915 and the birthplace of fascism in 1919. Barcelona was the industrial and commercial leader of Spain but also the centre of a somewhat distinct, rather than common or hegemonic, culture. It eventually became the focus of a centrifugal nationalist identity that had a crippling effect on the Spanish polity. Rural Castile lacked the social structure, economic base, or culture to foster a dynamic and modernizing Spanish nationalism. Resistance to Catalanism took the form not of positive Spanish nationalism but of a sterile and negative anti-Catalanism that further undermined the polity.

The nearest thing to a mood of nationalism was found in the traditionalist ultra-patriotic Catholicism of the traditionalist and clerical right. Religion had of course at the close of the Middle Ages provided the basis for Spanish identity. In the early twentieth century the national identity preached by Carlists, Integrists, and conservative Catholics was grounded on ultra-conservative religiosity, and completely lacked a dynamic, expansive or modernizing dimension. It also lacked any notable support, save in terms of the *status quo* politics of a portion of the Conservative party.

There was no real Spanish cultural equivalent of Italian neo-idealism and vitalist irrationalism. Spanish idealist philosophy largely remained faithful to its nineteenth-century foundations, and the political implications derived from it were almost unfailingly liberal and reformist. The Italian doctrine of systematic authoritarianism was preceded by the outright espousal of a kind of political amoralism as well. It was no accident that Italy's leading aesthetic amoralist, Gabriele d'Annunzio, became its most glamorous popularizer of political and militarist amoralism. Since the Spanish intelligentsia was less given to aesthetic d'Annuzianism, it was the less likely to produce political d'Annuzianism. A more traditionalist culture less influenced by European fads and slower to change had the initial advantage of being less subject to dehumanization. Irrationalism and vitalism found only limited voice in pure aesthetics, variants of anarchism, a sector of Catalan modernism (whose political connotations would be Catalanist rather than *españolista*) and the ambivalent but ultimately liberal élitism of José Ortega y Gasset. When a mystical sort of Spanish d'Annunzio finally appeared in the form of Ernesto Giménez Caballero in 1929, he was doomed to virtual isolation.

Denunciation of parliament became fairly widespread in Spain, and it is in this regard that Spanish moods might seem most closely to approximate prefascist currents in Italy. Even in this regard, there was a considerable difference both in degree and quality. Though antiparliamentarianism became widely diffused in both countries, it did not enjoy the sophisticated intellectual legitimization in Spain that some of the best minds of Italy gave it before 1922.[15]

In Spain's fin-de-siècle "disaster" literature, suggestions that corrupt parliamentarianism be replaced by a transition period of

149

authoritarian reformism were always vague and usually fleeting. Too much has been made of Joaquín Costa's famous phrase about the need for an "iron surgeon." [16] Costa never elaborated the concept and never worked out a precise political formula of any kind. He apparently ended his days a democratic republican.

In general, the antiparliamentary talk in Spain during the decade 1914–23 was mere negative criticism, without much theoretical foundation and with little or no suggestion of an alternative. Since the late nineteenth century, a few ideologues and propagandists of the ultra-right advanced vague notions of corporatism [17] but never clarified them or generated active new support. Moreover, some of the anti-establishment intellectuals who were most active in political criticism did not strive to undermine parliament but to reform and reinforce it through the Liga de Educación Política and the Reformist party. These two groups acquired a following among serious intellectuals without proportionate counterpart in any liberal reformist Italian group. Ortega y Gasset briefly came out for a corporatist alternative in newspaper articles during 1917–18, but afterward dropped the notion, returning to the concept of revitalized parliamentary liberalism on a broad national basis.[18]

Despite the lack of a conceptualized alternative, the prestige of Spanish parliamentary liberalism did reach a nadir between 1917 and 1923. The same thing was occurring at precisely the same time in Italy on an intensified scale. There political mobilization was much more extensive and political groupings more vigorously based, despite the fact that something approaching universal suffrage had been introduced only in 1913, a quarter-century later than Spain. Throughout the nineteenth century the formal institutionalization of Spanish liberalism had far outstripped the social and economic bases on which it rested. In Italy nearly the opposite occurred, for political institutionalization in terms of suffrage and party organization tended to lag behind social and cultural development.

It would be quite misleading to attempt a direct analogy between the Spanish and Italian political crises of 1919–23. Italy was by that point within the first phase of mass politics. Spain did not reach that level until after 1931. The Spanish crisis, if that is the word for it, of 1917–23 is in Italian history more analogous to the Italian phase of 1912–15. The political conflicts of both countries in those two phases were characterized by a new radicalization of politics touched off to a considerable extent by international events, an attempt at mass mobilization that could not be realized, growing stalemate of parliamentary politics, and an ineffectual groping for major new liberal alignments. Finally both phases were ended by the forced imposition of national unity to face war. In the case of Italy this meant the contrived entry into World War I; in the case of Spain, the contrived dictatorship of Primo de Rivera, whose principal *raison d'être* was the Moroccan War.[19]

Criticism of the Spanish parliament during 1917–23 resulted in depolitization and growing abstention among some sectors, but not to the rise of major extra-parliamentary groups. The sole exception was the rapid growth and decline of the CNT, (the anarchosyndicalist "National Confederation of Labor") but that was a half-coordinated mass nuisance, not an organized political force. The Spanish party sub-groupings of those years were exceedingly personalistic, status-oriented, envious and destructive of their potential allies; but that was not a necessary fault of the parliamentary system, which in fact represented the nearest thing to a consensus that existed in Spain before 1923. Despite the terrorism and counter-terrorism prevailing in several cities, basic civil liberties were for the most part preserved and a not inconsiderable amount of reform legislation was passed. The calibre of political leadership was not especially high, but fraud and corruption, at least on the national level, were rare. The country was registering measurable economic and cultural progress and, in view of Spain's overall level of development, the political system was functioning about as well in the face of multiple pressures as might have been expected.

Prior to 1933, a modern Spanish antiparliamentary right did not exist, whereas the modern Italian right emerged in 1910 and began to lay the groundwork for Fascism. Atavistic Carlism could not play such a role in Spain; in the early twentieth century it was relegated to an unimportant fringe position that merely contributed to political fractionalization without offering a viable modern alter-

151

native. The closest thing to a modern right in Spain were the "Maurist Youth" of 1914–23, yet they remained a small and nearly impotent group without clear definition. The Conservative leader Antonio Maura himself remained bound to a narrow, rigid, rule-of-law constitutionalism rather similar to Sidney Sonnino's conservatism in Italy. The politics of both men represented a paralysis of traditional liberalism rather than a replacement for it. Sonnino, however, was an active nationalist in foreign affairs, whereas Maura reflected Spanish diffidence in this area as well. Some of the Maurist Youth spokesmen did try vaguely to shift ground, and spoke of representing a higher synthesis of the best that was in both the left and the right. However, the Maurist Youth leaders only clearly emerged as the champions of a new reformist national authoritarianism after the collapse of the regular liberal system.[20]

Probably the chief reason why a Spanish right failed to emerge before it did was because a serious, organized Spanish left did not appear until 1931. No Spanish left of any consequence at all existed before 1917 and even in the hectic years following World War I mass anarchosyndicalism was unable to play the role of catalytic menace filled by revolutionary socialism. In 1913 Enrico Corradini, the central leader of radical Italian nationalism, asked the rhetorical question: "When and how were the new national doctrines born?" His own answer was: "There is no doubt that they were born in reaction against socialism." [21]

It might be added that though radical authoritarian Italian nationalism was developed in antithesis to Marxist socialism, it eventually broadened its base through the incorporation of part of the non-Marxist revolutionary left. Spanish anarchosyndicalism was not susceptible to the nationalistic orientation adopted by part of Italian anarchosyndicalism, though that was doubtless due in part to the complete absence of dynamic middle-class nationalism in Spain. It was apparently reinforced by the fact that Catalonia, the centre of middle-class regionalist dissociationism, was also the main home of working-class anarchist dissociationism.

In general, the Spanish parliamentary system was operating on a basis of "stalemate functionalism" in the years of 1918–23, involving low mobilization, high inter-factional cleavage and moderate success in reformist legislation. This situation, like that of Italy in 1910 or 1915 might have continued for some time and ultimately assumed the direction of evolutionary change had it not been for the intrusion of major foreign policy dilemmas: Libya and the World War in the case of Italy, Morocco in the case of Spain. Without the Moroccan quagmire and the danger of national military humiliation, the Primo de Rivera *pronunciamiento* could not possibly have taken place when it did, if indeed it could otherwise have occurred at all.

When Miguel Primo de Rivera took over government in 1923, he did not come to offer an alternative to liberal parliamentarianism, and altogether lacked the very theoretical idea of such a possibility. His "Dictatorship" was conceived in the classical sense as a temporary suspension of normal institutional functioning in order to resolve specific problems, which was also more or less the theory behind the granting of decree powers to João Franco in Portugal in 1906 and also of the short-lived establishment of the first direct dictatorship in the Hispanic peninsula during the twentieth century, the six-month Pimenta de Castro régime of 1915. This being the case, Primo vehemently denied that he was a real "dictator" in his first official press conference, and when asked at approximately the same time whether he had been inspired by Mussolini's "March on Rome," he replied:

> It has not been necessary to imitate the Fascists or the great figure of Mussolini, though their deeds have been a useful example for everyone. But in Spain we have the Somatén and we have had Prim, an admirable military and political figure.[22]

The Somatén was simply a moderate conservative middle-class Catalan militia, while General Juan Prim had been the most creative and forward-looking liberal among the major nineteenth-century pretorian caudillos of Spain. He had employed temporary military intervention in 1868 to reorganize and expand the processes of representative government.

Primo de Rivera had no ideology and no programme. Very nearly the same things might be said of Mussolini. The latter, however, had a mass movement, a genuine contempt for liberalism, and

153

also the means at hand to achieve an ideology and the institutionalization of an authoritarian régime through the Nationalist party, whom the Fascists incorporated in 1923.

After resolving the Moroccan affair with French assistance and restoring domestic order, Primo de Rivera was left in 1925 with a dictatorship in search of a political structure and theory. At that moment the most likely model was Italian Fascism, yet for several basic reasons it was impossible to copy it. First of all, the Fascist régime was just beginning to be institutionalized in 1925. Second, information in Spain about Italian Fascism tended to be quite vague. Third, the Fascist model could not be invoked without a mass party, and the recently organized Unión Patriótica completely failed to meet this need. It was not a political movement but a loose civic association formed for mutual advancement. Finally, the absence of serious "prefascist" culture and nationalism in Spain would have made it impossible midway through the 1920s to organize for such an end. It is true that Don Alfonso and Primo de Rivera had made their first and only formal state visit during the régime to Rome late in 1923, but the Spanish dictator seems at that time to have drawn little concrete inspiration from it and later opined that an explicitly institutionalized authoritarianism on the Fascist model would be impossible among so personalistic a people as the Spanish.[23] The establishment of the Fascist régime had apparently provided some stimulus to put an end to Spanish parliamentarianism,[24] but could not possibly serve at that time as an institutional model.

When the Unión Patriótica was formed in Valladolid in April 1924 it was intended to serve as the means for the reorganization of civic institutions on the basis of the existing constitution. Primo declared on April 15, 1924, that "there is room in the party for all those who respect the constitution of 1876." [25] In a set of programmatic norms issued on May 1, 1925, Angel Herrera, one of the UP's chief organizers, declared that its purpose was to serve as the transition "civil dictatorship" back to a somewhat modified constitutional parliamentarianism after the military dictatorship came to an end.[26]

154

Lacking clear goals, Primo's régime always tried to make a virtue of apoliticism and the want of ideology. Primo called the UP "an organized way of life" (*una conducta organizada*) [27] and stressed the maxim "first live, and then philosophize." [28] He bore heavily on the régime's "simplicity"—which was true enough—and his supporters used the terms "intuition" (*intuicismo*) and "intuitionism" (*intuicionismo*) to describe his subjective and nonanalytic approach to problems.[29]

It should be pointed out that the UP did eventually develop an ideology of sorts, or at least a set of principles. These included respect for established national institutions, support of the Catholic religion, an emphasis on Spanish patriotism that went only part way toward militant nationalism, corporative representation for the economic system, and local administrative decentralization.[30] The key note was conservatism and conservative traditionalism, and the main influence was conservative Catholic corporatism, not radical fascist statism.

Even that much went beyond Primo de Rivera's own outlook. He continued to insist on the broadly national and "apolitical" character of the UP, distinguishing it from any explicitly ideological or "doctrinaire, personalist" political organization. Down to the very end of his dictatorship he preferred to identify himself with the rather limited ideas and goals of early twentieth-century Spanish Regenerationism. At ceremonies inaugurating new school buildings in the Madrid working-class district of Vallecas in 1929, he said:

> *The régime is following the policy of the great Costa—marketing and schools, agriculture and elementary education—for which its concern was declared from the beginning. But since the dictatorship has been identified with Costa, he has become a secondary figure with the intellectual vanguardists.*[31]

Nonetheless, after Primo de Rivera committed himself to a continuation of the dictatorship in 1925, his régime had to attempt some form of institutional development. In general, its only policy was to try to substitute economic development for political representation, and in this it resembled the syncretic, a-ideological dictatorships of the Mediterranean and Hispanic world of the 1960s. The régime did give Spain its first national development policy.

Formation of a state labour and economic regulation system was a key part of this idea, and that meant corporative organization. Modern corporatist economic representation was apparently first advocated in Spain in 1872 by Eduardo Pérez Pujol, Professor of Law at the University of Valencia, to remedy the social tensions that came to the fore under the democratic monarchy of Don Amadeo. The Valencian chapter of the Sociedad Económica de Amigos del Pais, which in the late eighteenth century had together with its counterparts pressed for the elimination of the traditional guild system, in 1879 recommended a reorganized guild system to rectify the excesses of rampant individualism. From the time of Leo XIII some form of corporatism was often recommended by sectors of Spanish Catholicism, and the most prominent traditionalist politician of the early twentieth century, Vázquez de Mella, corresponded with Albert de Mun and preached corporative economic organization. Primo de Rivera's labour minister, Eduardo Aunós, had been a Maurist in his political youth and had subsequently figured in the Catalanist Lliga. Both those groups had favoured partial corporatist political representation on the local level. Even the Spanish Socialist party, after entering a new reformist phase in 1918–19, had urged the government to organize state labour regulation boards and mixed juries of worker and employer representatives.

In 1926 the Italian Fascist state had just begun to elaborate a general corporative system. Aunós later wrote that:

> The Dictator had the kindness to support my wish to observe the achievements being made in this regard in Italy and invited me to go there to gain a deeper understanding. Needless to say, I was received with the most open cordiality by Italian Fascists, who generously assisted my investigations. I went to Italy in April 1926 and was the recipient of high distinctions and immense satisfactions. Among these was being received by the Duce, who repeatedly expressed his warm sympathy for the régime and the men that were governing Spain.

156

(Giuseppe) Bottai, whom I had the honour to visit, extended himself to assist my search for information. I brought back a wealth of studies and observations that would serve to complete the ideal corporative project that I had already partially drawn up.[32]

The result was the Spanish decree law on economic corporations that was promulgated on November 26, 1926. This theoretically divided the entire economy into 27 corporations. Each was to be represented on the local level by freely-elected joint arbitration committees (in which management and labour were to be equally represented), similar committees on the provincial level, and, finally, corporation councils on the national level. Aunós liked to point out that this system was a theoretically more complete and hierarchical structure than that of Italy, and also more democratic.[33] It was also in a sense even more democratic than the recent Belgian arbitration and negotiation tribunals law of May 1926, according to which delegates had ultimately to be ratified by the state.

Yet, like the other institutions of the Primo de Rivera régime, the corporative system was never effectively developed. By May 1929 there had been formed a total of only 450 local joint arbitration committees representing approximately 320,000 workers and 100,000 employers.[34] This was only about 15 per cent of the total labour force in Spain and not even half the industrial workers, who were those primarily represented.

While this modest effort was being prosecuted, the dictator had to face the problem of political institutionalization. Strong encouragement for regularization of his government came from Rome.

. . . When Aunós returned from Italy (in April 1926) . . . the Duce, who is not an eminently political man in vain, transmitted through the former his resolute advice that Primo de Rivera convene a parliament. The system or procedure was not the important thing; in his judgment, what was essential was that it be begun and continue. "That is the costume which must be worn in international society", Mussolini said. This recommendation deeply impressed Primo de Rivera, not because he felt such extraordinary sympathy for the Italian

157

statesman but because the two régimes had a very similar origin and it was logical that they develop according to analogous norms. At first, Primo de Rivera decided to speed up elections. . . . However, advisers from the UP and perhaps one or two officious friends—some friends can be fatal—led him away from that path. [35]

Though encouraged in some quarters to hold regular direct elections, if only for a constitutional reform assembly, Primo de Rivera feared the results of any direct move, and in this his reluctance was strengthened by leaders of the UP. The eventual compromise was to convene a consultative "Parliamentary Assembly" in October 1927. Of its 400 members, part—such as 60 top officials of the Unión Patriótica—were declared *ex-officio* members by reason of their function or office, part were directly appointed by the government, and part were chosen by corporate elections in leading national organizations and professional associations. In 1928 a commission was finally charged with preparing the draft of a new constitution.

This commission was dominated by the ultra-conservative monarchists who formed the core of the UP and its draft project, officially presented in July 1929, provided for a great increase in royal executive power. Not merely was the king to be responsible for appointing the government, but his approval would be necessary for all legislation to become law, and parliamentary votes of confidence were proscribed. Elections would be based on direct, completely universal suffrage, with women for the first time having the right to vote and hold office. Prior censorship was prohibited. Though the Senate was eliminated, a new Council of the Realm was to exercise much the same functions and be composed in much the same way.

During the summer of 1929 the draft was subjected to extensive criticism in the Spanish press. Primo himself and some of his cabinet ministers, such as Calvo Sotelo, were dissatisfied with the proposal to institutionalize sweeping royal power. The king himself had earlier said that he would only accept institutional changes approved by a properly constituted legislature.[36] By the close of the year Primo had decided to scrap the entire constitutional draft.

Sick and prematurely ageing, he did not see his way clear to the institutionalization of a new régime, and his proposal of December 31 that a new assembly be chosen in mid-1930, half by direct election and half by corporative election and appointment, was rejected by the king.[37] By that point his political power was thoroughly exhausted.

Primo had failed to provide any alternative to liberal parliamentarianism. In the end he was groping toward a half-corporative, half-democratic concept that would apparently have further limited royal power and established the responsibility of the executive to parliament. On the lower levels of government, the dictatorship had suggested decentralization, partially corporative representation and procedural safeguards for fair elections, but had failed to institute these changes. Its reform programme was little more than a collection of some of the more salient proposals by members of the old Liberal and Conservative parties. Primo de Rivera was not only no prefascist, he was not even a consistent authoritarian, but rather a confused and impatient semiliberal whose political imagination could not fully transcend the categories of liberal constitutionalism.[38] Unfortunately the Spanish Cincinnatus not only failed to return to his plough with honours, he abrogated the basic constitutional structure of the state without being able either to restore or replace it.

During the period of the Primo de Rivera dictatorship one of the shrewdest efforts to grasp the character of the new authoritarian régimes of the 1920s was made by the Catalanist politician, Francesc Cambó. This took the form first of a series of newspaper articles, "Entorn del fexisme italià," published in *La Veu de Catalunya* in mid-1924, and then of a book *Las Dictaduras*, that appeared in 1929.[39] In his 1924 articles he observed that what was beginning to develop as the real ideology and structure of Italian Fascism was produced *ex post facto*, having been organized in a more conservative context after the formation of the Mussolini government and often in sharp contrast to Mussolini's own ideas prior to 1922. Like many others, Cambó doubted that it would be possible for Spain to institutionalize permanently a new kind of authoritarian régime. He conceded the validity of dictatorship only in the classic sense, as a temporary response to resolve a crisis. In his later book he advanced a general theory of the new nationalist authoritarian states of southern and east Europe as a product of relative backwardness, representing a kind of temporary phase of modernization, that should be completed as rapidly as possible.

The only attempt at a comparative analysis of the Primo de Rivera régime during the late 1920s and early 1930s that I have been able to find is a brief booklet by Wolfgang Scholz, *Die Lage des spanischen Staates vor der Revolution* (*unter Berücksichtigung ihres Verhältnisses zum italienischen Fascismus*) (*sic*) (Dresden, 1932). It drew the obvious distinctions between the institutionalization of the Italian régime and the failure to achieve an institutional structure in the Spanish régime, between the notable "idea world" of Italian Fascist culture and the lack of any ideology or active prefascist culture in Spain, between the existence of a broad Fascist or at least pro-Fascist intelligentsia in Italy and the almost exclusively liberal and anti-Primo de Rivera orientation of the Spanish intelligentsia.

The failure of *primorriverismo* exhausted what little energy the proponents of a modern Spanish right could muster, leaving the field almost exclusively to the forces of liberalism and the left. Had there been a seriously organized Spanish Republican liberal party able to take charge of the government in 1931 there would have been much less likelihood of provoking the emergence of a new Spanish right. However, once the idea of consensual, compromise constitutionalism—that is, genuine constitutional liberalism—was rejected by the new Republican left, particularly on the church issue, the emergence of a modern Spanish right was a foregone conclusion, and could have been discounted only by those so consumed with hubris as Manuel Azaña and his followers.

The nature and history of the CEDA (Spanish Confederation of Autonomous Rightist Groups) has been ably studied by Richard Robinson, and I would disagree with his analysis on only one point. It seems doubtful that Gil Robles can properly be described as a "Christian democrat." The reformist democratic parliamentarianism that has been accepted since 1945 as a final rather than transitory means was foreign to the thinking of the CEDA. There is no question as to the commitment of the CEDA leadership to parliamentary legalism as the means to power, but the ultimate goal of the CEDA was to transform Republican parliamentary democracy into a more fixed and corporatist system. Just as the Republican left denied equal civil rights to Catholics, monarchists, and other sectors of the right, so the Catholic right rejected inorganic parliamentary democracy as ultimately normative. The die was cast in 1934, even though the polarization was not yet absolutely complete and explicit.

By that time the word "fascist" was constantly in the air and was used *ad nauseam* by the enemies of the CEDA. The latter was not of course a fascist movement, but rather a conservative Catholic procorporatist party that merely from time to time, as the historian Ricardo de la Cierva has put it, "experienced the vertigo of fascism." No one analyzed the ambiguities of *cedismo* any more precisely than did José Antonio Primo de Rivera, who made clear why the party of Gil Robles could be considered neither "Christian democratic" nor "fascist," but rather an ambiguous interim movement. One of the great paradoxes of Spanish politics was that in the crucial beiennium 1934–36 when "communism" versus "fascism" began more and more to divide the body politic, genuine communism was comparatively weak and genuine fascism virtually nonexistent.

Fascist movements are, in Juan Linz's phrase, "latecomers" to a modern political spectrum and require a span of unoccupied space in order to develop a following. The Spanish fascist movement organized first by Ramiro Ledesma Ramos and then by José Antonio Primo de Rivera was unable to find that space. For three years the role of modern national opponent to the left was filled by the CEDA, making a fascist alternative seem irrelevant.

Fascist- and Nazi-type movements in the 1930s seem to have required a variety of factors to generate support. In addition to an atmosphere of national crisis, the existence of certain kinds of threatened or displaced social elements that were unrepresented or unorganized appear to have been essential. Until 1936 such a constellation of factors did not exist in Spain. This was clearly grasped by the leading revolutionary Marxist intellectual in the Socialist party, Luís Araquistain. In an article in the April 1934 number of the American journal *Foreign Affairs*, he pointed out that there seemed little danger of genuine fascism in Spain. There were no large numbers of unemployed veterans or university youths without a future, no huge proportion of urban unemployed, no strong sense of nationalism, and apparently no genuine fascist leaders of national importance. Thus when Ramiro Ledesma published his book on *Fascismo en Espana?* in the following year, he had perforce to put a question mark in the title.

For that matter, the JONS (Junta de Ofensiva Nacional-Sindicalistas) and Falangist leaders were given to ritualistic denials that they were "fascists," even though on an unofficial level the term was more often than not accepted. The main reason for this was that the chieftains of radical Spanish nationalism could not easily afford to admit that they were following in the footsteps of a foreign movement. That, after all, was what they always accused the liberals and the left of doing. Secondly, neither Ledesma nor Primo de Rivera were altogether enthusiastic about Fascist Italy. This was due especially to the latter's conservative aspects and the relative autonomy of Italian capitalism under Mussolini's régime. Ledesma was at first attracted by the genuine dynamism and radicalism of German Nazism,[40] and during his early phase was even given to combing his hair down over his forehead Hitler-style. Germanic racism, however, could scarcely form a model for Spanish nationalism, and José Antonio Primo de Rivera was genuinely repelled by some of the main features of Hitlerism, an attitude, it should be noted, that was also shared by Mussolini at least until 1935.[41]

Despite the concern of Falangist leaders to avoid the charge of mimesis, the doctrines of fascism provided the only viable model for their goals of radical and authoritarian nationalism in a still largely Catholic society that had just entered the age of mass mobilization and economic modernization. There are no significant discrepancies between the codified doctrine of mature Italian Fascism and the official programme and statements of Falangist leaders that were announced in 1934–35. Ideologically and structurally, historic Falangism was a generically fascist movement.

This was essentially the conclusion of contemporary Italian proponents of "universal fascism." . . . Many of the journals dealing with the expansion of fascism undertook to analyze these foreign movements case by case, in an attempt to ascertain which of them were worthy of inclusion in a Fascist International. At times the question was very difficult, since the journalists might decide that a movement claiming to be fascist was phoney, while some of the hierarchs in Rome felt otherwise. An even more perplexing problem involved the Spanish Falange, which claimed *not* to be fascist, but looked for all the world like a paradigm of a foreign fascism. (*Ottobre*, May 1, 1934). In a lengthy analysis for *Universalità Fascista* in 1936, Spinetti argued that the Falange was a true fascist movement because of its belief in the fascist trinity of "authority, hierarchy, order" and because of the "mysticism which raised Falangist principles to a universal plane." [42]

The weakness of Spanish fascism is graphically illustrated by the fact that as a national movement it had in the beginning almost to be incited by counter-revolutionary big business. At first glance the now rather famous meeting of "fascist candidates" in San Sebastián in August 1933 to discuss financing and propagation of a fascist-type movement would seem a classic verification of the standard Marxist interpretation of fascism. Such is not really the case, for a country in which fascism was to be developed as a shield for big business was a country in which there was virtually no real fascism. Ultimately Falangism did escape the clutches of the Bilbao bankers and assert its independence—albeit accepting later subsidies from the Italian Ministry of Press and Propaganda [43]—but this reinforced its impotence. By 1935 José Antonio had come largely to rely on the hope of direct military intervention, in itself a confession of political failure.

The party of conservative quasi-fascism which more nearly fits the stereotype of a front for big business was Calvo Sotelo's Bloque Nacional. The duality Falange/Bloque Nacional did not, however, parallel the rivalry between radical and conservative Fascist- or Nazi-type movements in other countries such as Austria, France, Hungary, Rumania, or even Belgium, for the Bloque Nacional was not a full-scale fascist movement. The ideological shift-

163

ing of Calvo Sotelo and his colleagues was even more recent and more syncretic than that of the Falangists. Calvo Sotelo only became directly associated with the radical right and fascism in France during 1932. The syncretic authoritarian nationalism of the Bloque Nacional was less systematic and in some respects more vague than the Falangist programme, but it was also more opportunistic and practical. That may have been because, to echo José Antonio's famous complaint about his father's finance minister, Calvo Sotelo had a head only for business and not poetry. Nonetheless, Calvo Sotelo's ideological grab-bag of radical, conservative, and practical reformist notions in some ways proved quite prescient. His postulates of a strongly authoritarian but not totalitarian régime (on which he shifted ground) and corporative parliamentary representation, state coordination of but comparatively little interference with capital and industry, respect for traditional culture, and reliance on the military with no effort to establish a mass revolutionary party, more nearly resembled the eventual form of the syncretic Franco régime than did José Antonio's formally doctrinaire party-based programme and poetic rhetoric.

Even when the great hour of opportunity for Falangism seemed to strike in 1936, the movement could not take advantage of it. The incipient collapse of the polity was not enough. Fascist- and Nazi-type movements burgeoned on crisis during the 1930s, but they required a crisis leading to stalemate conditions of frustrated revolution, together with the preservation of considerable liberty to organize. During the spring and summer of 1936 the Spanish revolutionary left seemed in little danger of frustration or defeat, as was the case with the Italian left in 1922 or the German left in 1933. For a fascist movement to achieve mass mobilization it had evidently to draw in part on disillusion with the possibilities of the revolutionary left through defeat or frustration as well as on direct opposition to the latter.[44] In addition to the Italian and German examples, it might be noted that in the other two countries with mass fascist or radical nationalist movements—Hungary and Rumania—the latter elements tended to take the place of a virtually nonexistent left. Such movements could then be presented as a different, superior fulfillment through national syndicalism or national socialism of the *révolution manquée*.

The situation faced by Falangism in Spain was entirely different. Just as the absence of nationalist spirit, military involvement or thoroughgoing middle-class secularization had earlier closed off the space on the right-centre and right, so the space on the left-centre and left remained fully occupied as the Spanish revolutionary left went on from apparent strength to strength. Moreover, the Falange could not take full advantage of the new support acquired from the right in 1936, for the movement was driven underground and more nearly resembled the organized chaos of the CNT in 1923 than the Italian Fascist party in 1922.

By mid-1936 the Spanish middle classes were not seeking a radical fascist solution to a prolonged and stalemated political crisis. As the polity collapsed, what they sought was counter-revolutionary leadership in the most direct sense, led by the army. Military counter-revolution is led by an Admiral Kolchak or a General Franco, not by political corporals like Hitler and Mussolini.

It may be objected that Franco did incorporate the Falangist doctrine and organization into his new state system, thereby making Franquism at least quasi-fascist. This is quite true. Though Spain was not so modern and socially-mobilized a country as Germany, it was not too far behind Italy and well ahead of the Balkans. The Franco régime required greater structure and organization than did that of Marshal Antonescu or General Metaxas. That structure was, however, one of syncretic authoritarianism based on limited pluralism in which fascistic Falangism was a major but not the dominant component. The dilution and withering away of the specifically fascist aspects of the Falange-Movimiento is a well-known story that need not be recounted here. It was to some extent at the mercy of the political and ideological context of international affairs. The only thing that might conceivably have led to a decisive Falangization of the Franco régime would have been a Nazi-Fascist victory in the Second World War. Since the preconditions for full-fledged fascism were lacking in Spain, they would have had to be established from the outside.

[1] Hannah Arendt, *Origins of Totalitarianism* (New York, 1951), and also Carl J. Friedrich, ed., *Totalitarianism* (Cambridge, Mass., 1954).

[2] *Varieties of Fascism* (New York, 1964).

[3] *Three Faces of Fascism* (New York, 1966); *Theorien über den Faschismus* (Cologne, 1967); and *Die Krise des liberalen Systems und die faschistischen Bewegungen* (Munich, 1968).

[4] In addition to Nolte, see Wilhelm Alff, *Der Begriff Faschismus und andere Aufsätze zur Zeitgeschichte* (Frankfurt, 1971).

[5] Renzo de Felice, *Il Fascismo. Le interpretazioni dei contemporanei e degli storici* (Bari, 1970), and De Felice, *et al.*, *Il problema storico del fascismo* (Florence, 1970).

[6] J. Plumyène and R. Lasierra, *Les Fascismes français 1923–63* (Paris, 1963), and Nicos Poulantzas, *Fascisme et dictature* (Paris, 1970).

[7] G. Mosse and W. Laqueur, eds., "International Fascism 1920–1945", *Journal of Contemporary History*, I:1 (1966); F. L. Carsten, *The Rise of Fascism* (Berkeley, 1967); and S. J. Woolf, ed., *European Fascism* (London, 1968), and *The Nature of Fascism* (London, 1968).

[8] H. Rogger and E. Weber, eds., *The European Right* (Berkeley-Los Angeles, 1966); P. F. Sugar, ed., *Native Fascism in the Successor States* (Santa Barbara, 1971); N. M. Nagy-Talavera, *The Green Shirts and the Others* (Stanford, 1970); and also Wolfgang Sauer, "National Socialism: Totalitarianism or Fascism?", *American Historical Review*, LXXIII:2 (Dec., 1967), 404–24.

[9] See Nolte's *Die Krise des liberalen Systems* (Munich, 1968).

[10] This is brought out in Michael Ledeen's *Universal Fascism* (New York, 1972).

[11] This distinction is basically similar to that drawn by Weber between fascist and national socialist movements—though our descriptive terminologies are somewhat different—and by Sauer between the West European fascist movements as distinct from Central and East European ones, though I disagree with his particular categorization of the latter.

[12] Starhemberg, the chief leader of the Heimwehr, joined the other side, and the Falange had no real leaders by 1940.

[13] The Fascists and Nationalists won only 9 per cent of the seats in the Italian elections of 1921, but their popular vote seems to have been somewhat greater.

[14] The PPF was organized only after the last general elections of the Third Republic, and hence I am extrapolating from the data in Dieter Wolf's *Die Doriot-Bewegung* (Stuttgart, 1967).

[15] This has been studied in the unpublished dissertation of Armand Patrucco, "Critics of the Italian Parliament" (Columbia University, 1969).

[16] Cf. E. Tierno Galván, *Costa y el regeneracionismo* (Barcelona, 1961). The authoritarian strain in Costa, such as it was, received one of its earliest treatments in Dionisio Pérez, *El enigma de Costa: revolucionario oligarca?* (Madrid, 1930). This was apparently provoked in part by Primo de Rivera's invocations of Costa.

[17] A brief summary of such ideas is given by Frederick B. Pike, *Hispanismo, 1898-1936* (Notre Dame, 1971), 255-62.

[18] See Gonzalo Redondo, *Las empresas políticas de José Ortega y Gasset* (Madrid, 1970), II.

[19] The only attempt that I have found to chart comparative phases of politico-social modernization in Italy and Spain is in Ludovico Garruccio's *L'Industrializzazione tra nazionalismo e rivoluzione* (Bologna, 1969), 299. It seems to me somewhat inaccurately conceived, and I would instead suggest the following:

Phase	Italy	Spain	Portugal
Elitist doctrinaire liberalism	1860–1876	1843–1881	1833–1857
Two-party/ trasformista liberalism	1876–1898	1881–1899	1857–1906
Pre-mass politics reformism	1899–1915	1899–1923	1910–1917
Authoritarian interlude	1915–1918	1923–1931	1917–1918
Convulsive mass politics	1919–1922	1931–1936	1919–1926

The last category does not, of course, fully fit Portugal, which never really knew a phase of genuine mass politics.

[20] Scattered references to Maurist Youth politics will be found in José Gutiérrez Rave, *Yo fui un joven maurista* (Madrid, 1946) and Manuel Pi y Navarro, *Los primeros veinticinco años de José Calvo Sotelo* (Zaragoza, 1961), 101-32.

[21] Enrico Corradini, *Il nazionalismo italiano* (Milan, 1914), quoted in Wilhelm Alff, "Die Associazione Nazionalista Italiana von 1910," in Alff's collection of studies *Der Begriff Faschismus* (Frankfurt, 1971), 78.

[22] Marqués de Cáceres, ed., *Dos años de Directorio Militar* (Madrid, 1926), 2-5.

[23] Jacinto Capella, *La verdad de Primo de Rivera* (Madrid, 1933), 19.

[24] This seems to have been essentially what he meant when he flattered Mussolini during the November 1923 visit by calling the latter "his inspirer and teacher." Gabriel Maura Gamazo, *Bosquejo histórico de la dictadura* (Madrid, 1930), I,

51–52. Further analysis of the formal relations between the Primo de Rivera régime and Fascist Italy may be found in Chapter One of John F. Coverdale's *Mussolini and Franco: Italian Intervention in the Spanish Civil War* (Princeton, 1975).

[25] *El pensamiento de Primo de Rivera* (Madrid, 1929), 109.

[26] N. González Ruíz and I. Martín Martínez, *Seglares en la historia del catolicismo español* (Madrid, 1968), 133.

[27] *La Nación*, Aug. 6, 1927.

[28] José Ma. Pemán, *El hecho y la idea de la Unión Patriótica* (Madrid, 1929), 113.

[29] José Pemartín, *Los valores históricos en la Dictadura española* (Madrid, 1929), 637.

[30] The most extensive exposition of the principles of the UP in its later phase is Pemán's book.

[31] Dionisio Pérez, ed., *La Dictadura a través de sus notas oficiosas* (Madrid, 1930), 257.

[32] Eduardo Aunós, *La política social de la Dictadura* (Madrid, 1944), 58–59.

[33] *Ibid.*, 64, and in Aunós' brief *Corporaciones de trabajo en el Estado moderno* (Madrid, 1928). The text of the decree and Aunós' explanation of it are given in his booklet, *Organisation corporative nationale* (Madrid, 1927). He explained his ideas further in *La organización corporativa del trabajo* (Madrid, 1929).

[34] These are the figures Aunós gave in a speech of May 3, 1929, *La organización corporativa y su posible desenvolvimiento* (Madrid, 1929).

[35] José Calvo Sotelo, *Mis servicios al Estado* (Madrid, 1931), 336.

[36] *Ibid.*, 118.

[37] *Ibid.*, 342–49.

[38] His son José Antonio noted the dictator's lack of "a great idea," that is, an alternative ideology, in his prologue to *La Dictadura de Primo de Rivera juzgada en el extranjero* (Madrid, 1931). Aunós was more explicit. On March 15, 1947, he gave a lecture in Madrid on "The ideology of General Primo de Rivera as chief obstacle to his work," declaring: "To no one is it a mystery that the Marqués de Estella was fundamentally a liberal. He passed his life amid principles, theories and facts of liberal significance." Eduardo Aunós, *Semblanza política del general Primo de Rivera* (Madrid, n.d.), 28–29.

[39] Hostile responses from the Marxist left were written by Andrés Nin, *Les dictadures dels nostres dies* (Barcelona 1930) and Joaquín Maurín, *Los hombres de la Dictadura* (Madrid, 1930), 73–100.

[40] Ledesma had aims in common with the early Italian anarchofascists and the "Nazi left." Cf. Reinhard Kühnl, *Die nationalsozialistische Linke 1925–1930* (Meisenheim am Glan, 1966).

[41] On May 26, 1934, Mussolini wrote that Nazi racism was opposed "yesterday to Christian civilization, today to Latin civilization and tomorrow to the civilization of the entire world," as quoted in K.-P. Hoepke, *Die deutsche Rechte und der italienische Faschismus* (Düsseldorf, 1968), 256.

[42] Ledeen, 100.

43 During the last seven months of 1935 it provided the Falange with 50,000 lire per month, while also subsidizing Marcel Bucard in France (Coverdale 40–41).

44 This point was brought out by Professor Juan Linz in a lecture on "The Social Basis of Fascism" at the University of Wisconsin in April 1970.

8

Was There a Russian Fascism?
The Union of Russian People

BY HANS ROGGER

Among the innovations which the revolution of 1905 produced in the political life of tsarist Russia, the appearance of a
number of movements and parties on the right of the political spectrum was certainly one of the most novel. The point can be made
that the entry of such groups onto the political scene marks a fundamental change in the relationship between the autocracy and the
state on the one hand and the conservative sector of opinion on the
other. The emergence of these groups marks both an unprecedented politicization of Russian conservatism and the splitting off
from its main body of an extremist right wing more political-
minded than traditional conservativism, which had tended to shun
political action and to consider it either a prerogative of the state or
the illegal activity of liberals and socialists. The post-1905 Right
was more militant, more demagogic, more intransigent vis-a-vis the
state and its officials than conservatives either wished or dared to
be. In this period, traditional conservatism was characterized by intellectual poverty and an unwillingness to descend into the political
arena. These characteristics stemmed not only from a distaste for
politics and a reluctance to see the larger public become involved in
it, not alone from the belief that the historic interests of the nation
would best be protected by established institutions and their servants, but also from the genuinely conservative inclination not to
bestir oneself, to leave things as they were, to let them take their
course, and hope that in time they would come out all right.[1]

The year 1905, and the unrest which had preceded it, de-

170

stroyed the faith of conservatives in the ability of the state to defend both itself and them. It also made a continued attitude of political abstinence difficult to maintain. In the face of growing popular discontent and the increasingly successful efforts of liberal and revolutionary parties to convert this discontent into political capital, some way had to be found for supporters of the status quo to demonstrate that popular sentiment was not all on the side of the opposition and that the state could count on allies in society if only it would resist the headlong rush to concession and innovation. The efforts made in this direction before October 1905—the staging or encouraging of pogroms and the organization of a number of monarchist organizations, mostly of local scope—were not notably successful. They failed to transform sporadic outbursts of popular passion or dynastic loyalty into sustained or organized political action; they were uncertain of their aims in the face of the government's own uncertainty, and they did not prevent the issuance of the October Manifesto which, with its promise of civil liberties, political rights, and a popularly elected legislative duma, made it all the more necessary that conservatives abandon their self-imposed restraint and bring a broadly based movement into the field against the liberals and radicals who had organized themselves into political parties long before October 1905. The realization of the need for a party or movement which could counter the opposition and yet develop a popular appeal, a party which would be free of an upper-class or bureaucratic taint and would give at least the appearance of independence while playing the role of stabilizer in the political maelstrom—this realization, and the existence of a few centers of popular conservatism, led in October 1905 to the formation of the Union of Russian People (*Soiuz Russkogo Naroda*). It was to become the most successful, the most numerous, the most noisy, intransigent, extremist and, withal, the most important of the Russian right-wing parties. For some years it dominated its end of the political spectrum and made URP practically synonymous with Right.[2]

Its importance derives not only from the role which the Union of Russian People (URP) played in Russian life; indeed, the significance of the URP derives in large measure from its introduction of a style of right-wing politics which was as novel for Russia as it was for much of Europe, and which gained for the Union the dubious distinction of being called, in a recent American text, "Europe's first fascist organization." [3] It was this also which led a Soviet biographer of V. M. Purishkevich, a leading figure of the URP, to write of him in 1925 that he was a fascist who set the style ten years before fascism arose as a political movement. [4] Even to those who did not wish to claim this "first" for Russia or burden her with it, it appeared that the URP constituted an emphatic break with the language and behavior that had commonly been regarded as typical of defenders of autocracy, orthodoxy, and nationality. The movement has been described as a Russian fascism, [5] a forerunner of fascism, [6] and as a Russian version of national socialism, [7] while in its own time it was called a rebellion or reaction [8] and a revolution from the right which pretended to act on conservative principles. [9] This was the view of Sergei Witte, chief minister from October 1905 to April 1906 and author of the October Manifesto, who had particular cause to be bitter about the URP, not only because it called him a traitor for having "extorted" the manifesto from the emperor, but more specifically because its agents tried to assassinate him in 1907. [10] It was also the view of some members of the URP itself. One of the few intellectuals in the URP, a part-time university lecturer, Boris Nikol'ski, confided to a friend in 1905 that "to be a conservative at this time means to be at least a radical or, rather, a revolutionary." [11]

The essential question here becomes whether it was the radicalism, the element of rebellion and revolution, or the conservatism of the URP that was the pretense, or whether we are not confronted with an indecisive mixture of the two. The question becomes all the more interesting in view of the fact that the ideas and methods of the URP are thought to have had a "tangible and substantial" impact on the origins of German National Socialism by way of Baltic and Russian emigres who found themselves in Germany after the Bolshevik revolution. [12] In order, therefore, to be able to decide these questions and to determine whether there was a Russian fascism or national socialism *avant le mot*, it is necessary

172

to have a closer look at the Union of Russian People, its origins, politics, and program.

To its proponents, the appearance of the URP in October 1905 always stood as a symbol of a national awakening which proceeded from the healthy national instincts of the healthy sectors of Russian society—that is, those who were not corrupted by Western liberal notions. It was the uncorrupted, not the educated, the privileged, the bureaucrats, the Westernized, who had come to the rescue of the state and imparted to it and its servants the determination to save themselves and their country. It had been the "grey and ignorant" popular masses who had first sensed the dangers which threatened the fatherland; only then had the classes, conscience-stricken over their former passivity, begun to join, to organize, to agitate, to stand up in word and deed.[13] The Union of Russian People, therefore, did not wish to be regarded as a political party, as an added element of division and contention, but as a spontaneous popular movement, as the people itself, a broadly based, million-voiced union for the defense of tsar, church, and fatherland.[14]

The enemies of the URP not only could not admit that it represented the nation or any significant number of its citizens; many of them saw in the new movement simply another concealed agency of the government, a pseudo-party called into being and maintained by the police department of the ministry of the interior. There was reason to doubt the genuineness and autonomy of an open, public organization which spoke on behalf of law and order against liberals and revolutionaries. The government had never encouraged independent political activity, not even on its own behalf, and the example of the *zubatovshchina*, the "police socialism" which in January 1905 had turned against its creators, was still fresh in people's minds. It seemed incredible that a discredited regime would not, after October 17, attempt to build a party for itself. This was, after all, what governments did everywhere when they wanted to influence opinion and the makeup of popularly elected assemblies. So thought a gendarme colonel who expressed his amazement to a member of the police department that nothing had

173

been done to call into being a popular ally for the government in the coming elections to the duma. So thought others, then and later, who viewed the URP as a direct creation of the police or at best a screen for the reactionary elements among the landed classes.[15]

From what we know of the origins of the URP, the impetus for its formation came for the most part from outside. There were no concerted efforts on the part of the administration to create for itself a popular ally. Witte was against such efforts because he wished to demonstrate the government's faithful adherence to the new rules of politics. His reactionary colleague in the ministry of the interior, P. N. Durnovo, believed that parties would be neither necessary nor allowed, because in the duma every deputy would vote according to his conscience. No parties were needed for that.[16] Genuine or not, this naïvete was not shared by the head of the police department's political section, who was in touch with individual members of the scattered "patriotic" organizations that had sprung up in the recent past. There was the Moscow Society of Religious Banner-Carriers and the Moscow Volunteer Okhrana; there was the St. Petersburg Russian Assembly (a patriotic organization of upper-class complexion, which was to furnish a hall for the early meetings of the URP and also supply some of its leaders) and a St. Petersburg circle of patriotic students; there were merchants, priests, and a union of teamsters; there were workers, shop clerks, cabmen, bathhouse attendants, and tradesmen.[17] At their meetings, there was also an occasional detective [18] and, above all, there was Dr. A. I. Dubrovin.

Dubrovin, a man of obscure antecedents, variously said to have given up a poor or a profitable medical practice, was a member of the St. Petersburg Russian Assembly and in touch also with the Moscow Banner-Carriers and other groups; it was he who helped bring them together and who emerged as the first chairman of the Union of Russian People, founded on October 22, 1905.[19] Dubrovin had been in contact also with a representative of the police department and the commander of the St. Petersburg Military District, but the official and the officer seem to have played only an auxiliary role. They encouraged Dubrovin; possibly they supported him in other ways; they, and some of their superiors, were probably glad to see such an organization come into being, but the URP cannot be said to have been their creation. The belief that it was stems from the irrefutable fact that at a later date the government supported the URP financially. At its inception, and, indeed, during the first months of its existence, the URP appears to have received no substantial help from the government, if any, and its financial support came mainly from members and well-wishers.[20] Its following was also the most "democratic" that had yet been assembled on the Right. While this was not fully reflected in its original leaders, who comprised engineers, lawyers, merchants, salesmen, a cattle-dealer, land-owners, ex-officers, a magistrate, and others, the URP had more claim to call itself an all-class organization than any of its predecessors on the Right, where titles and bureaucratic and military rank had figured prominently.[21] The social composition of its membership is difficult to determine from the available evidence, but even its enemies agreed that besides the *Lumpenproletariat* and disgruntled petty bourgeois, it was, in its early years, able to attract genuine peasant and proletarian elements.[22] In terms of its origin, the URP was indubitably something new and not irrevocably pledged to power and privilege. How the URP would interpret the interests of the Russian state and nation, for whose defense it had come into being, remained to be seen.

If independence of the government, financial and otherwise, is to be taken as a test of the Union's being an autonomous force on the Russian political scene and of its ability to strike out in new directions, it did not long pass that test. From the time that the government's hopes in the conservative instincts of the peasantry were disappointed by the elections to the first duma in March and April 1906 and the return of a solid oppositional majority, the administration gave various kinds of support to the URP. Most importantly, this took the form of financial subsidies to support its activities and publications. This was openly admitted by both donors and recipients afterward, though vigorously denied at the time.[23] The reasons for the government's denial are not far to seek: it wanted to appear to be above the political battle; it was also sup-

175

porting the Octobrist Party, which backed the reforms of October 1905 and which the URP fought; and, more importantly, it was not at all convinced of the advisability of supporting the URP. In this, as in so many other things, the administration was of divided mind, and even when it felt itself most threatened and most in need of aid from some social force, it was deeply distrustful of this rambunctious ally. S. E. Kryzhanovskii, Stolypin's associate in the ministry of the interior from 1906 to 1911, who handled financial disbursements to the URP and similar organizations, thought that these had adopted almost the same social program and propaganda techniques as the revolutionary parties. Indeed, he recalled in his memoirs that both Right and Left shared an economic and social program which promised the redistribution of private property to the masses; in the case of the Right it was to be carried out in the name of the autocratic tsar as the representative of the nation's interests and the defender of the poor from plutocratic oppression.[24]

It is hard to see how such a reading of the URP's intentions could arise on the part of a presumably well-informed official, though it was not infrequent among members of the URP.[25] It shows that the belief in the organization's essential conservatism was not universally shared, in spite of its commitment early in 1906 to the protection of private and public property and the avoidance of all violent means of political struggle. The conviction of the Union's radicalism must be presumed to stem from its attacks on the officials of the tsar, the bureaucrats, who were not serving him and the nation faithfully but usurping his power; from its denunciations of privilege, wealth, the ministries, the landlord class and, on occasion, the hierarchy of the church; from its promises to work for an increase in the holdings of land-poor peasants; from its expressed concern for the laboring classes in general and the hard plight of industrial workers in particular and the suggestion that relations between employers and employees be regulated legally.[26] Nor was all of this pretense. There were branches and members of the URP who took their "populism" seriously, and when, as a result of this, the subsidies were no longer forthcoming, there was often an increase of vehemence, especially at the local level, where

176

members were not always governed by the conduct of the URP's central organs.[27]

Like the government, the URP was not at one with itself on the issue of their mutual relations, and, with time, Dubrovin lost out to Purishkevich as the main recipient of official favors because the former refused to be reasonable. Purishkevich, it was said, had more sense and tact.[28] As late as July 1908, when the revolutionary danger had receded and the government was firmly in control, Dubrovin insisted that revolution had merely fled from the streets into the palaces and mansions. This was to him the meaning of Stolypin's collaboration with the Octobrists in the third duma.[29] The appearance of radical intransigence, whether it came from the head or the heart, was an intrinsic part of the URP's appeal, and that is why its leaders denied from the tribune of the duma that they were virtually pensioners of the state, and that is why the accusation was made.[30] But ministerial support was neither reliable nor adequate; it was never the expression of a definite commitment and it never made the financial situation of the URP secure.[31] It probably helped to tame and to moderate the extreme Right; it helped also to split and thereby to weaken it; it did not make it fully obedient or reliable.

This was most evident at the provincial level where national platforms were less important than local issues and where the relationship with the authorities took quite different forms than it did at the center. Here, in certain areas, particularly in provinces of mixed population where national and religious conflicts embittered existing political differences, the extreme Right found a broad scope for its activities. Here they could most easily be represented as being a defense of Russian national interests against Polish landlords and clerics, against Jewish traders and intellectuals, against Armenian nationalists. In such situations, the extremism of the URP, which took the form of street violence, strikebreaking, economic boycotts, and the organization of paramilitary organizations (such as the "Yellow shirts" in Odessa and secret combat groups, the *druzhiny*, which are reminiscent of the *fasci di combattimento*), could find a measure of approval among those of the local popula-

177

tion and authorities who shared the Union's prejudices. The governor of Ekaterinoslav *guberniiz*, for example, felt constrained to complain in March 1907 to the ministry of the interior about a captain of gendarmes whose "fanatic devotion to nationalistic and patriotic ideals" had not only led him to extend his protection to local branches of the URP but also to take a stand on the land and working-class questions which was dangerously close to that of the leftist parties and had gained for him a considerable influence among the workers. Altogether, the governor noted, the local authorities of his province were in too intimate relations with members of the URP and indulgent toward their less savory activities. The captain was transferred to another province.[32] It was not always that easy, and not all governors (or town commandants and chiefs of police) were as convinced as this one that the URP was deficient in its conservatism or necessarily disturbed by that fact, as long as they approved of the URP's targets. On such matters as the strict enforcement of restrictions on the Jewish population, in the proper celebration of patriotic festivals and resistance to "alien" economic oppression, in the spreading of loyal and nationalist propaganda, and in its electoral activity, the URP could afford to go quite far and still count on a measure of support, or at least benevolent neutrality, from local authorities in such important places as St. Petersburg (von der Launitz), Odessa (Tolmachev and Kaulbars), Yalta (Dumbadze), Kiev (Veretennikov) and others.[33]

The danger implicit in rousing the latent anarchist and revolutionary instincts of Russia's lower classes, even if they could be directed against approved targets, soon became worrisome to most of the Union's supporters at all levels of government, and from 1908–1909 those sections of society and the bureaucracy who had once supported or been favorable to it began to recoil from it with something approaching horror. The URP was not, after all, as an English journalist suggested at the time, a Russian version of the Primrose League,[34] but something much more frightening, something that no matter how inspired or motivated initially, was too uncomfortably like the many outbursts of resentment, envy, and social protest that throughout Russian history had taken the form of a "senseless and merciless Russian rising" (Pushkin), and that one could not be sure of controlling once it had been set in motion.[35] As a prominent rightist, V.V. Shul'gin, who eventually parted company with the URP over this issue, was to put it later: "A Jewish pogrom is the beginning of anarchy all around. It is the beginning of the so-called 'black rebellion.' They will begin with the Jews, but they will most certainly end by knocking out all there is of culture, and by smashing that which with such very great labour we have succeeded in setting up." [36] It is this viewpoint also which led him ultimately to desert the government itself over the Beilis ritual murder trial which the URP and its allies had persuaded the ministers of justice and interior to stage in 1913. The Russian ruling class was not prepared to entrust the defense of its interests to a movement whose shock troops were recruited from the bottom of the social ladder by appeals to their grievances.

One indication of the ultimate direction the URP might take came from the concentration of much of its propaganda on the liberals and the Constitutional Democratic (Kadet) party as the country's worst enemies because they were nearest the levers of real power and gave the appearance of respectability. "The Kadet party," wrote a URP pamphleteer in 1907, "is the most dangerous and the most powerful of all our parties;" its members are mostly rich people; a large number of them have titles and large estates; there are many ex-bureaucrats in their midst, an equally large number of lawyers, not a few charlatan professors and rich merchants. "They all have too much money and free time." That was the explanation for their interest in politics. The socialists, whether Social Revolutionaries or Social Democrats, were not by themselves a real threat; they merely did the bidding of the more powerful secret forces (Jewish and/or liberal) standing behind them.[37] On socialist subservience to liberal command the URP was not, however, consistent, for it threatened at times to join forces with the socialists either to torpedo the duma or as the only way to beat the Kadets (from whom, supposedly, the socialists were indistinguishable) at the polls.[38] On the party's proscription lists, liberal politicians figured prominently; two Kadet deputies, Iollos and Gertsenshtein, fell victim to URP assassins, as did the laborite (*trudovik*) Karavaev; attempts on Miliukov, Gessen, and Witte

179

failed.[39] The Octobrists were also berated for their compromising stands and their defense of big-business interests,[40] but the heavier fire of URP propaganda was directed against the Kadets, and those ubiquitous allies of liberalism—wealth and cunning. For moderation the URP, like other extremists, had little tolerance.

While the URP both stirred up and made use of envy, fear, and mass passions, and although this was quite novel and daring for a party which proclaimed its commitment to the forces of law and order and bears a striking resemblance to tactics employed by right-wing extremists elsewhere, none of this could be said to amount to a program. And to build more than a loose, ephemeral association, to build an effective movement, some kind of program, the setting of certain goals, either very specific or very general goals, is necessary. It was very difficult for the URP to develop such a program. It had, after all, come into being to defend the state, the monarchy, and the church at a time of dissolution and disorder, so that at least with part of its being it was dedicated to the preservation of the status quo. On the other hand, its very existence and nature were also testimony to the belief that the state was no longer a healthy organism, that it had been infected with the liberal virus and had to be saved from itself by the truly Russian elements of the population. And these, it was implied more than once, were not to be found near the top of the social ladder. It was simple burghers (*meshchane*) and peasants who were the true Russia.[41] The problem is further complicated by the fact that it is difficult to tell who, if anyone, could speak with authority on behalf of the organization as a whole. In spite of elaborate rules designed to assure unity and control of branches from the center, there was neither unity nor unanimity, and even within certain branches there were important and unresolved differences on aims and policies. The URP was never a monolith, and after 1908 it split first into two and then three different organizations.[42] These might still collaborate at the local level or even in the duma, but the extreme Right could no longer claim to speak with a single voice. Even when it had appeared to do so, the political, economic, and social aims of the URP had not been distinguished for system, coherence, or consistency. Ideologically, the extreme Right in Russia was not much of an advance over Russian conservatism, certainly not in the political parts of its program.

In its dedication to the autocracy as a God-given, historically justified and proven, popularly approved institution, the URP constituted no break with the past. But unlike other parties of the Right (the Monarchists, for example) it did not think autocracy incompatible with an assembly of elected people's representatives. On the contrary, such an assembly, in loyal union with the supreme power and informing it of the people's needs, could only strengthen autocracy. It would make possible the closer supervision of a bureaucracy which tsar and nation distrusted and which was at one and the same time too arbitrary in its treatment of the people and too receptive to the liberal views that had spread among the upper classes.[43] This view of the duma as a latter-day Assembly of the Land (*zemskii sobor*) and of the manifesto which created it as returning to the people a part of their rights, the expectation that it would diminish the ministerial-bureaucratic regime which stood between tsar and people, did not long outlast the failure of the Union and the whole of the Right in the elections to the first two dumas—there were no rightist deputies at all in the first and some ten (out of a total of 518) in the second.[44]

In the second duma, URP deputies had bent every effort to undermine the assembly's work from within and without by creating scandals, siding with the Left, trying to keep the duma from any productive work, and organizing a campaign of letters and telegrams to the emperor asking for its dissolution. Doubts were now expressed as to whether the October Manifesto and the duma as constituted were after all compatible with autocracy, whether they did not infringe its rights and prerogatives and whether, in fact, the monarch had had the right to share what he had inherited intact from his ancestors.[45]

Dedication to undiminished autocracy and hostility to the duma which had been granted, or rather ordered, by the autocrat placed the URP in an extremely awkward position. If it fought against the duma for a restoration of the sovereign's full rights, it admitted what it had long denied: that the October Manifesto was, in fact, a constitutional document and that by issuing it the monarch had limited and shared his power. To attack the manifesto would mean to go against his expressed will and against the decrees creating the new institutions which he had vowed to maintain. To fight the tsar's government in the name of the tsar seemed impossible, and to suggest that he had been tricked into making unnecessary concessions by unscrupulous advisers (such as Witte) was not very flattering. It was possible, however, to try to convert the duma into something else by changing the electoral law. Once that was done, and the oppositionist majorities safely reduced, it would be possible to live with the quasi-constitutional regime created in 1905 and 1906 and strive to keep alive sound sentiments and organized strength for a time of need. And the best arena for doing so, according to N. E. Markov, the URP's leader after Dubrovin, was the parliamentary one.[46] This was no principled commitment to the idea of representative government; but unless the extreme Right were willing to go unequivocally into opposition, deny itself the platform of the duma, and risk losing what governmental favors it might obtain by offering or withholding votes, there was no other way. So the extreme Right, represented at the opening of the third duma by fifty-one deputies (of whom at least thirty-two, headed by Purishkevich and Markov, belonged formally to the URP), joined sixty-five other deputies of the duma's right wing in an address to the emperor which thanked him for having, through the duma, re-established the long-desired and long-broken union of people and sovereign.[47]

The problem of a legislative body which implied by its very existence a diminution of autocracy was simply ignored by speaking of it in terms that were meant to evoke the image of the Muscovite assembly of estates, the purely consultative *zemskii sobor*, without specifically demanding a change of the fundamental laws of 1906 and the duma's functions. Purishkevich, for example, before the elections to the third duma, gave no indication that he was against the institution as such; he merely insisted that unlike its predecessors it be composed of loyal, non-revolutionary elements; otherwise it too would be dissolved.[48] Dubrovin, who along with other elements of the URP had wished to boycott the elections, saw the flaw in this position. He opposed the third duma as he had the second, arguing that instead of bringing the tsar and his people closer, it would erect between them still another barrier. It would be better, his side argued, if the duma were entirely oppositional. Then the question of its true nature would have to be faced and the fundamental laws changed to make it a purely advisory body. Dubrovin withdrew his own candidacy, though this may have been due to fear of failure; he and other opponents of participation in the elections were told by their rightist friends that this meant opposing the will of the tsar.[49] Markov himself, in the emigration, seems to have been converted to Dubrovin's view when he said that the opening of the third duma in the autumn of 1907 marked the beginning of the constitutional period of Russia's history and the preparation for revolution and final defeat.[50] But to an investigating commission of the provisional government in 1917 he insisted that, unlike Dubrovin, he and his wing of the URP had accepted the duma as proposed in October 1905 and had worked within its rules to strengthen the monarch's powers.[51]

The splits within the URP and the muddying of the issues of the duma and the imperial prerogative reflected deep uncertainties on both scores. It is certainly accurate to say that the URP was against parliamentary government, against party politics and the infringement of the emperor's authority. These were the devices which it had inscribed on its banners, but it does not appear to have done so with any confident assurance or belief in their essential rightness or political value. The very arguments for which the whole Right embraced autocracy—firm leadership above factions; the interests of the whole nation given impartial expression by one man; restoration of the communion between ruler and ruled; and the restraint of rapacious and selfish officials—were each undermined by the character and conduct of the occupant of the throne. The autocratic principle is hardest to uphold in the abstract, and the entire Right realized with despair that Nicholas was its worst possible embodiment. Viewed in that light, the many petitions and loyal addresses to Nicholas, insisting that the fullness of power was still his to use as he saw fit, sound rather like anxious pleas than confident assertions, sound more like wishes than statements of fact. What other meaning could petitions for the "restoration" of

183

autocracy have when all along the insistence had been that it had never ceased to exist? There were even threats that the people would not stand for its surrender.[52] The hope was for firm and decisive leadership from some source, even for a military dictatorship exercised not by, but in the name of, the tsar; autocracy seems to have been the weak, traditional formula used to describe the object of that hope.[53]

Lev Tikhomirov, the erstwhile revolutionary turned speaker and pamphleteer for the URP and other rightist groups, remarked in February 1906 that it would be better to admit once and for all that the autocracy was gone than to compromise it further by quarrels over how much of it was left intact, especially since the tsar himself furnished no clear answer to the question and made contradictory statements to different deputations. He either could not or would not speak out. Without him, the 1905 revolution would not have taken place; with him, there was not much hope for the cause of autocracy.[54] The view was even expressed that no government at all would be better than the present one; presumably, its disappearance would relieve the extreme Right of much embarrassment and free it for truly militant action.[55] There were rumors that the Right disliked the emperor even more than did the Left and that there were those in its midst who wished to be rid of him.[56]

The autocrat could not be relied upon to uphold autocracy, and in the normal course of events no one else could play that role; Stolypin, the only possible candidate for the role of strong man, wished to cooperate with the duma and free himself of dependence on the Right. Thus there was little left to do, short of creating a revolutionary opposition, but to play the abhorrent game of politics for whatever benefits it might bring, supplement it with direct action where that seemed promising, and hope in this fashion to exercise some pressure on the government and even, though this was not made explicit, on the tsar. Deprived of the possibility of a sweeping indictment of the existing political and social order, unwilling to go into true opposition, most of the URP came by the autumn of 1907 to a factual acceptance of the situation created by the October Manifesto and the fundamental laws of 1906. And in that situation of political contest it faced again what had been a most troublesome question from its inception—the content of its social and economic program.

Nothing illustrates better both the genuinely popular complexion of the membership which the Union had been able to attract and the problems this created for its leaders than the discussions which took place at the fourth Congress of the United Russian People in April 1907 at a time when the second duma, even more oppositionist than the first, was in session. Attended by some 500 delegates of the URP and allied organizations, of student clubs and workingmen's guilds, the congress, when it turned to the discussion of the program to be adopted, was barely kept by its organizers from disintegrating in a violent burst of dissension. The peasant members, spurred on by the fanatic monk Iliodor, who took his own words so seriously that his ecclesiastical superiors were ordered by the government to discipline him, demanded the compulsory alienation (with compensation) of private lands and proposed a delegation to the tsar to submit this demand to him. Worker delegates succeeded in having their demands and grievances incorporated in a resolution that had to be carefully edited behind the scenes in order to cleanse it of its socialist overtones. Altogether, it appears that the leadership was hard put to it to restrain its followers, though we cannot be sure that it was unanimous in wishing to do so. Its original intention of having the congress ask for a dictatorship was quite lost sight of in the stress which the resolutions adopted put on social and economic issues. A direct confrontation of the agrarian question, which the peasants had so insistently raised, was avoided only by a compromise which admitted the need for more land but reserved a final solution to the emperor and a *zemskii sobor*, to be drawn from all estates of the Orthodox Russian population with one peasant representing each *uezd*. In the meantime, the administration was asked to take all possible measures to keep peasant lands from passing into the possession of other classes, of ethnic non-Russians and Jews, to assist resettlement and to extend liberal agrarian credits. While the peasant commune was to be preserved as the only safeguard against landlessness, peasant farmsteads were to be individually owned within the commune. Exit from it was possible if the allotment was

185

sold to the commune or to one of its members.[57] How a *zemskii sobor* could be summoned without a change in the fundamental laws which had intrusted the duma and the council of state with all legislative activity was not made clear. Nor did the political resolution, which asked for conversion of the duma into a purely consultative organ, explain whether it was to continue to exist alongside an assembly of estates. A change in the electoral law was also demanded: deputies should be chosen by a combination of election, lot, and imperial appointment.[58]

The coming electoral campaign for the third duma, and reports from provincial branches that the Union was losing peasant support [59] because its agrarian program failed to meet the needs even of the most moderate and well-disposed peasants, led to no revisions of the URP stand on the peasant question. A July 1907 meeting of chairmen of provincial and district branches of the URP and allied parties again recognized the peasant need for land but held that it must be met in a just, peaceful, and lawful way, without damage to the rights of other classes, with full regard to local conditions and the laws regarding private property. This was even vaguer than the April congress had been. Concern for workers and lower-level employees was expressed in a demand for legislation to improve their lot, again with proper attention to the "unshakable rights of property." [60] On this issue, too, the April congress had at least been more specific: the softened resolution it finally adopted spoke of the situation of the working classes as especially difficult, of poor working conditions in shops and factories; mentioned unemployment, the need for old-age pensions, factory legislation, and inspection. Blame for this parlous state of affairs was, it is true, placed primarily on foreign employers and Jews, but in its general tone the resolution was far less cautious than it was on the question of land. In the unequal battle between capital and labor, the state and the URP were to assist the Russian worker and craftsman by the organization of marketing organizations, the provision of credit, mutual aid societies (with, of course, purely economic goals), and remedial legislation.[61]

The URP always found it easier to sound an anticapitalist and antiindustrial note than an antilandlord one, since capitalism, industry, the whole mysterious world of finance and business could be represented as being in essence un-Russian, of benefit only to Jews and foreigners, and could even be held responsible in a vague way for the agrarian problem. There were denunciations of the government's financial conservatism; demands for easy credit and a paper ruble not backed by gold—"for the issue of paper notes depends on the will of the Tsar and the needs of the people" [62]— for state capital to aid Russian entrepreneurs in their battle against foreigners and Jews, for making the state bank independent of foreign money markets, and for including in its directorate representatives of small and large trade and industry.[63] But here, too, there was no fundamental challenge to the economic system of the country, and there could not be without seeming to enbrace parts of the socialist program. Attacks on the Jews were the surrogate for a frontal attack on capitalism because of the role they were said to play in the national economy. They were to be eliminated from it as fully as possible, by legislation, economic boycott, and finally by expulsion to Palestine.[64]

The electoral law of June 3, 1907, which had been promulgated by decree after the dissolution of the second duma, was designed to assure for its successor a more loyal and conservative representation. This was achieved by the weighting of votes on the basis of property qualifications, by a further division of the electorate into curias and (in certain localities) nationality groups, as well as by a complex electoral procedure by stages. The outcome was, from the government's point of view, a vast improvement, but it was hardly a triumph for the URP and its allies, who elected fifty-one deputies or 11.5 per cent of the total duma membership.[65] The new electoral law made a special appeal to the economic and social grievances of workers and peasants less urgent than had been the case earlier, a fact which may account for the more moderate tone adopted by the July congress as compared with that of April. The increasing conservatism of the URP in these areas manifested itself in a variety of ways. Its leaders in the duma, Markov and Purishkevich, although they were still capable of shrill attacks on "liberal" ministers, Jews, the universities, and the press, came to a *modus vivendi* with the government and the conservatives in the duma, moved closer to the organization of landowners, the Congress of the United Nobility, and further away from their erstwhile leader, Dr. Dubrovin. Both men established their own organizations. Purishkevich's called itself the Union of the Archangel Michael, and in certain localities the Union of Russian People of the Archangel Michael; Markov retained the name, much of the membership, and the organizational apparatus of the URP. Dr. Dubrovin was left with a splinter and the organization's newspaper *Russkoe Znamia;* a small number of branches, apparently the more "radical" ones, stayed with him. But he had not sufficient character or funds to retain a following of real consequence; none of the duma deputies appears to have remained loyal to him. He tried to suggest in *Russkoe Znamia,* and with the help of scattered individuals and branches, that he alone was carrying on the tradition of a truly popular monarchism against those who had sold out to the powers that be.[66] After 1908, his was a barely audible voice. After that date the organization which he had created lost in importance and numbers in all its sectors. The country was tired of being exhorted; and the government, thanks to Stolypin, once again felt firm ground under its feet.

It seems beyond dispute that the URP was not politically, socially, or economically radical. What made it appear to be so in Russian conditions was its willingness to employ a degree of violence and the fact that, unlike earlier defenders of autocracy, orthodoxy, and nationality, the URP realized that in the conditions created by 1905, resistance to political liberalization had to find support in broader strata of the population and therefore take some account of their grievances and aspirations. It is revealing that it was, for the most part, conservatives who regarded the URP as a form of right-wing radicalism, people who were fearful of mass politics, afraid that once the masses had been summoned to battle against political liberalism, there might be no turning them away from further attacks on the economic and social order. These fears were justified. The disintegration of the URP after the first years of its existence was the result of much of the membership's inclination to take seriously the populism of the URP and its claim to represent the true Russia and its interests, the true Russia being that of

188

peasants, artisans, and small traders as opposed to that of big business, industry, the stock exchange, international finance, and bureaucracy. But the main point of attack for the URP always remained political liberalism, the facade which capitalism, Jews, and selfish interests of all kinds had erected to do their sinister work. And when political liberalism appeared to be safely contained by firm governmental action, the main body of the URP lost interest in developing an economic and social program that would appeal to the vast majority of Russians—peasants, petty traders, and workmen—who were not very much interested in the forms of politics.

It may be argued that there is no such thing as a radicalism of the Right, that the Right is always and everywhere incapable of developing genuine social and economic appeals. Without debating the essential nature of Italian Fascism and German National Socialism, it must be conceded that it was not, in the final analysis, with the radicalism of their economic and social programs that Nazis and Fascists outbid communists and socialists. So that even if the URP was not genuinely radical, it might still perhaps be regarded as fascist or national socialist. These movements rejected, it is true, political *and* economic liberalism and individualism; spoke of the twentieth century as the century of collectivism (Mussolini); denied that private property was an absolute right; demanded that property be made responsible to the community (Hitler); asked for the abolition of incomes not earned by work, the nationalization of trusts, profit-sharing in wholesale trade, land confiscation for communal purposes, measures against usurers, profiteers, and speculators (Program of the National Socialist German Workers' Party, 1920). It is true also that the URP rarely, if ever, spoke of the bourgeois-capitalist order with such unmistakable hostility. But it is not the failure of the URP to draw a sharper line between itself and the old regime in social and economic terms, not its compromises on the agrarian or working-class questions that make the URP ineligible for consideration as the first fascist movement or even as a prototype. Italian Fascism and German National Socialism, in spite of their denunciations of the bourgeois order, also compromised with it, accepted its support, moderated their egalitarianism, and brought about no revolutionary transformation of the economy. Italian Fascism, which at the outset, in its ideological sweep, in the development of corporatism and the idea of the totalitarian state, threatened or promised a radical alteration of Italian society, turned out to be in practice a fairly traditional regime of one-party dictatorship. And even Hitler's state did not reveal the full extent of its radicalism (if criminal nihilism can be called that) until the war years when its energies were directed not so much to the reorganization or reformation of German society as to its racial purification and that of most of the continent.

Although both Fascists and Nazis claimed to stand equally against Reds and reaction (in the words of the Horst Wessel song), they, too, like the URP, collaborated on occasion with forces of the old order which they wished to displace—industry, the army, the churches, the monarchy. The difference between them and the URP does not lie primarily in any objective measurements applied to their respective party programs and their radical content but in the differing opportunities which different societies in different stages of historical development presented and the uses which were made of these opportunities.

Italian Fascism and German National Socialism were radical in the sense that they were broad indictments of their respective societies, their values, and institutions. They addressed themselves not simply to specific issues of politics or economics about which they were purposely vague. They were responses to a deeper malaise of modern civilization, a malaise which Russia had not yet fully felt (as she had not yet experienced its benefits) and which was not borne in upon Europe with full force until after World War I. It was that war that made Europeans question the validity and blessings of the whole complex of political and economic liberalism by which they had lived; it was the war that habituated a whole continent to the practice of violence. It was the war also that created a deep schism between the generation which had come to maturity under its impact and the generation which had held Europe's destiny in its hands when the war began. Nothing after it was ever the same; nothing after it was quite right, least of all in

190

Germany and Italy. The attack Fascism and Nazism made on the old order was thus made in the name of youth against age, of the new against the old, of the fighters and producers against those who had stayed home and governed badly and profited too well. In Italy and Germany the old order was in disarray, under attack from everywhere. It was easy to proclaim that the twentieth century would be the century of Fascism, that National Socialism was the wave of the future, that movement toward that future was in itself good. The common perception that the old order was in decay was shared and heightened by men like Mussolini and Hitler, who saw in it their opportunity and were prepared to act on it. Their will to power was not mere rhetoric; their conception of the Fascist and Nazi movements as something essentially novel, not another political party but as *the* political organization and government of the entire nation was, as Mussolini claimed, new to history.

The Union of Russian People, though it too claimed to be not a political party but the expression of a nation's aspirations, of a historical outlook and way of life, was a political party of a much more conventional kind. It arose in response not so much to a crisis of civilization as to fulfil a specific and limited political task. Most Russians were not ready to abandon an experiment which had not yet been tried. They had no perception that the standards and values by which Europe had been governed for almost a century needed thorough replacement. They were still, for the most part, prepared to regard as desirable and beneficial for Russia what Germany and Italy would a decade or two later blame for their troubles. They still believed that reform rather than a total upheaval was the answer to their problems. In such a situation, the URP could not claim to speak for youth against age, for an entirely new order against an old one which had shown its failings and deserved only to be swept away. Unable to ride the wave of a future which they could not yet perceive, or to speak in the name of a new historical phase, the men of the URP were condemned to compete in the political arena on the same terms as other political parties, and in that competition they could never be successful. The middle class which might have looked to them as their defenders against

191

peasant and proletarian demands was in Russia neither sufficiently numerous nor sufficiently fearful of threats from that direction to resist substantial concessions and to turn for help to the extreme Right. There were elements to the right of the bulk of the middle classes—large landowners, bureaucrats, some clerics—who saw in the URP a defense of their interests, but who wished that such an ally were not necessary and abandoned it when the regular forces of authority recovered their nerve. Russia seemed to be in a half-way house between authoritarian monarchy and a constitutional representative system where both the older privileged classes and the forces of political and economic liberalism seemed for the moment willing to reside, hopeful that either a balance could be kept or a gradual and cautious transition be made to a fully constitutional regime without opening the floodgates to revolution. In such a situation, extremism found it difficult to operate, and the URP became within three or four years of its foundation precisely the opposite of what it had always claimed to be—a political party in the very narrowest sense of the term, a tool for its leaders to launch themselves into some kind of prominence and prosperity. And none of the leaders of the URP, neither Dubrovin, nor Purishkevich, and least of all Markov, were men of sufficient personal stature, probity, or magnetism to make up for their party's lack of a program.

But for that, they were not alone responsible. They could not become the leaders or the creators of a national revolution as long as the monarchy survived and as long as they proclaimed their loyalty to it and to its head. They might privately chafe under such a restraint, but they had to reckon with it. And that simple yet overwhelming fact deprived them of the possibility and the will of power. Not even their shrill chauvinism, which in a multinational state tended rather to work against than for them, could make up for this fundamental disability. Without the possibility of power, they were also without the dynamism which the struggle for power and the belief of its accessibility confers, a dynamism which more than any program helps to swell the ranks of political movements. Such a dynamism can develop for the Right only when the job of freeing it of the paralyzing embrace of an old regime has already been performed for it, and when it can stand as a new and vital force against the "old" discredited regime of political and economic liberalism, democracy, or socialism. By that test, there could be no fascism or national socialism in tsarist Russia.

[1] General surveys of the Russian Right (i.e., of parties to the right of the Octobrists and the Party of Peaceful Renovation), and of its origins in the pre-1905 period, are contained in the following: V. Levitskii, "Pravye partii," in L. Martov *et al.* (eds.), *Obshchestvennoe dvizhenie v Rossii s nachala XX veka* (St. Petersburg, 1914), III, 347–462; V. Mech, *Sily reaktsii* (Moscow, 1907); L-ch, "Momenty kontr-revoliutsii," in *Itogy i perspektivy* (Moscow, 1906); L. Slonimskii, "Nashi monarkhisty i ikh programmy," *Vestnik Evropy*, No. 5 (May 1907), pp. 250–72; V. N. Zalezhskii, *Monarkhisty* (2d ed.; Khar'kov, 1930); Horst Jablonowski, "Die russischen Rechtsparteien, 1905–1917," in *Russland Studien, Gedenkschrift für Otto Hötzsch* ("Schriftenreihe Osteuropa," No. 3 [Stuttgart, 1957]), pp. 43–55; N. D. Noskov, *Okhranitel'nye i reaktsionnye partii v Rossii* (St. Petersburg, 1906); see also my article, "The formation of the Russian Right, 1900–1906," in Nicholas Riasanovsky and Gleb Struve (eds.), *California Slavic studies*, III (Berkeley, Calif., 1964), 66–94.

[2] Russian journalists and political commentators of the period were not always very discriminating in their use of such terms as "right" or "conservative" and at times used them interchangeably. Thus, e.g., L. Martov's *Politicheskiia partii v Rossii* (St. Petersburg, 1906), p. 4, has this, not very helpful but inclusive, chapter heading: "Right reactionary-conservative parties." More often, distinctions were made (by Martov and others) between conservatives and the Right (sometimes called "extreme"), with the latter referred to as "Black Hundreds." But the "Black Hundreds" were not so much a specific political movement as perpetrators of antiliberal and antisocialist violence and Jewish pogroms. Since many members of the URP and its allies (the Monarchist party, the Union of Russian Men, the Kursk People's party, and others) were disposed to view such outbursts as justified expressions of popular indignation and to encourage them, it is not incorrect to include them under the general heading of "Black Hundredism" (*chernosotenstvo*). But *chernosotenstvo* was a broad, amorphous phenomenon and descriptive rather of outbursts of violence than of political organizations. During the period treated by this article, from the end of 1905 to the beginning of 1908, Right, extreme Right, and URP may be regarded as synonymous.

[3] Geoffrey Brunn and Victor S. Mamatey, *The world in the 20th century* (4th ed.; Boston, 1962), p. 891.

[4] S. B. Liubosh, *Russkii fashist Vl. Purishkevich* (Leningrad, 1925), p. 29.

[5] V. A. Maevskii, *Revoliutsioner-monarkhist; pamiati L've Tikhomirova* (Novi Sad, 1934), pp. 74, 81.

[6] Alfred Levin, *The second duma* (New Haven, Conn., 1940), p. 27.

[7] G. P. Fedotov, "Russia and freedom," *Review of politics*, VII (1946), 31.

194

[8] "Zhurnal'noe obozrenie," *Russkaia Mysl'*, XXVII, No. 5 (May 1906), p. 201.

[9] S. Iu. Vitte, *Vospominaniia*, ed. A. L. Sidorov (Moscow, 1960), I, 282–83.

[10] *Ibid.*, III, 414–40.

[11] Sh. M. Levin, "Materialy dlia kharakteristiki kontr-revoliutsii 1905 g.," *Byloe*, No. 21 (1923), p. 161.

[12] Walter Z. Laqueur, "Russia and Germany," *Survey* (London), No. 44–45 (Oct. 1962), p. 91.

[13] Ia. Demchenka, *Evreiskoe ravnopravie ili russkoe poraboshchenie* (2d ed.; Kiev, 1907), pp. 6–7.

[14] Leader from *Moskovskie Vedomosti* (No. 131), quoted in "Vnutrennee obozrenie," *Vestnik Evropy*, No. 8 (Aug. 1907), p. 751. See also *Russkii Vestnik*, LI, No. 5 (May 1906), p. 330; and *Russkoe Znamia*, Nos. 212 and 365 (1906), quoted by Sherman D. Spector, "The doctrine and program of the Union of Russian People in 1906" (unpublished Master's thesis, Russian Institute, Columbia University, 1952), p. 89. No absolutely reliable statistics on URP membership are available. URP sources mention anywhere from 900 to 3,500 branches and from 600,000 to 3,000,000 members. It is impossible to tell what the basis for these figures is and what criteria were used in arriving at them. The maximum estimated by a hostile student of the Right is about 100 branches with 10,000–20,000 members (Levitskii, "Pravye partii," p. 406). If accurate, this would be evidence of considerable organized strength. There is no doubt that the URP was numerically and organizationally the strongest of the rightist parties until it split.

[15] Levin, *Second duma*, p. 27; O. O. Gruzenberg, *Vchera* (Paris, 1928), p. 133; V. P. Viktorov and A. Chernovskii (eds.), *Soiuz russkogo naroda* (Moscow-Leningrad, 1929), pp. 8, 84.

[16] Vitte, *Vospominaniia*, III, 356–57; Alexander Gerassimoff, *Der Kampf gegen die erste russische Revolution; Erinnerungen*, trans. E. Thalmann (Leipzig, 1934), p. 80.

[17] Boris Nikol'skii, "Dnevnik," *Krasnyi Arkhiv*, No. 63 (1934), II, 88; L. A. Tikhomirov, "25 let nazad; iz dnevnika L. Tikhomirova," *ibid.*, No. 40 (1930), p. 84; Levitskii, "Pravye partii," pp. 380–83, 394, 408.

[18] Nikol'skii, "Dnevnik," p. 87.

[19] *Ibid.*, p. 88; Viktorov and Chernovskii, *Soiuz*, pp. 29, 34.

[20] *Ibid.*, pp. 35–37; S. E. Kryzhanovskii, *Vospominaniia* (Berlin, 1938), pp. 100–103; V. I. Gurko, *Features and figures of the past—government and opinion in the reign of Nicolas II*, ed. J. E. Wallace Sterling *et al.*, trans. Laura Matveev (Stanford, Calif., 1939), p. 435.

[21] Viktorov and Chernovskii, *Soiuz*, p. 32; Spector, "Doctrine and program," p. 23.

[22] Levitskii, "Pravye Partii," pp. 410–12; *Vestnik Narodnoi Svobody*, No. 33/34, Aug. 30, 1907, cols. 1569–70, and No. 30, Oct. 1, 1906, col. 1627; Viktorov and Chernovskii, *Soiuz*, pp. 374, 395; K. Avgustovskii, "V soiuze russkogo naroda," *Sovremennyi Mir*, IX, part 2 (1907), pp. 61–63.

[23] Kryzhanovskii, *Vospominaniia*, pp. 155–57; Interrogation of N.E. Markov

195

in P. E. Shchegolev, ed., *Padenie tsarskogo rezhima* (Leningrad, 1926), VI, 179; "Obshchestvennaia khronika," *Vestnik Evropy*, No. 2 (Feb. 1907), p. 889.

[24] Kryzhanovskii, *Vospominaniia*, pp. 153–54.

[25] Avgustovskii in *Sovremenny Mir*, pp. 61 ff.; and P. Timofeev, "V chainoi SRN," *Russkoe bogatstvo*, No. 2 (Feb. 1907), pp. 76–77.

[26] V. Ivanovich, *Rossiiskiia partii, soiuzy i ligi* (St. Petersburg, 1906), pp. 118–22, contains the URP program of early 1906; for attacks on the rich, the educated, and the powerful see Spector, "Doctrine and program," p. 54 (against liberalism in the church hierarchy); Ivan Kashkarov, "Kak sanovniki podryvaiut Samoderzhavnuiu vlast'," *Mirnyi Trud*, No. 7 (Sep. 1906), pp. 171–95, on bureaucratic subversion of imperial authority; V. N. Zalezhskii, *Monarkhisty* (2d ed.; Khar'kov, 1930), p. 26, has examples of denunciations of ministers and of demands for the accountability of all public servants; "Khronika vnutrennei zhizni," *Russkoe bogatstvo*, No. 4 (Apr. 1908), p. 66, cites URP attacks on judicial authorities, higher educational institutions, and ecclesiastical seminaries and academies for helping to undermine authority. The examples could be multiplied.

[27] Avgustovskii, in *Sovremennyi Mir*, pp. 63–66, 72; Viktorov and Chernovskii, *Soiuz*, pp. 379–80, 398–99.

[28] Kryzhanovskii, *Vospominaniia*, p. 156.

[29] Viktorov and Chernovskii, *Soiuz*, pp. 401–3.

[30] Shchegolev, *Padenie*, VI, 179.

[31] At an Aug. 20, 1907, session of the council of the URP, its treasury was described as almost empty and the further existence of its newspaper, *Russkoe Znamia*, called in question (see *Vestnik Narodnoi Svovobody*, No. 33/34, Aug. 30, 907, col. 1568; and Alfred Levin, "The reactionary tradition in the election campaign to the third duma," *Oklahoma State University Publication*, LIX, No. 16 [June 1, 1962], p. 13).

[32] Viktorov and Chernovskii, *Soiuz*, p. 391.

[33] Levin, "The reactionary tradition," p. 25; Gerassimoff, *Der Kampf*, pp. 212, 216; A. A. Kizevetter, *Na rubezhe dvukh stoletii* (Prague, 1929), p. 508; L. Bernstein, *Les Cent Noires ou les nationalistes russes* (Paris, 1907), pp. 43–48.

[34] Rothay Reynolds, *My Russian year* (London, 1913), p. 139, speaks of numbers of "nice" Russian women who joined the URP—"just as numbers of nice English women become members of the Primrose League"—but then became dismayed by its terrorist methods and the ruffians in its midst.

[35] Gurko, *Features and figures*, pp. 436–37: "In normal times, no government should use methods employed by revolutionists, for in its hands such methods become double-edged weapons. But during times of revolutionary unrest, when the people are in the grip of mass psychosis, the government must support individual organizations that spring up to support it. In 1905 the URP was such an organization."

[36] From "The sleeping car," a section of *Tri Stolitsy*, translated by Bernard Pares in *The Slavonic and east European review*, V, No. 15 (Mar. 1927), p. 475.

[37] B. V. Nazarevskii, *Osnovy parlamentskogo stroia* (Moscow, 1907), pp. 16–18; and Levitskii, "Pravye partii," p. 402.

[38] P. N. Miliukov, *Vospominaniia* (New York, 1955), I, 421, and *Vestnik Narodnoi Svobody*, No. 6, Feb. 8, 1907, col. 431.

[39] Viktorov and Chernovskii, *Soiuz*, p. 87; Gruzenberg, *Vchera*, p. 133; "Chernosotenstvo," in *Bol'shaia sovetskaia entsiklopediia*, LXI (Moscow, 1934), 356, also mentions the Bolshevik Bauman as a victim of URP assassins.

[40] Spector, "Doctrine and program," pp. 35, 38, 40; Levitskii, "Pravye partii," p. 445; Viktorov and Chernovskii, *Soiuz*, pp. 401–3.

[41] Mech, *Sily reaktsii*, p. 85; Timofeev in *Russkoe Bogatstvo*, p. 76.

[42] See the testimony by Markov in Shchegolev, *Padenie*, VI, 176–77.

[43] N. D. Noskov, *Okhranitel'nye i reaktsionnye partii*, p. 40; *Russkii Vestnik*, LI, No. 3 (Mar. 1906), p. 305. See also N. E. Markov, *Voiny temnykh sil* (Paris, 1928), p. 129.

[44] Levin, *Second duma*, p. 67; Levitskii, "Pravye partii," p. 460.

[45] G. V. Butmi, *Rossiia na rasput'i: kabala ili svoboda?* (8th ed.; St. Petersburg, 1906), pp. 33–34.

[46] Markov, *Voiny temnykh sil*, pp. 134–35.

[47] For the text of the address see *Vestnik narodnoi svobody*, No. 46, Nov. 25, 1907, cols. 1980–81; for the electoral statistics, Levin, Reactionary tradition," p. 45.

[48] *Ibid.*, p. 32.

[49] *Ibid.*, pp. 31–32; Viktorov and Chernovskii, *Soiuz*, 402–3; A. S. Izgoev, "Pered tretei Dumoi," *Russkaia Mysl'*, XXVIII, No. 10 (Oct. 1907), p. 210.

[50] Markov, *Voiny temnykh sil*, p. 138.

[51] Shchegolev, *Padenie*, VI, 175.

[52] One deputation to the tsar, whose spokesman was Boris Nikol'skii of the URP, was so insistent on this point that the ministry of the court prohibited the publication of his address to the emperor. See Levin, "Materialy," *Byloe*, No. 21 (1923), pp. 168–69, 184; W. W. Schulgin (V. V. Shul'gin), *Tage; Memoiren aus der russischen Revolution*, ed. George v. Reutern, trans. Marissa von Reutern (Berlin, 1928), pp. 219–23, describes the visit of the Volhynian branch of the URP to the emperor and its petition for the retention of autocracy.

[53] Levitskii, "Pravye partii," p. 422; Lev Tikhomirov in *Krasnyi Arkhiv*, No. 61 (1933), p. 103.

[54] *Ibid.*, No. 41/42 (1930), pp. 130–32. In a letter of July 2, 1906, Nikol'skii referred to Nicholas as an idiot and predicted that the dynasty would be removed "in the Serbian manner" by Siberian officers (Levin, "Materialy," p. 185).

[55] Levitskii, "Pravye partii," p. 422.

[56] S. R. Mintslov, *Petersburg v 1903–1910 godakh* (Riga, 1931), pp. 111, 231; Vitte, *Vospominania*, II, 555.

[57] *Vestnik narodnoi svobody*, No. 20, May 24, 1907, cols. 1227–28.

[58] *Ibid.*, col. 1223.

[59] *Ibid.*, No. 33/34, Aug. 30, 1907, col. 1569.

[60] *Ibid.*, No. 39/40, Aug. 2, 1907, col. 1481.

[61] *Ibid.*, No. 20, May 24, 1907, cols. 1228–32.

[62] Butmi, *Rossiia na rasput'i*, p. 44; see also Mech, *Sily reaktsii*, p. 86.

[63] *Ruskii Vestnik*, LI, No. 11 (Nov. 1906), p. 315.

[64] Mech, *Sily reaktsii*, p. 86; *Vestnik narodnoi svobody*, No. 20 (May 24, 1907), col. 1235; Bernstein, *Les Cent Noirs*, pp. 9–12; Levin, "The reactionary tradition," pp. 18–19.

[65] *Ibid.*, p. 45.

[66] N. Zhedenov, *Margarinovye monarkhisty* (St. Petersburg, 1912); *Vasileostrovsty o glavnosovetchikakh; k vserossiiskomu s'ezdu SRN v g. Moskve, 21-ogo noiabria 1911 g; doklad Vasileostrovskago otdela SRN* . . . (St. Petersburg, 1911), pp. i–iv, 147–52.

198

9

A New Look at the Problem of "Japanese Fascism"

BY GEORGE MACKLIN WILSON

In the decade and a half from 1931 to 1945 Japan confronted a series of domestic and international crises culminating in the national disaster of World War II. Many authors—both Japanese and Western—have portrayed this period in terms of the labeling generalization "fascism," suggesting that Japan's experience ran parallel to that of such European countries as Italy under Mussolini and Germany during the Third Reich.[1] My object here, after first attempting to explain how and why this interpretation arose, is to take issue with it, but in criticizing the use of the label fascism I do not mean to fall back to the position that what happened was simply *sui generis*, a somehow "unique" Japanese response to the troublesome developments of the interwar world. Fascism has the virtue of being a comparative concept, and if we throw it out we need to seek other comparative concepts to test as possible replacements.

There are basically two lines of interpretation which have yielded the conclusion that Japan became a fascist state during the nineteen-thirties. One is the Marxist approach, the second what I will call the "authoritarian modernization" thesis.

Since the early thirties Marxist theoreticians have contended that the appearance in Japan, first of fascist movements, then of a full-blown fascist regime, was a function of objective class conditions and a desperate form of last-ditch defense on the part of Japanese capitalism against the menace of social and economic revolution. This is the same interpretation which Marxists apply to Fascist Italy and Nazi Germany,[2] and it holds that Japan's "fas-

199

cists," whether or not they used the word and no matter how they subjectively viewed their own role, objectively represented the interests of monopoly finance capital. Today we may look with bemusement at the notion that someone like Kita Ikki, for instance, was "objectively" serving finance capital or bureaucratic and military reaction—both of which he condemned repeatedly in all of his writings as barriers against national and popular progress.[3] But in the Marxist scheme of things this simply makes no difference. As Karl Radek put it thirty years ago in his theoretical introduction to the book by Soviet authors Tanin and Yohan, *Militarism and Fascism in Japan*, Marxist analysis is of course concerned with the social composition of a given movement, but this is irrelevant in the end; what counts are the class interests which a movement ultimately benefits, and since Japan had become a capitalist and imperialist nation, whatever its particular historical development might be, movements opposed to bourgeois liberalism and socialist revolution were *ipso facto* fascist.[4]

Since World War II, Soviet scholarship has echoed the general Marxist interpretation of fascism laid down three decades ago. A book on "the bourgeois state" during the interwar period, for example, summarizes its definition of fascism as follows: "Fascism, appearing as an open terroristic dictatorship of the most reactionary, most chauvinistic, and most imperialistic elements of finance capital, shakes off all the 'democratic' cloaks masking the subordination of the state apparatus to the monopolies."[5] In another study, one which deals with Japan on the eve of the War in the Pacific, I.A. Latyshev concludes that the Japanese government was an "openly terroristic fascist regime" having a "purely class, purely antipopular character . . . as a dictatorship of monopolists and landlords."[6] There is nevertheless a tendency among Soviet scholars to look for a special label to delineate the Japanese experience. Latyshev writes: "The specific character of the . . . fascist regime in Japan lay in that absolute monarchy was its form, while the leaders of the Japanese military came forward in the role of fascist dictators [and were] the most ardent servants of the zaibatsu and landlords, the cruelest butchers of the Japanese people. Therefore, in order to set off and underline the specific character of the fascist dictatorship in Japan, [we may] call it monarcho-fascist dictatorship, or military-fascist dictatorship." [7]

Postwar Japanese Marxists have not been of one mind on the question of Japanese fascism. During the Occupation years a debate, whose roots trace back to the major intellectual controversy of the nineteen-thirties, arose about the character of the Meiji Restoration of 1868 and the subsequent development of Japanese capitalism.[8] At that time, one school of thought held that the Restoration was a full-fledged bourgeois revolution, while other writers of the so-called "Kōza faction" contended that it was an incomplete bourgeois revolution which had led to "absolutism." [9] The Kōza interpretation has dominated postwar thinking on this subject, and some Kōza writers deny that Japan ever had a genuine fascist period because, as they see it, the presence of "feudal" holdovers in prewar Japanese absolutism meant that the bourgeoisie—without whose predominance "modern" fascism cannot appear—had not yet completed their rise to full power.[10] But most postwar "neo-Kōza" scholarship agrees that the fascist label does apply to early Shōwa Japan, although it was a peculiar Japanese form of fascism. A typical statement of the neo-Kōza position is this one recently delivered by Inoue Kiyoshi: "The proponents of military dictatorship . . . in Japan, whatever their subjective view might be as they cried out against the zaibatsu and actually did kill some representatives of the zaibatsu, [wanted] to fuse monopoly capital with the state and have the military—the nucleus of the absolutist emperor-system structure—seize the state's dictatorial power, seeking [thereby] to resolve the crisis of Japanese imperialism. Therefore this is called emperor-system fascism." [11]

Despite the neo-Kōza emphasis on the special or peculiar nature of Japanese fascism, scholars of this persuasion all reaffirm the fundamental Marxist belief that the substance of fascism lies in monopoly capital dictatorship. Tanaka Sōgorō, for instance, writes that "fascism is one form of dictatorship attempted at the time when capitalist society stands at the brink of disaster." In his view, fascism came to Japan as it did to Italy and Germany because these

201

were "middle countries, strong enough to be able to undertake fascism's basic actions—internal repression and external aggression—but not great powers." [12]

The Marxist assessment of fascism, for Japan as elsewhere, stands on metaphysical or at least transhistorical grounds, and as such ordinary historical analysis can scarcely challenge it. The imputation of a class basis to diverse groups which themselves were usually supra-class in conscious ("subjective") orientation, and especially the dogmatic conclusion that the wartime regime from 1937 to 1945 was serving the interests of monopoly capitalism and the landlords, are hypotheses unsupported by available documentation which one must therefore either accept on faith or reject out of hand as unrealistic. Even if we should allow that the capitalists benefited—temporarily—from the government's actions, the Marxist approach creates an imbalance by stressing only the real and presumed connections linking bureaucrats and generals with capitalists and landlords while ignoring broader questions about what was actually taking place in Japanese society and politics.

More compelling and harder to reject is the second approach I have referred to—the authoritarian-modernization thesis of Japanese fascism. The general premise underlying this thesis is that in the interwar decades there was a world-wide trend among industrial nations toward the emergence of fascist movements and regimes, particularly in countries like Germany and Japan where rapid modernization spurred on by the power of the state had brought a relatively high level of development but also severe social and economic dislocations. Is it not proper, this argument asks, to label as fascist all those governments which, in the process of rapid and paternalistic industrialization, encounter domestic and foreign crises that lead them to pursue policies of repression at home and aggressive expansion abroad?

This thesis has found many able exponents among both Western and Japanese scholars. Robert Scalapino and Richard Storry; [13] Maruyama Masao, Ishida Takeshi, Hata Ikuhiko,[14] and others have established a persuasive non-Marxist case for a peculiarly "Japanese" form of fascism—different from the European variety chiefly in that it came not from below through successful mass mobilization but from above, by transforming the existing state structure into an "emperor-system" or "military-bureaucratic" fascism which acted in the main like its European counterparts, suppressing liberalism and socialism and cementing state authority over all aspects of national life. By substituting the army for the fascist party, the symbolic force of the emperor for the fascist "leader," and drawing other similar analogies, the conclusion emerges that Japan had a fascist system, particularly after 1936.

Most persuasive among advocates of this "Japanese" fascism is Maruyama Masao, whose argument runs as follows: [15] In a Japan lacking the tradition of a bourgeois-democratic revolution, fascism had to develop from above since mass energy, having never before been a main force in political change, could not serve to bring it to power. But, as in Europe, there was a mass social base for fascism among the "pseudo-intellectuals" of the middle class who felt threatened by liberalism and were willing to support Japan's mission of expansion in Asia.

Confronted with the objection that by 1936 or 1937, when Japan left off simply having fascist movements and presumably became a fascist state, the nation was already deeply involved in war, whereas when Italy and Germany became fascist they were not at war, the counter-argument from Maruyama's viewpoint is that this is just one more reason why Japanese fascism had to proceed from above, that a war crisis brings more rapid fascist consolidation from the top. If Germany had been at war in the early thirties, or on the verge of it, probably the Wehrmacht would have taken a more important part in the process of "fascization." [16]

There is an inclusive logic in this interpretation which effectively blunts the "concrete facts" approach of a writer like Nakamura Kikuo, who argues that "Japanese fascism" is a misnomer.[17] When Nakamura points out that in actual fact Japan witnessed no successful takeover of power from below and no formal change in the existing Meiji constitutional order, no pogroms and no *Gleichschaltung*,[18] the rejoinder is that these were never necessary; the existing machinery of state was convertible to operation as a fascist system without recourse to total "homogenization" of the populace or formal institutional change. Indeed, Maruyama holds that fascism's precise organizational form is irrelevant—it varies according to differences in the "concrete circumstances of the revolutionary situation"; where the potential for revolution is limited, but the ruling circles *think* the situation is assuming crisis proportions, "fascization from above" will likely proceed under the existing formal-legal structure.[19]

The inclusiveness of this argument makes it difficult to challenge, but two related answers to it do suggest themselves. First, the authoritarian-modernization thesis plays down the severity of the differences between European and "Japanese" fascism. In terms of political *process*, we may or may not wish to emphasize the fact that the Italian-German pattern of mass mobilization and seizure of power from below had no parallel in Japan. If one accepts as reasonable the proposition that a fascist structure could come into being through a variety of procedural routes, it is relatively unimportant that the Japanese process was grossly dissimilar to the German and Italian. But it is crucial to note the differences in the character and function of political *institutions*. There were in Japan no parallels for the Nazi and Fascist parties, their party armies, and their heroic "leaders," the Führer and Duce. Japanese government operated as before under the control of the same elites, chosen largely from among Tokyo Imperial University graduates and, in the military, from among regular staff officers, who had gradually become dominant early in the twentieth century. Neither the civil nor the military bureaucracy changed its role, nor were significant numbers of high-level officials recruited from previous non-elites such as the membership of a popular mass movement, as happened in the Nazi and Fascist experience. One can, it appears, remove the terms "fascist" and "fascism" at every point where they occur in the authoritarian-modernization thesis, and the resulting analysis is an impressive demonstration of the fundamental continuity of Japanese political life in modern times. Such a conclusion is particularly apt with respect to Maruyama's work. He repeatedly stresses the continuity of Shōwa leadership elites with their Meiji and Taishō predecessors.[20] In addition, he views all three of the "distinctive characteristics" of Japanese fascist ideology in his schema—familism (*kazokushugi*), agrarianism, (*nōhonshugi*), and pan-Asianism (*dai-Ajiashugi*)—as permanent features of the post-Restoration scene.[21]

The related second answer to the authoritarian-modernization thesis is that there should be no need to qualify fascism in Japan as something distinctively or uniquely Japanese if the concept of fascism is to have general applicability. Proponents of the authoritarian-modernization thesis are always careful to make just this kind of qualification: [22] it was a special form, a "Japanese" fascism, different in important particulars from that of Italy and Germany since it came from above and manifested a high degree of military involvement in political interest-articulation. For a comparative concept to be useful, however, only minor distinctions among concrete situations should be required.[23] Karl Radek was aware of this problem when he chided and even rebuked Soviet experts Tanin and Yohan for suggesting that what they called the "Japanese reactionary-chauvinist movement" differed considerably from European fascist movements.[24] In short, if Japan is properly labeled fascist, the qualifying adjectives should be dispensable.

Suppose we sought to resolve these difficulties by constructing an ideal-typical model of a fascist system against which to test the Japanese case. Epistemological limitations suggest that there are only two ways to do it. On the one hand, if we assume that there *is* something generically identifiable as cross-national fascism in Europe, we can put together a model by relying solely on the European experience.[25] We could, on the other hand, build our model by combining the principal attributes of European fascism with the outstanding features of the Japanese situation, but then what we will have done, in effect, is to "take an average" in which Japan must necessarily figure as a variant but recognizable species of the fascist genus as a whole.

I submit that this latter operation is what the advocates of the authoritarian-modernization thesis have unwittingly performed. In other words, they *assume* that the Japanese experience belongs in any model of fascism. Why do we find such an assumption? It results, I think, from two psychological attitudes which Western observers and Japanese intellectuals, for the most part, have shared with respect to the history of modern Japan. One is an understandable and poignant sense of bitterness at the suppression of freedom in wartime Japan, which reversed earlier trends toward the expansion of liberal ideas and institutions. The other is an almost intuitive conviction that Japan's rapid evolution from "feudalism" to "absolutism" and "capitalism" indicates the proximity of Japanese historical development to the pattern of early modern and modern Western history. This conviction has led some to conclude that Japan's history should have followed a pattern practically identical to that of modern Europe were it not for certain "peculiarities." [26]

From Meiji times to the present Japanese writers have taken the very terminology for periodizing their history from European historical categories, but they certainly have no monopoly on the attitudes I have described. Contemporary Western visitors have professed to see striking similarities between Japanese and European history ever since the Jesuit padres of the sixteenth century found castles and knightly warfare on Kyushu and the diplomats of the Bakumatsu (ca. 1853–1867) and early Meiji era declaimed about the seemingly laboratory-like resemblance between the land of the Mikado and earlier European feudal society. Such thinking has persisted into the twentieth century: in the thirties both Japanese and Western writers were quick to fasten on fascism as a label for the extremist patriotic groups—civilian and military—that were appearing on the scene.[27] And it is especially notable since World War II as Japan's modernization continues to go forward at so dynamic a pace. The expectation that study will turn up profound likenesses as well as specific differences between Japanese and Western political processes, whether these are greeted with approval or dismay, goes on today as we try to assess the future of the postwar parliamentary order, and it is usually the specific differences that both Westerners and Japanese tend to disapprove as "deviations" from the norm.[28]

One need not deny the historical analogies in order to counter this argument. On the contrary, there are probably substantial similarities in the evolution of human society wherever man has settled and organized his communities, although, to be sure, there are differences as well. I would suggest, however, that instead of

206

interpreting Japanese history so single-mindedly in terms of Western patterns, we should reach out occasionally to compare it with the historical development of the non-Western societies, of which Japan is obviously one. It is a simple but nonetheless meaningful truism that if, when Commodore Perry came calling in 1853, Bakumatsu Japan had instead been *sengoku* Japan of the fifteenth or sixteenth century, its modernization would have followed a very different course indeed. Probably the absence of the widespread sense of national identity and the institutions of social communication and control that mark the Tokugawa scene [29] would have rendered Japan easy prey for the sort of colonialism which the nineteenth century witnessed on so broad a scale in other parts of the non-Western world. Early twentieth-century Japan might then have produced a nationalist independence movement on the order of the Chinese, the Indonesian, the Tunisian, or any of a host of others.

Although mid-nineteenth-century Japan had not attained the institutional and technological level of the more advanced Western nations of the time, it is plain enough that the Japanese were far ahead of most Asian and African societies, particularly so, for our purposes here, in the capacity for effective exercise and extension of central political control. The regime that emerged from the Meiji Restoration came to power in order to guarantee national independence and security and to foster modernization so that national security could not again be threatened. Twentieth-century independence movements in Asia and Africa have stressed these very same goals. In this respect it is useful to think of the Meiji state as a forerunner of the nationalist regimes that have flowered so profusely in our own time.

At this point we may borrow terminology from the thesis advanced by Robert C. Tucker that there is a genus of twentieth-century political systems definable as "the revolutionary massmovement regime under single-party auspices," or, for short, the "movement-regime." [30] Tucker's taxonomy of this genus discloses three subordinate species: communist, fascist, and nationalist. The former two are "totalitarian" regimes,[31] while the nationalist species is apt to become totalitarian only when it undergoes "metamorphosis" to a communist or fascist form. In contrast to the utopian goal of totally transforming society which provides the "revolutionary dynamic" of the latter two, the nationalist movement-regime's goals are those of promoting national independence and initiating a process of rapid modernization. As a result, these nationalist regimes have a tendency to become "extinct," that is, to lose the dynamism which propelled them into power once they achieve their original goals.[32] The regime is no longer responsive to new challenges for which it was neither established nor equipped to handle.

We may characterize the Meiji system as a nineteenth-century forerunner or precursor of this sort of twentieth-century nationalist mass-movement regime.[33] Although the masses assuredly played no significant part in bringing it to power, the government moved quickly to harness the energies of all within the realm in order to make Japan secure and keep it that way. The "emperor-system" ideology gave legitimacy to the process of tapping all available talents and resources in support of national goals. In place of the one-party, charismatic-leader trait marking full-blown examples of such regimes, as in Kuomintang China, Nasser's Egypt, or Bourguiba's Tunisia among others, we find the Meiji oligarchy, which shed the cocoon of local interests that nurtured it—chiefly those of Chōshū and Satsuma—and acted in the over-all national interest. In diplomacy, war, law, politics, and the economy, oligarchic initiative produced a secure and modern Japanese nation, but the institutions built by the oligarchs were to prove insufficiently responsive to the challenges which the modernization process set in motion. The first third of the twentieth century brought the gradual rise of new forces which severely taxed the capacities of the system erected in the last third of the nineteenth.

The earliest wave of these new forces began to gather strength after 1890 and centered on political liberalism amidst the growing urban-industrial sector of society. Urbanism in particular contributed to the politicization of more and more of the populace, confronting the government with the necessity of adaptation to popular political demands through incorporating the parliamentary system into the decision-making process. "Taishō democracy" represented the peak of this liberal wave, but during and especially

208

after World War I a second wave washed over Japan—a wave of radical "nativist" discontent standing in opposition to the "alien" Western quality of the great cities, the new industrial empires, and parliamentary politics.

Movements embodying this nativist tendency bear comparison with certain forms of reaction against the European or American presence in colonial areas, but they also approximate the function of early fascist movements in Europe, which, again as Tucker phrases it,[34] gained momentum at times of crisis by inveighing against a status quo that they treated *as if* it were foreign—what the Nazis condemned as a "West European" parliamentary system in Germany, for instance, or democracy and socialism in Italy. When Japanese agrarian supremacists such as Gondō Seikyō railed against the cities, or civilian activists like Ōkawa Shūmei joined hands with army officers belonging to Lieutenant Colonel Hashimoto Kingorō's Sakurakai (Society of the Cherry) in 1931 and 1932 to attack the parliamentary principle, they were reflecting a kind of patriotic despair over Japan's condition—something akin to the feelings of political and cultural despair that gave impetus to early European fascist movements.[35] In Shōwa Japan, however, such fascist-like representatives of nativism stood little chance of coming to power in the face of the entrenched authority and legitimacy held by the existing regime. Suppression of the young officers' insurrection in February 1936, as is often noted,[36] brought an end to this "fascism from below," such as it was, which in any event enjoyed no substantial base of mass support.

Challenged less by socialists or communists than by nascent fascist movements such as these, the government eventually moved to block both sets of forces. Instead of "metamorphosis" to a fascist or communist movement-regime, the bureaucratic, political-party, and military elites who had emerged from the Meiji state composed their differences as best they could and acted as a conservative coalition to maintain the system they had inherited. The war crisis of the thirties and, after 1937, the war itself, only added urgency to their efforts, but did not change the basic conservative character of their rule.

In conclusion, I would offer again the reflection that we shall

209

not adequately understand the nineteen-thirties in Japan through reference to fascism and other European historical patterns, helpful as these commonly are for the sake of comparison. Nor can we do so by abandoning comparative perspective altogether and suggesting that there was some sort of atavistic reversion to the Tokugawa preëminence of Bushido ideology and the samurai caste, or by contending that what happened was all part of an epic "war against the West" uniquely waged by Japan on behalf of Asia, as Hayashi Fusao would have it.[37]

Instead I have recommended turning to the possibility of drawing enlightenment from comparisons with the late-developing non-Western nations.[38] Along this line I have argued that it is useful to view interwar Japan as proceeding developmentally from the political stage represented by the precursory Meiji nationalist "movement-regime" to a point where the "extinction" of that regime's original dynamism, coupled however with the tenacity of its institutions and the onset of total war, brought a reassertion of authoritarian tendencies and a corollary restraint on the exercise of liberalism and individual freedoms. Distressing as these developments are, they do not add up to "fascism." If we wish to find fault with the conservative leaders of early Shōwa Japan, we might do so not because they were "fascists" but, paradoxically, because of the inflexibility of their very commitment to the institutional framework and national security conceptions that grew out of the Meiji system.[39]

¹ A compendium of readings both pro and con on the question of whether "fascism" applies to Japan is Ivan Morris, ed., *Japan 1939–1945: Militarism, Fascism, Japanism?* (Boston, D.C. Heath, 1963).

² The classic statement of the Marxist position on fascism is perhaps R. Palme Dutt, *Fascism and Social Revolution* (New York, International Publishers, 1934).

³ See George M. Wilson, "Kita Ikki's Theory of Revolution," *Journal of Asian Studies*, XXVI.1 (Nov. 1966), pp. 94–96.

⁴ O. Tanin and E. Yohan [pseuds.], *Militarism and Fascism in Japan* (New York, International Publishers, 1934), pp. 21–22.

⁵ Yu. I. Avdeyev and V. N. Strunnikov, *Burzhuaznoe gosudarstvo v period 1919–1939 gg.* (Moscow, Izdatel'stvo Instituta mezhdunarodnykh otnoshenii, 1962), p. 409. There have been remarkably few Soviet studies of European fascism; some of the reasons why are explored in Walter Laqueur, *Russia and Germany* (Boston, Little Brown, 1965), pp. 196–251.

⁶ I. A. Latyshev, *Vnutrenniaia politika iaponskogo imperializma nakanune voiny na Tikhom okeane, 1931–1941* (Moscow, Gospolitizdat, 1955), pp. 3–4.

⁷ Latyshev, pp. 215–216; see also Avdeyev and Strunnikov, p. 285 n. 54. Another more recent Soviet study of modern Japan that takes much the same line as Latyshev is L. N. Kutakov, *Ocherki noveishei istorii Iaponii 1918–1963* (Moscow, Izdatel'stvo prosveshchenie, 1965).

⁸ There is a vast literature on the capitalism controversy (*Nihon shihonshugi ronsō*); one reliable and straightforward introduction to the historiography of the controversy is the section called "Meiji ishin kenkyū no rekishi" in *Nihon no rekishi* (Tokyo, Yomiuri shimbunsha, 1963), X, pp. 246–251. In English, see George M. Beckmann, "Japanese Adaptations of Marx-Leninism—Modernization and History," *Asian Cultural Studies*, III (International Christian University, Tokyo; Oct. 1962), pp. 103–114. On the controversy's application to the problem of Japanese fascism, see Tōyama Shigeki and Satō Shin'ichi, eds., *Nihonshi kenkyū nyūmon*, I (Tokyo, Tōkyō daigaku shuppankai, 1954), pp. 362–367; II (1962), pp. 268–279.

⁹ *Kōza* (Symposium) comes from the title of a famous multi-volume series of essays on the history of Japanese capitalism (*Nihon shihonshugi hattatsushi kōza* [Tokyo, Iwanami shoten, 1932–1933]); the opponents of the *Kōza* faction, i.e., those who believed that the Meiji Restoration *was* a bourgeois revolution, were known as the *Rōnō* (Worker-farmer) faction, after the title of a magazine put out by a group of Marxist intellectuals.

¹⁰ Kamiyama Shigeo is the most prominent advocate of this minority position; see his *Tennōsei ni kansuru rironteki shomondai* (Tokyo, Minshu hyōronsha, 1947).

211

[11] Inoue Kiyoshi, *Nihon no rekishi,* III (Tokyo, Iwanami shoten, 1966), p. 188.

[12] Tanaka Sōgorō, *Nihon fuashizumu shi* (Tokyo, Kawade shobō shinsha, 1960), pp. 3–4.

[13] Robert A. Scalapino, *Democracy and the Party Movement in Prewar Japan* (Berkeley, University of California Press, 1953); Richard Storry, *The Double Patriots* (Boston, Houghton Mifflin, 1957) and "Japanese Fascism in the Thirties," *Wiener Library Bulletin,* XX.4 (Autumn 1966), pp. 1–7.

[14] Maruyama Masao, *Thought and Behaviour in Modern Japanese Politics,* Ivan Morris, ed. (London, Oxford University Press, 1963); Ishida Takeshi, *Kindai Nihon seiji kōzō no kenkyū* (Tokyo, Miraisha, 1956); Hata Ikuhiko, *Gun fuashizumu undōshi* (Tokyo, Kawade shobō shinsha, 1962).

[15] Maruyama, pp. 57–66, 76–77, 80 (from "Ideology and Dynamics of Japanese Fascism," pp. 25–83).

[16] Maruyama, p. 172 (from "Fascism—Some Problems: A Consideration of its Political Dynamics," pp. 157–176).

[17] Nakamura Kikuo, "Tennōsei fuashizumu wa atta ka," *Jiyū,* No. 73 (Dec. 1965), pp. 50–59 and *Manshū jihen* (Tokyo, Nihonkyōbunsha, 1965), pp. 194–202.

[18] Nakamura, *Jiyū,* No. 73, pp. 53–54.

[19] Maruyama, pp. 161–163.

[20] Maruyama, pp. 84–135 ("Thought and Behaviour Patterns of Japan's Wartime Leaders").

[21] Maruyama, *passim,* esp. pp. 36, 41, 51. Maruyama's stress on continuities makes it difficult to determine when or how Japan changed from being nationalist to being ultranationalist or "fascist," a point noted by Hashikawa Bunzō in his introduction to *Chōkokkashugi* (= *Gendai Nihon shisō taikei,* No. 31) (Tokyo, Chikuma shobō, 1964), p. 9.

[22] As indicated above, the neo-*Kōza* school of postwar Japanese Marxist historians also generally insists on this sort of qualification, although such writers hew more closely to the original Marxist assessment of fascism than do the advocates of the authoritarian-modernization thesis. Barrington Moore, Jr., whose comparative study of landlord-peasant relations and modernization covers Japan as well as numerous other countries, represents a variation on the usual authoritarian-modernization thesis of Japanese fascism since he offers no significant qualification and refers to Japan as having followed the "capitalist and reactionary" route to the modern world, resulting, as it did also in Germany, in "fascism." See *Social Origins of Dictatorship and Democracy* (Boston, Beacon Press, 1966), pp. xv, 159–161, 228–313. But Moore defines fascism at an extremely high level of generalization as "conservative modernization through revolution from above" (p. 436) or "an attempt to make reaction and conservatism popular and plebeian" (p. 447). This is tantamount to asserting that any form of paternalism or authoritarianism for purposes of industrialization equals fascism, a reading that would make "fascists" even of Bismarck and the Meiji oligarchs.

[23] John W. Hall makes this point in examining the relevance of feudalism as

an explanatory generalization for aspects of earlier Japanese history; "Feudalism in Japan—a Reassessment," *Comparative Studies in Society and History*, V.1 (Oct. 1962), pp. 20–24.

[24] Tanin and Yohan, pp. 7–22.

[25] For building this model, one would have to add to earlier studies at least three major contributions of the nineteen-sixties to the comparative study of fascism in Europe. First there is Seymour M. Lipset's thesis, in *Political Man* (Garden City, N.Y., Doubleday, 1960), that fascism represents the extremism of the usually moderate and liberal middle class due to prolonged and severe economic aggravation, which Lipset bases on an analysis of voting patterns in Germany and other Western countries. Second is the ideological taxonomy of fascism by Ernst Nolte in *Three Faces of Fascism* (New York, Holt, Rinehart and Winston, 1966), according to which fascism arises out of a philosophical revolt against the modern world; Nolte holds that fascism appropriates the ideas of Marxism but turns them against the Marxists for the glory and benefit of the nation. Finally, there is Wolfgang Sauer's article "National Socialism: Totalitarianism or Fascism?" in *The American Historical Review*, LXXIII.2 (Dec. 1967), pp. 404–424, which supplements Nolte's philosophical analysis by using economic-growth theory in order to provide a socio-economic dimension to the non-Marxist interpretation of fascism.

[26] For an epitomatic statement reflecting both of these attitudes, see Maruyama Masao, *Nihon seiji shisōshi kenkyū* (Tokyo, Tōkyō daigaku shuppankai, 1952), "Atogaki," pp. i–xii. His "Author's Introduction to the English Edition" in *Thought and Behaviour*, pp. xi–xvii indicates a similar line of thought.

[27] As examples see Sakuzo Yoshino, "Fascism in Japan," *Contemporary Japan*, I.2 (Sept. 1932), pp. 185–197 and T. A. Bisson, "The Rise of Fascism in Japan," *Foreign Policy Reports*, VIII.17 (Oct. 26, 1932), pp. 196–206.

[28] Consider, for instance, Robert A. Scalapino and Masumi Junnosuke, *Parties and Politics in Contemporary Japan* (Berkeley, University of California Press, 1962).

[29] See John W. Hall and Richard K. Beardsley, *Twelve Doors to Japan* (New York, McGraw-Hill, 1965), p. 159.

[30] Robert C. Tucker, "Towards a Comparative Politics of Movement-Regimes," *American Political Science Review*, LV.2 (June 1961), pp. 281–289. The definition appears in italicized form on p. 283. I am grateful to William E. Steslicke for calling my attention to Tucker's concept.

[31] "Totalitarian" in the sense elaborated by such theorists as Hannah Arendt in *The Origins of Totalitarianism* (New York, Harcourt Brace, 1951) and Carl J. Friedrich and Zbigniew Brzezinski in *Totalitarian Dictatorship and Autocracy* (Cambridge, Harvard University Press, 1956).

[32] Tucker, *American Political Science Review*, LV.2, pp. 286–287. Examples of this kind of "extinction" include Chiang Kai-shek's Republic of China, Rhee's regime in Korea, and, apparently, Sukarno's in Indonesia.

[33] Tucker points out (*American Political Science Review*, LV.2, p. 284) that Mazzini in Italy conceived a precursory idea of this sort of national-liberation mass movement.

213

[34] Tucker, *American Political Science Review*, LV.2, p. 283.

[35] See Fritz Stern, *The Politics of Cultural Despair* (Berkeley, University of California Press, 1961). Ōkawa Shūmei, of course, was no mere cultural conservative such as Arthur Moeller van den Bruck in Weimar Germany (see Stern, pp. 231–325). Ōkawa's organizational skills and political ambitions led to several plots against the existing constitutional order. He was a leading conspirator until he went to jail following the failure of the *Putsch* of May 15, 1932.

[36] *Inter alia*, see Maruyama, *Thought and Behaviour*, pp. 33, 66; Storry, *Wiener Library Bulletin*, XX.4,3.

[37] Hayashi Fusao, *Daitōa sensō kōteiron*, 2 vols. (Tokyo, Banchō shobō, 1964–1965).

[38] George Akita holds that the Meiji experience cannot serve as a model for today's emerging nations because of the different circumstances of the mid-twentieth century, which he feels vitiate comparisons with what Meiji leaders confronted; see *Foundations of Constitutional Government in Modern Japan* (Cambridge, Harvard University Press, 1967), pp. 161, 175. Different as conditions may be, however, the internal problems of social control and building industry are major concerns for these nations today, just as they were for Meiji Japan.

[39] See James B. Crowley, *Japan's Quest for Autonomy* (Princeton, Princeton University Press, 1966).

10

The Fascist Mentality—
Drieu la Rochelle

BY RENEE WINEGARTEN

An observer might have noticed at various times between 1927 and 1943 two men walking along a street in Paris, deep in discussion. They share an admiration of Maurras, though both in their different ways have passed beyond it. They are fascinated by T.E. Lawrence. Both are exponents of self-realization and the cult of risk in the manner of Barrès' "free man." Above all, they are steeped in Nietzsche.

The younger of them is André Malraux (born in 1901), the erstwhile Gaullist Minister for Cultural Affairs, novelist, noted anti-fascist, organizer of a volunteer air squadron for the Spanish Republic, commander in the Resistance movement. The elder is Pierre Drieu la Rochelle (born in 1893), novelist, supporter of Jacques Doriot and member of his fascist *Parti Populaire Français*, who killed himself in 1945 rather than stand trial for collaborating with the Germans.

Drieu profoundly admired Malraux and his work, not least because the author of *La Condition Humaine* was a man of action as well as an intellectual, who had contrived to escape from the constricting and debilitating atmosphere of France between the wars. This atmosphere, Drieu felt, was what forced him to write satirically about the anti-heroic tenor of modern life, whereas he longed only to stretch his spirit in heroic spheres like Malraux. One of Drieu's last wishes was for Malraux to be present at his funeral; while Malraux was later to say of his friend, "Drieu fought for France. Until death." [1] And this mutual respect, this complicity

215

between men apparently on opposite sides, may at first astonish, though they are both romantics haunted by the tragic sense of life.

There is something peculiarly intriguing about the confrontation of these key figures of an era. Do they represent the equivalence of totalitarian inclinations, at a time when there was considerable traffic between communism and fascism, and renegade adherents of the former (like Doriot himself) could be found among the latter faction? Were they essentially adventurers, risking their lives for causes in which they only half believed, and for the satisfaction of their private egos? In fine, were these opposite paths, if not the result of mere chance, ultimately interchangeable?

We cannot help being struck by the irony of a situation which led Malraux into the cabinet of General de Gaulle, while Drieu, when it was too late, asked himself whether de Gaulle was not the destined national leader he had desired for so long. Ironically, too, it is de Gaulle, himself deeply influenced by Nietzsche and Barrès, who has sought to put some of Drieu's views into practice: his notion of a united Europe as a world force (even if it is "l'Europe des patries" rather than Drieu's "l'Europe contre les patries"); his desire for reconciliation with Germany; his opposition to the hegemony of England and the United States. We are led to inquire what conjunction of character and circumstance was to bring about destinies so contrary in writers of similar intellectual background, leaving the name of one in ignominy while the other enjoys international respect. Could Drieu, in fact, have turned out differently?

If, as Malraux suggested, those who are at once active and pessimistic will inevitably be fascist unless they have some allegiance behind them, then the answer must be in the negative. When himself charged with fascism, Malraux always insisted that he could never be a fascist. In an interview, he declared in this connection that he is a pessimist as regards ideas, not human beings: "I have faith in people. . . ." [2] Here, surely, is the prime difference between them which goes a long way towards explaining the different course they took: for Drieu had faith in nothing, least of all in himself.

There is an illuminating glimpse of Drieu in Gide's journal for 1927. Gide met him on the boulevard and took him into a bar for a glass of wine, since he had announced he was about to get married. With a characteristic display of cynicism and self-belittlement, Drieu declared that marriage was an experiment he wanted to conduct. He wanted to know if he could last out, since he had never been able to keep up a love affair longer than six months. And Gide (who was certainly an authority on self-absorption) remarked how terribly self-absorbed the members of the younger generation all were. In his view, Barrès' teaching drove them to despairing boredom, and in order to escape it they threw themselves into religion or, like Drieu, into politics. He prophesied (rightly) that this trend would be severely judged in twenty years' time.

If, then, we feel that Drieu's fatal development was a logical one that could have been modified in degree rather than in direction, we realize at the same time that this dandy who frequented the Parisian night-clubs and brothels of the twenties, this perspicacious egoist whose principal subject is himself, this self-loathing and self-destructive nihilist serves as a valuable witness of his age, more revealing in this particular regard, perhaps, than many of his contemporaries of superior talent. Immersed in his epoch, sensitive to local undercurrents, at once troubled and exhilarated by vast new upheavals, he confesses his reactions with an almost bare simplicity, even at times with naïveté. As François Mauriac observed, he was "at the nerve-centre" [3] of everything that fascinated and tempted his generation.

Moreover, Drieu's case seems particularly interesting to us now, because of the striking affinity between his temperament and a certain aspect or tendency of his age. It is with this affinity that we are principally concerned here. There is a kind of pre-fascist inclination which in part grew out of romanticism, and which might or might not take the form of direct political partisanship, once fascism arose as a political force. Indeed, political partisanship might appear, as in Drieu, to be the rationalization of inner romantic tendencies. He is, in short, the fascist romantic *par excellence*, extremely well-equipped to figure in Paul Sérant's *Le Romantisme Fasciste*. For he is more interested in shattering existing political molds for the sake of his personal aesthetic and moral ideals of human plenitude and solitary heroism, than he is in the formation of any truly practical political structure.

Nonetheless, Drieu's concern with politics was not just the dilettantism of the man of letters: it was of long standing. He studied at the École des Sciences Politiques between 1910 and 1913, although he failed his examinations—a failure most bitter to him and one for which, perhaps, he spent the rest of his life trying to compensate. Thus it is quite absurd to speak of his political activity as "a comparatively slight aberration," [4] as did an anonymous reviewer in *The Times Literary Supplement* a few years ago. On the contrary, Drieu's political views and activity form an intrinsic part of his ideal style of life and a public extension of his private inclinations.

He believed, with other followers of Nietzsche like Malraux and Montherlant, that one must *live* first and foremost, and that to live fully one must be prepared to risk all. In an era when things were falling apart and the centre could not hold, when God was dead, when the conflict between political ideologies assumed the character of religious wars, political commitment finally appeared to him as a form of life-enhancing risk. He was perfectly conscious of what he was doing when he decided to commit himself, and he knew what was ultimately at stake: his head.

Significantly, at the core of his political views there lies neither a theory nor a system, but an immediate instinctive preference, a passionate emotional response. Frédéric Grover, who has done more than anyone for the current revival of interest in Drieu, makes this quite plain. And it is this very instinctive or emotional reaction in a romantic who located the dignity of man in the sincerity of his passions, which makes us feel that there is some point in examining the course he took, and in steeling ourselves to read a good deal that is both irksome and pernicious.

As he saw it, fascism was an expression of the innate romanticism of the lower middle class into which he was born. It was a movement aiming to defend a certain conception of heroic man against encroaching urbanization and the dehumanizing machine. Drieu's views are basically inspired by a romantic dream: the reluctant intellectual's aspiration to be an heroic man of action. Where

218

action was concerned, he received his flash of illumination on the battlefields of the First World War, in which he served at Charleroi, at Verdun and in the Dardanelles campaign.

It was at Charleroi in 1914 that a bayonet charge filled him with ecstasy, and that he suddenly perceived within himself the qualities of a leader of men. "All at once, I knew myself, I knew my life. So this was I, this strong, free, heroic man. . . . What suddenly spurted forth? A leader." [5] This was written in *La Comédie de Charleroi* (1934), but it may be taken to represent faithfully Drieu's emotions at the time he was twenty. The orgastic note, apparent here, becomes even more marked when he adds that a leader is a man who gives and takes "in the same ejaculation." [6] As he was to say of himself at this period, "I was a thorough fascist without knowing it." [7] That seems clear enough.

Drieu never recovered from this experience of action in war, which revealed to him (as it did to Hemingway and Montherlant) not only his own highest potentialities of virility, energy and courage, but also the hideous mechanistic face of the modern world. Exaltation of virility was doubtless a reaction against and almost a compensation for that dread mechanization. This was to him his finest hour (just as the horror of his experience is for us his sole tragic justification and excuse). He expressed his sensations in a collection of free verse, *Interrogation*, in 1917, which, though highly rhetorical, made his name.

And he was always trying to recapture that supreme moment without success, to impress his dream of virility and his vision of the atrocious new element in modern life, upon a society that did not seem to want to understand. He even thought he had found it once more on 6 February 1934 during the protest march of the war veterans and the ensuing riots which almost overthrew French democracy. He sent his protagonist, Gilles, to Spain to redeem himself by fighting for Franco in the Civil War. But for Gilles' creator there was to be no satisfactory way out through action.

Dream and action: Drieu's dream was rooted in the yearning to "sweep" men into action, to "destroy empires and build others." [8] He gave it complete imaginative expression in a poetic fable, *L'Homme à Cheval*, his penultimate novel. There, in a Bolivia of the imagination, in the second half of the last century, Felipe, a poet-guitarist, inspires an enigmatic officer named Jaime to seize power. These two figures represent the author's active and contemplative dream selves, the latter on occasion appearing totally detached and remote from the former.

As dictator, Jaime sets about reviving the lost empire of the Incas and their ancient religion. Unlike D.H. Lawrence's Mexicans who restore primitive Aztec ritual in *The Plumed Serpent*, he fails, but the virtue clearly lies in the attempt. In this novel which embodies both the grim and the absurd essence of fascist romanticism, Drieu obliquely conveys his own secret longings to be the prime mover in some vague vast enterprise, to be the inspiration behind those who seek by violent means to change the material and spiritual destinies of men.

So when Drieu decided to throw in his lot with Doriot in 1936, he was not just taking certain thoughts to their logical conclusion, he was also following the penchant of his nature and his imagination. As Ramon Fernandez said of Drieu's *Socialisme Fasciste*, what Drieu had produced was a document of poetico-political prophecy about a fascist Utopia that corresponded to nothing in reality. Fernandez aptly called Drieu's standpoint "poetical politics." [9] Indeed, Drieu admirably typifies the kind of writer, especially common between the wars, who naïvely carries over into the field of politics his literary reverie.

Drieu was therefore never really concerned with politics as the art of the possible, only as an emotional outlet, as a means of fulfilling his dreams, desires and aspirations. While he could distrust the militant nationalism of the Nazis, at the same time he could comment with shattering irresponsibility on the Nuremberg rally of 1935: "I have experienced nothing like it for artistic emotion since the Russian ballet." [10] A blend between aestheticism and the love of force (whose feminine sexual character he himself accurately perceived) was to provide the basis of his public stand.

The disastrous consequences of Nietzsche's influence on the weak can be seen particularly clearly in the feeble eponymous hero of *Gilles*, who acts chiefly as a projection of the negative qualities in

Drieu himself. For there is no correlation between Gilles' ideal conception of himself and of the world, and the debauched and futile life he leads. This long, uneven satirical novel, in the form of a triptych and epilogue, is a savage onslaught on the literary and political coteries of the Third Republic. The sterility of Gilles' sexual life is intended to coincide with the sterility of French society between the wars.

Returning from the Front, and while engaging in numerous casual sexual encounters, Gilles marries a Jewess for her money and through her family's influence obtains a post in the Quai d'Orsay. (This section is by far the most effective.) After their divorce, he hovers—like Drieu himself—on the fringe of the surrealist and communist avant-garde, which he despises, and has an affair with a wealthy American married woman who jilts him. He willingly marries a former prostitute when she is about to bear his child, but she falls ill and dies of cancer after an abortion. Disgusted with political corruption, indifference and apathy which reflect his own ineffectualness and disease of will, in desperation he proposes an alliance of communists and nationalists: "Yes, anything," he cries, "so long as that old shack over there by the water (i.e. the Chamber of Deputies) cracks up"; [11] anything that will make a clean sweep of all he fears and loathes in the modern world.

The sheer hollowness at the core of Drieu's life and work is fully exposed here, for this cry expresses his own reaction. In spite of the high-flown gestures of the would-be heroic superior figure who thinks he knows better than anyone else, in spite of the reams of words (over thirty published volumes and the source of his posthumous writings shows no signs of drying up), there is simply nothing there but an attitude: violence, hatred and self-hatred. "Mystery of humanity which gives itself for nothing, to nothing!" [12] one of his characters exclaimed in words that seem to epitomize the standpoint of the writer himself.

Drieu confessed that he had no sense of being, no sense of matter. The lack of grip on people and life that runs throughout his work, and was apparent in his remarks to Gide, haunts *Le Feu Follet* (published in 1931, eight years earlier than *Gilles*). This novel is based on the suicide of his friend Rigaut, but the theme of a weak man deliberately choosing to pursue his own destruction is essentially Drieu's own, for he himself was fascinated by suicide. He had thought of doing away with himself more than once, the idea having occurred to him when he suffered an attack of venereal disease and at moments of failure before he was twenty.

Alain, the drug-addict of *Le Feu Follet*, would have liked to captivate and hold people, but they and everything else always slipped from him. It is no use advising people like Alain to exert will-power when their very disease is lack of will. For them, self-destruction is the only "noble deed" they are capable of: "Suicide is an act, the act of those who could not accomplish any other." [13] The fascination of the abyss, the overwhelming attraction of a destructive nothingness (of which Drieu speaks, like so many of his contemporaries, as if it were something positive), these lie at the heart of his writings.

For if, as he thought, paraphrasing Nietzsche, man is a mere accident in a world of accidents, if the world has no meaning other than that we give it for the development of our passions and actions, then where is one to look for a stay on the solitary and dizzy heights? Of Alain in *Le Feu Follet* he wrote: "Thus, because it was not upheld by ideas, the world was so unsubstantial that it offered him no support." [14] Drieu himself found some buttress against all-invading nothingness in his political opinions and activity. He also sought it, largely in vain, in friendship and especially in his association with a considerable number of women apart from his two wives. Unable to find any solid prop within himself, Drieu was disinclined to fashion some fictitious positive persona, unlike Montherlant who wrote: "I have only my idea of myself to sustain me on the seas of nothingness." [15]

Perhaps Drieu's personal tragedy lay in the fact that he was ready to settle for a partisan answer, and in so doing he betrayed the openness essential to the artist if he is to achieve real stature. He preferred Stendhalian dirty hands to the ivory tower, or to that prudent (if not always timely) withdrawal which was his principal objection to the position adopted by Montherlant. To live is above all to compromise oneself, said Drieu; whereas Montherlant always managed somehow to keep open a door through which he could make his escape.

In Montherlant's eyes, Drieu was one of those writers who, like Barrès, erroneously devoted to political and social questions the time they should have been devoting to the perfection of their art. That was a mistake Montherlant had no intention of making, even if he made others. This refusal is what helps Montherlant to appear superior to Drieu as an artist, and it is curious that Drieu once revealingly observed how the fact that Montherlant existed more than half dispensed him from doing so.

It is hardly surprising that in the end none of the causes to which Drieu committed himself really satisfied him, for not only was there an evident lack of connection between this dreamer and political reality, there was even a split between his contemplative self and the self busy in the arena. Symptomatic of this gap, perhaps, is the fact that he neither sought nor obtained political office and power. He became disillusioned with Doriot, and left the *Parti Populaire Français* in January 1939. And although warned by Otto Abetz from the beginning about the likely consequences of his choice when there was no pressing obligation for it, he threw himself into the cause of collaboration with the Nazis, editing *La Nouvelle Revue Française* during the Occupation.

This action may have been partly the result of a movement of despair and anger with his compatriots during the débâcle of 1940, not dissimilar to that which led Montherlant to write the distasteful indictment of *Le Solstice de Juin*. Realizing his mistake fairly early, after the battle of El Alamein, and thoroughly disenchanted with the Nazis, who were not doing what he expected to stimulate national rehabilitation or to further the cause of fascism in France, he could easily have made his escape in time. He remained, possibly out of pride, but more especially (one imagines) out of a private urge to contribute to his own ruin, like so many of his fictional heroes.

If we want some idea of what was passing in his mind during the latter part of the Occupation, we could do no better than read his last completed novel, *Les Chiens de Paille*, published in 1944, but written in the spring of 1943. The epigraph is taken from Lao-Tsu:

in the eyes of the gods, human beings are no more than straw dogs used in religious sacrifices. Life has become for him a tale told by an idiot.

The action of the book takes place during the Occupation. The central figure, Constant Trubert, is a battered, sex-weary, world-weary adventurer, owing allegiance to none. He is not in the least averse to coolly drawing blood from the thigh of a naked woman, who has disrobed for another purpose, in order to elicit information from her—a scene in harmony with the worst sadistic lucubrations of the romantic agony.

A mysterious Corsican black-marketeer, Susini, places him in charge of a deserted house near the northern seaboard, with an arms depot concealed in its grounds. There, Constant attracts the attention of the warring factions of the district who all covet the hidden arms. Scorning everyone, the Germans (who are serving their own interests), the collaborators (who are serving those of Germany), the Gaullists (who are serving those of England and the United States), and the communists (who are serving those of Russia), he feels a modicum of sympathy for a group of outmoded young French nationalists, who care only for France.

In the end, he decides to blow up the arms depot, together with himself, Cormont the nationalist leader and Susini the black-marketeer (who is part-Jewish and turns out to represent the forthcoming postwar triumph of international Jewry). Before he can do so, however, an English plane drops a random bomb which destroys them all. The book leaves the reader in no doubt about Drieu's mania for destruction, as well as his final bankruptcy, hysteria and despair.

Les Chiens de Paille represents the grand culmination of Drieu's defeatism. Exasperated by his countrymen's lack of fibre, he had (like Montherlant) more than once contemplated abandoning France to her sorry fate. Here, Constant reflects at length on the idea of treason, regarding himself as a Judas figure (who, as he sees it, served Christ by his very betrayal). In other words, he would betray France as it were for her own good, so that she might eventually rise again in some obscure Heraclitean movement of flux and reflux.

224

There is evidently in Drieu a tension between the pained nationalist patriot and the person who thinks he has passed beyond nationalism, a tension that is never reconciled. Drieu had travelled too widely—in South America, Algeria, Greece, England, Russia, Germany and elsewhere—to be intellectually content with a narrow nationalism, but emotionally he still related everything he saw to France. Indeed, all Drieu's hopes for a supra-national European *bloc* were really founded in an exasperated and disappointed nationalism that he had never fully eradicated in himself.

Like other Frenchmen of his intellectual upbringing, he inwardly preferred France in the abstract to his compatriots in the flesh. It is essential to remember that he had breathed the polluted air of defeatism for as long as he could remember, hearing talk of nothing but defeat—Sedan and Fashoda, if not Waterloo. His grandfather's pessimism, his father's resentment, were part of a heritage that he was never able to throw off. France might be victorious in 1918, but he was convinced this victory was meaningless, especially when he perceived what little use was being made of it.

The corrupting notion of decadence pervades Drieu's work: it is the "crushing fact" [16] of which he spoke in the preface to *Gilles*, but already in *Genève ou Moscou?*, written in 1926–7, published in 1928, he had devoted a sizeable appendix to this theme. It was not just that for him, a witness of the intrigues and scandals of the Third Republic, France appeared as degenerate, but that he believed in the Spenglerian decadence of the West, to say nothing of the decadence of the very planet itself.

Everywhere he saw forces hostile to meaningful life as he conceived it, and he was able to describe these destructive forces with some power because he felt so many of them within himself: he regarded himself as the victim of the ills he denounced. As he put it, "I pitilessly scourged the age in myself. . . ." [17] The worst anyone can say of him he had already masochistically said of himself; and to this extent, the vitriolic comments made about him by that other self-loathing bourgeois, Sartre, may be regarded as otiose.

Certainly, when one comes to examine his ideas as such, one

225

finds that the best this representative member of the French lower middle class could propose was a restoration of aristocratic values, the creation of a world where there was to be a proletariat for production and an élite for contemplation. Along with so many of his generation, he yearned for a return to a mythical medievalism where the cult figure would be a combination of warrior-hero and saint, as in the *Bhagavad Gita*. In common with the modern trend, the more disgruntled and disillusioned he became with the modern world and with his own conduct, the more he devoted his attention to a study of esoteric religion, evidently preferring Hindu and Arab mysticism to the *Zohar*.

His only contribution to ideas which seems of any interest and relevance to us now is his view of Europe. In a period of intense nationalism, he proclaimed the end of the nation-state, and as early as 1918 he urged the establishment of a united Europe that would be able to stand up against the two great *blocs* that he saw emerging: Soviet Russia with its new barbarism, and the United States with its facile concept of material happiness. In 1922, in *Mesure de la France*, he wrote: "Europe will federate or will devour herself, or will be devoured." [18] The theme of the economic and political unification of Europe was his King Charles's head. He went on reiterating this idea when it was thoroughly compromised after 1940 as a tool of German hegemony.

Having accepted without demur Maurras' critique of democracy, Drieu constantly denigrated the bourgeois liberal parliamentary system, which in his opinion was a moribund relic of the nineteenth century. For him, "the new fact" [19] of the twentieth century which French democracy persisted in ignoring, was the rise of totalitarianism. He dated this from Lenin's formation of the Bolshevik party in 1903. As Nazi defeat drew nearer, he confessed in his diary, published after his death in *Récit Secret*, that he now believed in the triumph of communism, but felt he was too old to change his coat. In short, where he was concerned, the solution had to be a totalitarian one.

The development of Drieu's anti-Semitism forms part of his ever-increasing distaste for democracy. The Jews seem to him a fermenting element in the middle-class rationalism and decadence he detests, and democracy the milieu in which they thrive. At first, he showed little sign of racialism. He could graciously acknowledge the sacrifice of a Jewish comrade during the Great War, while at the same time appearing somewhat patronizing towards the patriotism of French Jews. "What is a Jew? Nobody knows,"[20] he wrote, rather ambiguously, in *La Comédie de Charleroi*. At one moment in the twenties he even thought the French ought to become the Jews of a united Europe, that is, mercantile rather than military.

His first wife is said to have been Jewish in origin though Catholic by religion. He saved her life during the Occupation and she sheltered him at the Liberation. After their divorce, he had made at least two unsuccessful attempts to marry Jewish heiresses. Indeed, he seems to have grown to dislike Jews largely because when they were rich they tempted him by dangling before him what he wanted—money and luxury—at the same time as he professed an ascetic ideal. To this extent, they could be regarded by him as a corrupting influence.

Later on, however, after his link with Doriot, after the rise to power of Léon Blum, and the influx of refugees fleeing from Nazi tyranny, anti-Semitism became a positive obsession. By then, it was difficult for him to speak of a Jewess without calling her, in Baudelaire's phrase, *une affreuse juive*. He was thoroughly convinced that the Jews would "get him" at the Liberation, if no one else did.

For some years after Drieu's suicide, silence descended upon him and his works. One of the most curious developments in French cultural activity in recent years has been his steady rehabilitation, which has taken some critics by surprise. This revival (which tends to play down his anti-Semitism) has involved a popular film, the reprinting of some of his novels in cheap editions, the collection and editing of unpublished or scattered material and the publication of a number of monographs. In 1959, Louis Aragon, the communist poet and novelist who was once Drieu's friend (they quarrelled in 1925), remarked that people were busily engaged in fostering a Drieu legend. Why?

The obvious answer might be sought in his suicide, since for some odd reason suicide is supposed to add to the romance sur-

rounding dead writers, as witness the supreme example of Chatter-
ton. His self-contradictory personality certainly stimulates curios-
ity. More properly, the answer might be looked for in his literary
merit. But on the whole I think these are secondary considerations.
Whatever historical interest Drieu may have as a painter of his age
and of a particular sensibility and state of mind, he is, from an artistic point of view, a profoundly flawed and minor figure. A novelist of undoubted talent, he nevertheless lacks the range and depth,
the control and command of either Malraux or Montherlant, with
whom he was fond of comparing himself. Moreover, for the most
part, no great claims are being made for him as a writer.

What really arouses so many of his French readers today is
that he expresses their own obscure yearnings and disappointments
in life, their immersion in a life of pleasure that ultimately fails to
satisfy their secret aspirations for something nobler and more lofty.
To a generation that was too young to have experienced the Second
World War, but which has known humiliating defeats and savage
losses in Indochina and Algeria, Drieu has much to say. (His restoration roughly coincides with the aftermath of the Algerian war
and the terrorist activities of the *OAS*). Many of those who belong
to this generation believe (like him) that they have fought in vain
and that their comrades have been sacrificed for nothing. His nihilism feeds theirs. Besides, some of his prophecies appear to them to
have been fulfilled; and one of his new admirers declared that the
world comes more and more to resemble what he had foretold.[21]

If, as we have tried to show here, fascism of Drieu's type is to
be seen primarily as a subjective view of the world, as an aesthetic
outlook, as the conjunction of sensibility and circumstance rather
than as a set of ideological doctrines and dogmas, then it is not
solely an historical phenomenon that we have done with. On the
contrary, it seems only too clear that such romanticism as his may
survive or revive, whether under its own or under some different
name. The anti-heroic current flowing so strongly now is surely
likely to provoke a reaction.

At a time when nothing seems to go right, when people are
confused and are looking for a leader, when they feel lost in a too
rapidly changing universe, and are prepared to convince themselves

of their own decadence by denigrating parliamentary democracy, Drieu appears to us as an exemplary warning. That is why I feel he is particularly relevant at the moment, less for what he was, an instinctive rather than an ideological fascist typical of his age, than for what he represents.

[1] Gaëtan Picon, *Malraux par lui-même* (Paris, 1959), p. 90.

[2] Interview in *L'événement*, September 1967, p. 61.

[3] Quoted in Frédéric Grover, *Drieu la Rochelle* (Paris, 1962), p. 84.

[4] *Times Literary Supplement* (London), 26 April 1963.

[5] Drieu, *La Comédie de Charleroi* (Paris, 1934), p. 57.

[6] Grover, *op. cit.*, p. 76.

[7] *Ibid.*, p. 77.

[8] Drieu, *La Comédie de Charleroi*, p. 28.

[9] Ramon Fernandez, "Literature and Politics" in *N.R.F.*, ed. Justin O'Brien (London, 1958), pp. 314, 317.

[10] Grover, *op. cit.*, p. 42.

[11] Drieu, *Gilles* (Paris, 1967), p. 432.

[12] Drieu, *L'Homme à cheval* (Paris, 1965), p. 52.

[13] Drieu, *Le Feu Follet* (Paris, 1967), p. 164.

[14] *Ibid.*, p. 33.

[15] Henry de Montherlant, "Chevalerie du néant," in his *Service inutile* (Paris, 1935), p. 61.

[16] Drieu, preface to *Gilles*, p. 5.

[17] *Ibid.*, p. 7.

[18] Grover, *op. cit.*, p. 175.

[19] "The New Fact of the Twentieth Century" in *N.R.F.*, ed. O'Brien, p. 377.

[20] Quoted by Paul Sérant, *Le Romantisme fasciste* (Paris, 1959), p. 82.

[21] Jean Mabire, *Drieu parmi nous* (Paris, 1963), p. 248.

AIDS FOR
FURTHER READING

Most of the publications on fascism as a generic phenomenon are referred to in the notes to the selections in this volume, so that no additional bibliographical listing is necessary. There are, however, several useful bibliographies that can be recommended. For example, the history of the concept of fascism as well as the development of writing on the subject is perceptively analyzed, with extensive bibliographical references, in Wolfgang Schieder, "Fascism," in *Marxism, Communism and Western Society. A Comparative Encyclopedia*, ed. by C. D. Kernig, vol. III (New York, 1972), 282–302. See also A. James Gregor, "Fascism: The Classic Interpretations of the Interwar Period," and "Fascism: The Contemporary Interpretations," in *University Programs Modular Studies* (General Learning Press: Morristown, N.J., 1973). On Italian Fascism, see Geneviève Bibes, "Le fascisme italien. Etat des travaux depuis 1945," in *Revue française de science politique*, XVIII (1968), 1191–1241; also the bibliographies in A. James Gregor, *The Ideology of Fascism: the Rationale of Totalitarianism* (New York, 1969) and Roland Sarti, (ed.), *The Ax Within. Italian Fascism in Action* (New York, 1974). For an excellent and extensive bibliography on German National Socialism, see Karl Dietrich Bracher, *The German Dictatorship* (New York, 1970).

INDEX

Abyssinia, 102
Action Française, 2–25, 26–42, 81ff., 102, 104
Albania, 18
Alexander, king of Yugoslavia, 7
Anarchism, 16, 149, 178
Anarchosyndicalism, 152
Anti-Semitism, 4, 5, 9, 13, 14, 16, 21, 22, 34, 35, 36, 70f., 73, 79, 81, 82, 84, 99, 104, 108, 116 n. 35, 177, 178, 179, 185, 186, 187, 189, 194 n. 2, 221, 224, 226, 227
Antonescu, Ion, 85, 146, 165
Araquistain, Luís, 162
Argentina. *See* Perón, Juan
Arrow Cross (Hungarian), 34, 80, 147
Aunós, Eduardo, 156, 157
Austria, 49, 53, 79f., 85, 104, 145f., 163
Austria-Hungary, 48
Austrian Nazi party, 80
Azaña, Manuel, 160

Barrès, Maurice, 215, 216, 217

Belgium, 81, 83, 85, 145, 147, 157, 163
  See also Rexists
Bismarck, Otto von, 19, 47, 48, 212 n. 22
Blomberg, Werner von, 109, 116 n. 34
Blum, Léon, 227
Bottai, Giuseppe, 157
Bourguiba, Habib, 208
British Union of Fascists, 84
  See also Mosley, Oswald
Bucard, Marcel, 169 n. 43

Cambó, Francesc, 159
Camelots du Roi, 16
Capitalism, 31, 36, 37, 38, 39, 71, 78, 94, 99, 100, 101, 108, 122, 128, 163, 164, 180, 186, 187, 189, 199, 200, 201, 202
Catholic Center party (Germany), 59
Catholicism, 15, 16, 30, 36, 53, 55, 74, 77, 78, 85, 97, 111, 148, 149, 155, 156, 161, 162
Chamberlain, Houston Stewart, 16

233